THE MARGINAL SELF

The Marginal Self

An Existential Inquiry into Narcissism

René J. Muller

Humanities Press International, Inc.
Atlantic Highlands, NJ

First published 1987 in the United States of America by
Humanities Press International, Inc., Atlantic Highlands, NJ
07716
Reprinted 1989, 1992
©1987, Humanities Press International, Inc.

Library of Congress Cataloging-in-Publication Data

Muller, René J.
  The marginal self.

  Bibliography: p.
  Includes index.
  1. Self (Philosophy) 2. Existentialism.
3. Narcissism. I. Title
BD450.M775   1987   126   86–2880
ISBN 0–391–03374–3
ISBN 0–391–03423–5 (pbk.)

MANUFACTURED IN THE UNITED STATES OF AMERICA

To Ralph Harper,
with Gratitude

The best spirits of the twentieth century have thus expressed their conviction that the original innocence, which to earlier periods was a sinful conceit, the new center, which can be held even as communities disintegrate, is the self.

—Philip Rieff, *The Triumph of the Therapeutic*

Contents

Preface

It is not enough to write about what you know, as Henry James recommended; the trick is to write about what you know that no one else knows—or, at any rate, has gotten around to putting into writing. I wrote this book to say something that, as far as I can tell, no one else has said. I wrote it to describe a phenomenon I first experienced and then thematized as the "marginal self."

I see the marginal self as someone who is not adequate to the demands of his or her new condition—i.e., living in a world where the transcendent absolutes of religion and reason, which for two thousand years gave men and women their bearings on this earth, are being repealed. Because religion and reason no longer fulfill an integrating and therapeutic role, we are being confronted for the first time since the ancient Greeks with our limits *as people*. We are being thrown back on our own and made to ask ultimate questions, when there are no longer ultimate answers. During this time of limited resources for many and what seem like unlimited resources for others, an inadequate response to our new condition—the response of the marginal self—is a common denominator, although at times this may be masked by concern for economic survival.

The world we know today, the one that has recently gone sour on us, is a legacy of Judeo-Christian religion and post-Socratic thought. In the last century, two writers appeared who claimed that this world had been constructed on illusions, that it was, in short, a false world: they were Kierkegaard and Nietzsche. They were the first modern existentialists, the first modern thinkers to insist that a person's *existence* (how he or she lives) was more important than that person's *essence* (what he or she is). Kierkegaard and Nietzsche laid the foundation for the existential revolt that was continued later by Heidegger, Jaspers, Sartre, Camus, Unamuno, Ortega, Marcel, Tillich, Buber, and others. Time has caught up with the existentialists, which is to say their time has come. We would do well to pay attention now to what they have been saying, because their questions have become our questions. That is why I turned to the existentialists for help in characterizing what I see as the marginal self.

How does one write about a "lack" of something? To describe the phenomenon of the marginal self it was necessary to first make palpable the notion of self, to say something about how self is acquired and lost. "Self" is a word we use to talk about our experience, interior and exterior, vis-à-vis others and the world. We use this inadequate word in the hope of grasping something of the flow of our experience in the Life-World. Nothing we say or write can do full justice to lived experience; our sentences are always a distillation and, therefore, a distortion. But that is the price we pay for attempting to turn experience into words.

The emphasis in what I have written here is on the self-pole of the self-other-world interrelationship and totality. This is in no way meant to downplay the importance of the other and the world, without which the self is inconceivable. Nor am I advocating an isolated, solipsistic, or narcissistic self. What I have done is to look at the self-other-world totality principally from the *perspective* of self. I feel justified in this approach because I believe that when people choose another person or something from the world, what they are choosing, ultimately, is themselves. Moreover, as I have tried to show here, without an adequate self there can be no relationship with another person or relation to the world that is worth very much. There can be no genuine *We* without an adequate *I*.

Implicit in how I have gone about describing and characterizing the marginal self is what I have come to think of as the primacy of the *I*. While there can be no *I* without others and the world, it must be acknowledged also that the *We* of relationship very often dissolves, as does our relation to the world—our identity—leaving the *I* at least partially isolated and alone. New relationships develop and new identities form, but it is the *I* that endures, changing as it does. People can break with others and discontinue their projects, but they cannot get rid of themselves.

What I describe as the marginal self has much in common with the narcissistic self—hence, the subtitle, *An Existential Inquiry into Narcissism*. Narcissism can be seen as one specific variation of the marginal self. This is most apparent in Chapters 6 through 9. I invite the reader to integrate the phenomenological descriptions of the marginal self given here with the more technical (and sometimes limiting) language of clinical psychoanalysis. I have tried to unveil the marginality behind the psychopathology. The narcissism I describe, but do not specifically name, is not so much pathological narcissism or the narcissistic personality disorder as a "milder" form that seems endemic to Western culture. (I look into the mirror and constitute myself according to an image of myself shaped largely by the expectations and judgments of others, and of the culture I live in.) To do this is to deceive oneself and to act inauthentically. It is a "marginalizing" capitulation of the self to what Heidegger calls the "they."

It is a pleasure to acknowledge the help and encouragement of Ralph Harper in getting this project off the ground and bringing it to completion.

Baltimore, Maryland
November 1986

1

Existential Shock:

Can Man Be Man?

What sense has our whole being, if it does not mean that in our own
selves that will for truth has come to its own consciousness *as a
problem?*—By reason of this attainment of self-consciousness on the
part of the will for truth, [Christian] morality from henceforward—
there is no doubt about it—goes *to pieces*: this is that great hundred-act
play that is reserved for the next two centuries of Europe, the most
terrible, the most mysterious, and perhaps also the most hopeful of all
plays.

—Nietzsche, *The Genealogy of Morals*

Sometime between 1960 and 1970, a corner was turned in the course
of the West. It is not possible to pinpoint a specific year, but it was
probably closer to the end of the decade than the beginning that
something fundamental happened to the psyche of American, indeed all
Western, society. It is difficult to be precise about what it was, but it
cannot be denied that it has happened, for the results are in evidence all
around us.

In *Howards End* E. M. Forster envisioned, with the coming of World
War I, an end to a way of life that Europe had known for almost a century.
To the extent that the beginning and end of an epoch can be sketched with
broad strokes, it appears as though we are now straddling another
cultural and historical discontinuity, that we have passed from the modern to what it seems appropriate to call the postmodern world.

From the birth of Christ to the Middle Ages, into the Renaissance and
through the doldrums of the Reformation, through war, famine, pesti-

lence, and about every other form of tribulation we know today, there was, in the Western world, a sustaining credo that gave a man, however high or low his station, a sense of what he was and what his ultimate fate would be. This belief was an acceptance, although sometimes questioned, of God as Creator and benefactor. A man of position could plunder, rape, or kill, but if he repented, he was assured of being forgiven and meriting a place in the next world. A serf, no matter how little of this world's largess he had, could, if he maintained his faith and adhered to the laws of God and the Church, look forward to an existence in eternity which would surpass that of any earthly king. The appearance and existence of man in this world (why we are here and not not here) was explained through the belief that there was one Being—God—whose existence was necessary, whose very essence it was to exist. Man existed because there was a Supreme Being who willed that this be so and had the power to make it so.

But starting in the seventeenth century, belief in God and the accompanying guarantee of happiness in the world to come was replaced as the *summum bonum* (ultimate good) for many of Europe's most eminent philosophers and scientists by belief in reason and progress. The most significant and lasting effect of the Enlightenment was to change the direction of man's gaze from heaven toward earth. The hierarchic, Scholastic, metaphysical system originated by Thomas Aquinas during the thirteenth century—a system that placed God at the top of the pyramid of Being, man farther down, and the animals and the plants lower still—was superseded in the nineteenth century by Hegel's system of the dialectic, with "Absolute Knowledge" as the ultimate metaphysical and historical goal. This is not to say that the best educated people of the nineteenth century had necessarily read Hegel (any more than the best educated people of the medieval period were directly acquainted with the writings of Aquinas), but they were influenced indirectly by what had become the world view of the time.

From the beginning of the Enlightenment, there was a strong current of belief among the intelligentsia that all aspects of life were improving with time, although this view was by no means universal. In Hegel's system, for example, it was assumed that there were answers to all questions, that they just had to be found, and that with perseverance they *would* be found. The feeling was that the rational, well-trained mind could solve any problem. To see that this was an extremely optimistic world view one need only recall that conflict, the quintessence of which is war, was presumed to result always in progress, an advance. In turn, each advance meant that the next conflict, caused by a clash of thesis with antithesis, would lead to a synthesis at a still higher level. The theorists projected a heaven on earth underpinned by reason, while on the practical side the benefits accruing from the Industrial Revolution were plainly visible.

Until the twentieth century, the new "religion" of reason and progress was almost exclusively for the intelligentsia. Most people still pinned their ultimate hope on the promise of a better existence in a life beyond this life. But as the century advanced, a large number of people, aided by easier access to higher education, progressed from a level of slightly more than subsistence to a level approaching what we now call affluence. After World War II, the rate of educational and economic progress became so rapid that a middle-class intelligentsia was generated, and the fruits of a secular golden age came to be expected by more people than at any previous time.

In *The Courage to Be*, published in 1952, Paul Tillich recognized the juggernaut of progress as a form of transcendence, a kind of immanent divinity. He characterized it as "the courage to be as a part [of something outside of oneself, as distinguished from the courage to be as oneself] in the productive process of history . . . the affirmation of oneself as a participant in the creative development of mankind."[1]

> It is not the tools and gadgets that are the *telos*, the inner aim of production; it is the production itself. The means are more than means; they are felt as creations, as symbols of the infinite possibilities implied in man's productivity. Being-itself is essentially productive. The way in which the originally religious word "creative" is applied without hesitation by Christian, and non-Christian, alike to man's productive activities indicates that the creative process of history is felt as divine. As such it includes the courage to be as a part of it.[2]

THE DEATH OF REASON (AS IMMANENT GOD)

But the attainment of a goal does not guarantee the satisfaction anticipated during its pursuit. When, in the 1950s, the generation of Americans that started out during the Great Depression achieved the economic security it had pursued so singlemindedly, there was a palpable hollowness in the victory. Success was bittersweet. For some reason, the affluent society didn't *feel good* about what it had accomplished. Once the striving

for success was over, it was left to the affluent society to *live* with its
success, and that proved to be more difficult than the ascent of the
mountain.

Although there was a widespread feeling of disquietude in the 1950s,
the values of the American way of life were not seriously questioned by the
middle class itself. (There was, however, criticism from the Academy,
typified by books such as William H. Whyte Jr.'s *The Organization Man*
and David Riesman's *The Lonely Crowd*.) Then, suddenly, in the 1960s,
young doctors, lawyers, academicians, and many who were preparing for
these careers—the sons and daughters of the depression generation—
began questioning the value of their work, something that had previously
seemed beyond question. Scholarship and research, up to this time so
bountifully subsidized and highly prized, in themselves and for what they
contributed to the American way of life, now seemed not as important and
in some cases even suspect. This is not to say that people stopped
working—and "progressing." Work, whether that of a farmer, businessman, or scholar, has always been valued highly in American society. For
many, work had once been a form of prayer, where the elect succeeded
and those out of favor with the Almighty did not. But during this time,
work became a less effective escape from and substitute for self. The tacitly
assumed congruence of working and living began to slip a little.*

Those who had reached and were reaching maturity in the 1960s
constituted the first American generation to *grow up* in affluence, having
been freed by their parents' success from the need to win it. This was,
therefore, the first generation to expect all the imagined benefits of
affluence. But working, succeeding, and "progressing" did not bring
happiness and fulfillment for many of these young people, any more than
it had for their parents. Unlike their parents, who had chafed and suffered
in silence during the fifties, they found this letdown intolerable. Triggered
by the awareness of the injustice of the Vietnam war (and, probably, even
more significantly by the prospect of having to put their own lives on the
line in that war), the disenchantment of a "critical mass" of the younger
generation became the foundation for a cultural revolt. And once the
insurrection began, it was joined, at least in spirit, by many of the
previous generation. Parents aped the life-style of their teenage children,
and college professors that of their students.

---

*The question of work and self will be considered in Chapter 7.

When the expectations of the golden age were not realized, the assumptions from which the goal had been projected—the supremacy of reason and progress, the advancement of knowledge, and so on—themselves became suspect. Walker Percy trenchantly and prophetically caught the sense of this epiphany in his novel *The Moviegoer*, published in 1960. The narrator, Binx Bolling, is speaking here:

> Until recent years, I read only "fundamental" books, that is, key books on key subjects, such as *War and Peace*, the novel of novels; *A Study of History*, the solution of the problem of time; Schroedinger's *What Is Life?*, Einstein's *The Universe as I See It*, and such. During those years I stood outside the universe and sought to understand it. I lived in my room as Anyone living Anywhere and read fundamental books and only for diversion took walks around the neighborhood and saw an occasional movie. Certainly it did not matter to me where I was when I read such a book as *The Expanding Universe*. The greatest success of this enterprise, which I call my vertical search, came one night when I sat in a hotel room in Birmingham and read a book called *The Chemistry of Life*. When I finished it, it seemed to me that the main goals of my search were reached or were in principle reachable, whereupon I went out and saw a movie called *It Happened One Night* which was itself very good. The only difficulty was although the universe had been disposed of, I myself was left over. There I lay in my hotel room with my search over yet still obliged to draw one breath and then the next. But now I have undertaken a different kind of search, a horizontal search. As a consequence, what takes place in my room is less important. What is important is what I shall find when I leave my room and wander in the neighborhood. Before I wandered as a diversion. Now I wander seriously and sit and read as a diversion.[3]

Binx Bolling came to realize that the rewards of the "vertical search"—essentially, the search of the intellectual, the pursuit of what William James called "knowledge about" as contrasted with "knowledge by acquaintance"—were limited, and that although he could master the "fundamental books" without too much difficulty, this was not the same as mastering himself. After putting the books down, *He* was "left over." At this point, Binx acquired a sense of the particularity of time and place, i.e., the particularity of *his* existing at a given instant. Sunlight, wind, clouds, and the smell of things became important to him because they were part of what made a day (and an instant) unique.

During the 1960s, Binx Bolling's discovery was made on a massive scale in this country. People began to realize that although they had been successful in the "vertical search," *they* had been "left over." It was not long before the disenchantment and emotional stress that accompanied this discovery crystallized as the counterculture movement, which was, in essence, an attempt to begin the "horizontal search"—the search for self.*

Another fictional search for the ineffable, "left over" self was initiated by Phaedrus, the protagonist of Robert M. Pirsig's *Zen and the Art of Motorcycle Maintenance* (1974). Precocious but emotionally unstable, Phaedrus starts college early, as a science major. He becomes absorbed in his work to the exclusion of everything else, and tries to use the abstract method of science to define and shape his most subjective feelings. In other words, he tries to extrapolate the method of scientific abstraction to what Husserl designated as the Life-World, the world that is lived through and felt prior to conceptualizing or philosophizing. Not surprisingly, he encounters only frustration and failure. After two years, Phaedrus is forced to drop out of school because of a nervous breakdown brought on by what he eventually recognizes as his obsessive concern with "hypotheses as entities in themselves." (Phaedrus tells his story in retrospect during a motorcycle trip from Minnesota to California. He is accompanied on the trip by two friends and his twelve-year-old son, Chris.)

Phaedrus later returns to college to study philosophy, looking for what he is able to express in words at this point only as "Quality." But he does not find this in his reading. What he is looking for is not in the books of Socrates, Plato, and the other analytical philosophers through Hegel. After finishing college, Phaedrus enrolls in a graduate program at the University of Chicago. But several years of formal study there bring him no closer to this elusive "Quality." Then, by chance, he picks up H. D. F. Kitto's book, *The Greeks*—for fifty cents!—and reads a commentary on the section of the *Iliad* where Hector is telling his wife, Andromache, why he will go into battle against the Achaeans, although it means certain death for him and subsequent enslavement for her. Kitto says that Hector's

---

*Traditionally, the term "vertical search" has been used to specify the search for God. For Binx Bolling, the vertical search was not a search for the Christian God, but for the god of Reason—i.e., knowledge.

motivation was not duty toward Troy or any other person, but primarily "duty toward himself." The Greeks called this *arete*, which we translate as "virtue," but which meant "excellence" to them. Suddenly ("Lightning hits!"), Phaedrus recognizes that Hector's courage was not just an *act* of courage, but an externalization and example of the "Quality" Phaedrus had pursued for so long and he was now able to express verbally as the "wholeness or oneness of life." The passage in Kitto's book that crystallizes this recognition for Phaedrus is the following:

> Thus the hero of the *Odyssey* is a great fighter, a wily schemer, a ready speaker, a man of stout heart and broad wisdom who knows that he must endure without too much complaining what the gods send; and he can both build and sail a boat, drive a furrow as straight as anyone, beat a young braggart at throwing the discus, challenge the Pheacian youth at boxing, wrestling or running; flay, skin, cut up and cook an ox, and be moved to tears by a song. He is in fact an excellent all-rounder; he has surpassing *arete*.
>
> *Arete* implies a respect for the wholeness or oneness of life, and a consequent dislike of specialization. It implies a contempt for efficiency—or rather a much higher idea of efficiency, an efficiency which exists not in one department of life but in life itself.[4]

That is what Phaedrus could not find in the writings of the analytical philosophers. And it had been there, in the sense that it had been "incarnated" through Homer's writing, at least five centuries before the dialecticians turned their backs on it, before it had been lost (in "word-traps")—no, thrown away—by Socrates et al. Phaedrus now sees that the object-subject, matter-mind, causality-freedom dichotomies that he had tried to integrate with the help of the analytical philosophers were not *inherent* in life, but *were put there by the analytical philosophers themselves*, and that within an existing human being, these polarities could be *distinguished*, but not *separated*. In language that could be Kierkegaard's, he concludes that "Quality" cannot be systematized and grasped through reason: "Any attempt to develop an organized reason around an undefined quality defeats its own purpose. The organization of reason itself defeats the quality." At this point, Phaedrus would have been able to understand what Unamuno meant in *Tragic Sense of Life* when he said of the *Discourse on Method* that its defect lay in Descartes's "resolution to begin by *emptying himself of himself*, of Descartes, of the real man, the man of flesh and bone, the man who does not want to die, in order that he might be a mere thinker—that is, an abstraction" (emphasis added). Phaedrus was looking for "himself" in a series of philosophical systems that had been "emptied" of the notion of self from the outset. Finally, he comes to realize that his search has been a "fool's mission to begin with." Phaedrus's search was very much like the "horizontal search" of Binx Bolling in *The Moviegoer*, although it was more systematic and more agonizing. Phaedrus, too, was looking for the *He* that had been "left over."

During the 1960s, the god of Reason—i.e., the transcendent value placed on the powers of reason, work, progress, analytical philosophy, and other manifestations of the supremacy of the intellect that originated largely with the Enlightenment—died for many in this country, as well as in the rest of the Western world. Reason was not abandoned, but it was dethroned as *summum bonum*. People did not stop thinking, working, and "progressing," they just came to feel that thinking, working, and "progressing" were not ultimate ends in themselves, that they did not constitute a raison d'être. To an appreciable extent, the transcendence of self through the god of Reason ceased. What Tillich called the "courage to be as a part of the productive process" lost its nerve, and thus its muscle.

But Reason was not the only deity to fall in the 1960s. Another god, far more powerful, longer established, and more widely worshiped, would not survive the decade either.

THE DEATH OF GOD

At the same time that so many of the growing middle class were finding a place within the affluent society, there was an erosion, first gradual, then drastic, of adherence to the traditional religious values. During the 1960s, the Jesuit theologian John Courtney Murray remarked that people were just "too damn busy" to be concerned about God. But that explanation, to say the least, was incomplete. On the cover of the 8 April 1966 issue of *Time* Magazine, the question was asked forthrightly: "Is God Dead?" (To understand just how much of a break with the ethos of the recent past this represented, try to imagine the same cover story appearing ten years earlier, in 1956, about halfway through the Eisenhower years.) An equally forthright answer to the question had already been given in the form of an obituary carried by the Methodist student magazine *motive*:

ATLANTA, Ga., Nov. 9—God, creator of the universe, principal deity of the world's Jews, ultimate reality of Christians, and most eminent of all divinities, died late yesterday during major surgery undertaken to correct a massive diminishing influence.

Reaction from the world's great and from the man in the street was uniformly incredulous . . . From Independence, Mo., former President Harry S. Truman, who received the news in his Kansas City barbershop, said "I'm always sorry to hear somebody is dead. It's a damn shame."

God, of course, is the lifeblood of theologians, and they did their best, even after surgery failed, to keep him alive. The brain waves were flat, but they refused to pull the plug. God was now comatose, "silent," "hidden." Another Jesuit, Karl Rahner, suggested that God had become an "anonymous presence." The German theologian Gerhard Ebeling opined that the problem might be a linguistic one: if language is an imperfect means of communicating, even when one man speaks to another, is it not reasonable that language should be inadequate to express the relationship of man and his Creator? And then Schubert Ogden suggested that instead of thinking of God as the immutable Prime Mover of the universe (*Ens causa sui*), he might be thought of as a process, the "ultimate effect," the "eminently relative One, whose openness to change contingently on the actions of others is literally boundless."[5] But perhaps that *is* pulling the plug!

What it comes down to, really, is faith. It no longer seems *possible* to believe in God. Why, now, after nearly two thousand years, is the Christian God falling from his throne?* "Christian incredulity," Camus wrote in 1943, "no longer leans on science and religion. It no longer is the skepticism of reason concerning the miracle. It is a passionate unbelief" (*incroyance passionnée*). Camus is not speaking here of anti-clericism or the kind of dissatisfaction with the institutional Church that Garry Wills describes in *Bare Ruined Choirs*. His "passionate unbelief" is directed at the heart of the Christian ethos, the claim of the Incarnation.

---

*Really, the Judeo-Christian God. Christianity was a logical outgrowth of Judaism as well as a counter-movement against it. The term "Judeo-Christian" signifies the continuity of the Jewish and Christian religions (see Friedrich Nietzsche, *The Anti-Christ*, trans. R. J. Hollingdale [Harmondsworth, Middlesex, England: Penguin Books Ltd., 1968], pp. 134–41).

Science has not killed God—quite the contrary. It is clearer now than ever that what we can learn from science is limited to what is abstract and quantifiable. Because of what science has achieved, the unresolved (and undoubtedly unresolvable) dilemmas of what Unamuno called the "man of flesh and bone; the man who is born, suffers, and dies—above all, who dies" are more poignant, the mysteries deeper. God is needed now more than ever before. Nietzsche felt it was man's need for God that "created" him in the first place (*Deus ex machina*). From what he called the "retrospective inference . . . the inference from the work to its author, from the deed to its doer, from the ideal to him who *needs* it, from every mode of thinking and valuing to the imperative *want* behind it," Nietzsche asks, "Has hunger or superfluity become creative here?"

While Nietzsche understood that the need for God (for transcendence) was undiminished, he recognized that European theism was declining. In *Beyond Good and Evil*, he wrote that "though the religious instinct is in vigorous growth, it rejects the theistic satisfaction with profound distrust." Because, during times of personal stress and cultural breakdown, people flock to the churches does not mean they are deriving genuine satisfaction from this religious activity. The febrile ceremonies of the Pentecostal movement, for example, seem more like a "last hurrah" than a return to the fervid Christianity of the catacombs. As Philip Rieff notes in *The Triumph of the Therapeutic*, "There will be more singing and more listening. People will continue to genuflect and read the Bible . . ."[6] But, Rieff points out, it is the therapist and not the priest who is looked to for the final word now.*

The notion of the dead God is new to us, but Nietzsche recognized more than a century ago that Christianity would lose its power over the imagination of Western man. The following is an excerpt—the parable of "The Madman"—from *Joyful Wisdom*, written in 1882, where Nietzsche announced the Death of God, as well as the perils that would face those who were to live in a world without him:

> Have you ever heard of the madman who on a bright morning lighted a lantern and ran to the market-place calling out unceas-

---

*Let us be fair about this. The churches *are* attempting to insert reality into their teaching. But the irony is that the farther they go in this direction, the more truly secular they are becoming. The farther they move into the real world, the less sound the foundation of the religious world appears.

ingly: "I seek God! I seek God!"—As there were many people standing about who did not believe in God, he caused a great deal of amusement. Why? is he lost? said one. Has he strayed away like a child? said another. Or does he keep himself hidden? Is he afraid of us? Has he taken a sea-voyage? Has he emigrated?—the people cried out laughingly, all in a hubbub. The insane man jumped into their midst and transfixed them with his glances. "Where is God gone?" he called out. "I mean to tell you! *We have killed him,*—you and I! We are all his murderers! But how have we done it? How were we able to drink up the sea? Who gave us the sponge to wipe away the whole horizon? What did we do when we loosened this earth from its sun? Whither does it now move? Whither do we move? Away from all suns? Do we not dash on unceasingly? Backwards, sideways, forwards, in all directions? Is there still an above and below? Do we not stray as through infinite nothingness? Does not empty space breathe upon us? Has it not become colder? Does not night come on continually, darker and darker? Shall we not have to light lanterns in the morning? Do we not hear the noise of the grave-diggers who are burying God? Do we not smell the divine putrefaction?—for even Gods putrefy! God is dead! God remains dead! And we have killed him! How shall we console ourselves, the most murderous of all murderers? The holiest and the mightiest that the world has hitherto possessed, has bled to death under our knife,—who will wipe the blood from us? With what water could we cleanse ourselves? What lustrums, what sacred games shall we have to devise? Is not the magnitude of this deed too great for us? Shall we not ourselves have to become Gods, merely to seem worthy of it? There never was a greater event,—and on account of it, all who are born after us belong to a higher history than any history hitherto!"—Here the madman was silent and looked again at his hearers; they also were silent and looked at him in surprise. At last he threw his lantern on the ground, so that it broke in pieces and was extinguished. "I come too early," he then said, "I am not yet at the right time. This prodigious event is still on its way, and is travelling,—it has not yet reached men's ears. Lightning and thunder need time, the light of the stars needs time, deeds need time, even after they are done, to be seen and heard. This deed is as yet further from them than the furthest star,—*and yet they have done it!*"—It is further stated that the madman made his way into different churches on the same day, and there intoned his *Requiem aeternam deo.* When led out and called to account, he always gave the reply: "What are these churches now, if they are not the tombs and monuments of God?"[7]

Nietzsche, indeed, had "come too early." The event was "still on its way." But the time required for his madman to appear not only sane but also right on the mark has elapsed, as inevitably as it does with the sound of thunder and the light of stars. Nietzsche foresaw that the world without God would be very different from what it had been with him. In his book *Existentialism*, Ralph Harper explains how Christianity added another facet to "the tragic sense of life" already known to the Greeks:

> Christianity has offered to guarantee the infinite worth of each person—not just humanity—by the appearance on earth of God himself, and by Christ's promises to leave us his gift of the Holy Ghost, the Comforter. Even if Christianity is—as many suspect—a sham and a mirage, we can recognize that its promises have been printed into the nerve of our Western attitudes towards life. As long as one can say there may be time and a chance to overcome the seemingly ineradicable tragedy of human life, "the eternal wound of existence," as Nietzsche put it, hope will remain, and inversely, frustration wax more bitter.[8]

As long as someone who has lost his faith in the promise of Christianity, either totally or in part, cannot overcome the *desire* that the promise be fulfilled, he will remain, as Harper says, "infected." In Percy's novel *The Moviegoer*, Binx Bolling lives in a world where faith in a transcendent, omnipotent Being has been lost, while the nostalgia for transcendence remains unabated. Nostalgia for the absolute is rooted deeply in the human heart and, once lodged there, is not easily quenched.

The problem of the Death of God goes beyond getting over the "broken promise" of immortality. The Christian was told that because his human nature was derivative of the divine nature, he was to act in accordance with certain rules set down by God and by the Church. If God is dead, however, these rules no longer have any meaning, and one must hence-forth make his own rules and determine his own values. This all sounds rather heady, but is at least as difficult and painful as it is exhilarating. In a world without God, Sartre says, we are "condemned to freedom" and, therefore, to the anguish of responsibility which that freedom demands: "I am *abandoned* in the world not in the sense that I might remain abandoned and passive in a hostile universe like a board floating on the water, but rather in the sense that I find myself suddenly alone and without help, engaged in a world for which I bear the whole responsibility without being able whatever I do, to tear myself away from this responsibility for an instant."[9]

There are, of course, some whose lives have never been touched by religion, or by *any* notion of God. For them the Death of God is a non-event.*

NO "*SUMMUM BONUM*"

If either the Death of God or the Death of Reason—the widespread recognition of the limits of reason and progress—had occurred without the other, that would have been one thing. But during the ten years between 1960 and 1970, the crisis of religious belief peaked almost simultaneously with the trembling of the Temple of Reason. The problem now is that it has become increasingly difficult for a growing number of people to pin their ultimate hope on either the promises of religious faith *or* the immanent "gods" of reason, work, and progress. There is now no *summum bonum*, no final desiderative value that seems secure. That so many people, such a large fraction of the population of the West, should suddenly find themselves bereft of any access to transcendence (other than self-transcendence) is without precedent, and nothing less than a major discontinuity in Western cultural history.

---

*We have been stating the extreme case here. Even for those who still "believe" in a transcendent divinity, the *degree* of transcendence (sustenance) made possible by religious belief is considerably less now than it was up to, say, 1960. Many people are now experiencing what could be thought of as the "dying" of God, rather than the "death" of God.

The appearance of the Charismatics, the Pentecostals, the Born Again Christians, the Moonies, the faith healers, and other similar groups has been interpreted by some as a rebirth of religious sentiment. Rather, it seems that this frenetic activity at the fringes is replacing the traditional religious center, which is not holding. In Germany and France during the 1920s and 1930s, a similar and short-lived explosion of interest in the mystical and the occult occurred. Other manifestations of this phenomenon have appeared throughout history during periods of cultural instability (see C. G. Jung, *Modern Man in Search of a Soul*, Chapter 10, trans. by W. S. Dell and Carry F. Baynes [New York: Harcourt, Brace & World, Inc., 1933]).

Roger Quillot sees our situation this way: "A universe which is deprived or freed of God, but not resigned to this fact, and which is looking for the moon in a thousand places."

A striking manifestation of this cultural discontinuity occurred in 1970 with the publication of Charles Reich's book *The Greening of America*. The revelation did not come so much from the substance of the book, although there were epiphanies, as from the reaction of middle-class American adults to it. Reich had touched a nerve, and the twinge was felt everywhere from the op-ed page of the *New York Times* to the Women's Club of Roland Park in Baltimore. The tenor of the reviews was that Reich had asked the right questions, but was wrong about many of the answers. Particularly ingenuous was the book's main theme—that the revolution of consciousness occurring among young Americans would, as its denouement, change the political structure of the country. One reviewer suggested that more of value to the understanding of the current cultural crisis had come from the discussion triggered by the book than from the book itself. But whatever the shortcomings of the guided tour through Consciousness I, II, and III, it must be credited to Reich that his verdancy gave voice to the pain for many who otherwise would not have known how to express it.

At about the time *The Greening of America* was published, several other writers came out with books that attempted to fathom the causes of the cultural crisis. In *Future Shock* Alvin Toffler tried to explain the new trauma as a kind of culture shock: progress had been so rapid—things had changed so fast, especially since the end of the World War II—that Americans were unable to adapt to the change and had lost their bearings. Then there was a book by Philip Slater called *The Pursuit of Loneliness*, which was not as widely read as the books by Reich and Toffler, but which received considerable critical attention. Slater's theme was that individualism, i.e., the pursuit of individual interests, was at the core of the problem, and that the "new culture" (what Reich called Consciousness III) would reverse this trend by subordinating the interests of the individual to the "common good."

Probably the finest analysis of the cultural discontinuity that surfaced during the 1960s was Theodore Roszak's book *The Making of a Counter Culture*. Unlike those of Reich and Slater, Roszak's analysis was not marred by an uncritical advocacy of the counterculture movement and a sycophancy toward the motivations of the young. He diagnosed correctly the cause of the crisis (as did Reich) as a dichotomy of self—the rending within the self of reason and passion, intellect and feeling, the head and the heart: ". . . at the ethical level of discussion, the choice comes down most often to one between two styles of conduct. One pursues a rational style of life, we say, if one's behavior is characterized by dispassionate restraint, unfailing deliberateness, and an articulated logicality. Conversely, one is irrational if one's conduct forsakes dispassion in favor of an intense and overt emotionalism, deliberation in favor of impulsiveness, articulation and logic in favor of rhapsodic declamation or some manner of non-verbal expression." Roszak had no trouble seeing that in the current technocratic society, reason, intellect, and the head had taken hegemony over passion, feeling, and the heart. "The capacity of our emerging technocratic paradise to denature the imagination by appropriating to itself the whole meaning of Reason, Reality, Progress, and Knowledge," he said, "will render it impossible for men to give any name to their bothersomely unfilled potentialities but that of madness."

In his analysis of the counterculture revolt, Roszak cited primarily the work of contemporary social critics such as Herbert Marcuse, Norman Brown, Allen Ginsberg, Alan Watts, Timothy Leary, and Paul Goodman, all of whom had questioned and found lacking the values of the current technological world view. But Roszak's book has two significant shortcomings. First, although he identified the dichotomy of self in Western society and skillfully characterized the antinomies of the head and the heart, the emphasis of his thought was often against the ethos of the time to such an extent—he was, after all, writing about a *counter*culture—that the "heart side" of the dichotomy predominated at the expense of the "head side." The second shortcoming (and this is not unrelated to the first) is that Roszak failed to take note of an earlier and more profound revolt, a reaction fired by the split in Western philosophical thought, which became manifest in all Western culture, between the intellect and, let us say, the rest of what makes us what we are. That dichotomy originated with Plato, widened with the Scholasticism of the Middle Ages, and became all but complete with Descartes's declaration "*Cogito ergo sum*" and Hegel's system of objective idealism. This philosophical and literary revolt began in the nineteenth century (although Augustine and Pascal, thirteen centuries apart, had sounded the call much earlier), and eventually became known as existentialism. The term derives from the emphasis of the existential—the unique, *existing* human being—over the essential, a more general and abstract consideration of man's essence.*

---

* This distinction between existence and essence requires some further elaboration. "Essence" here is identified with philosophical idealism, and is not the essence of the phenomenological reduction, which will be considered later.

(*Who* am I as contrasted with *What* is man?) The Jesuit philosopher Hunter Guthrie pointed out just what it was that the existentialists revolted against:

> The history of Western philosophy presents a striking phenomenon: since its first memories, from the time of Plato and Aristotle, men have exercised their ingenuity in fashioning a philosophy of *essence*. Through the centuries, essential man (never existential man) has been studied, analyzed, dissected, and afterwards reconstructed in the domain of thought . . . Ideal man has taken the place of real man. So most of the conclusions of the history of philosophy bear on a being which does not exist at all . . . These conclusions, placed beside living and tumultuous reality, presented the curious but futile spectacle of a portrait of man taking the place of man himself. It only lacks life.[10]

Guthrie has put his finger right on the problem: "Ideal man [i.e., inauthentically transcendent man] has taken the place of real man." We have lost ourselves (*our selves*) in delusions and abstractions—the delusion of a divine heritage (Guthrie would not have agreed with this) and the abstractions of reason (as an immanent god), which cut us off from the rest of what we could have become. But the "portrait of man taking the place of man himself" is no longer an adequate substitute for the real thing. The escapes from self (inauthentic transcendences) that were successful in the past do not have the same assuasive effect as before. The Emperor is naked, i.e., *we* are naked. The center has not held: Yeats's rough beasts whose time has come slouch toward Bethlehem at an ever-increasing rate, only to die there ever more rapidly. What is needed, as Guthrie said, is a philosophical activity of *life itself*—the philosophical counterpart of the Museum without Walls of the plastic arts—"an activity produced directly from the warmth and turbulence of existence, [the] analysis of which would give us a secret vision of the true personal reality."

This is what the existential revolt was and continues to be about. A brief definition would be risky, but this one by Hwa Yol Jung is useful, since it bears directly on our theme here: "Existentialism is a philosophy of revolt against mass man who lost his authentic selfhood in modern technology and industrial culture."[11] If a father of existentialism must be named it is Kierkegaard, perhaps with Nietzsche as correspondent. The progeny, just to cite some of the principal and best-known names, include Husserl, Kafka, Heidegger, Jaspers, Unamuno, Ortega, Merleau-Ponty, Buber, Berdyaev, Marcel, Tillich, Camus, and Sartre.

EXISTENTIAL SHOCK AND THE MARGINAL SELF

The sense of anomie (homelessness) that has been experienced and articulated by Camus, Sartre, Beckett, and other writers of the past generation—as well as by Kierkegaard, Nietzsche, and Heidegger before them—has, during the last few years, come to be felt by the middle-class American adult, and perhaps even more painfully by his children. The Death of God–Death of Reason trauma, what it seems appropriate to call "existential shock," is just now beginning to affect the man in the street, the "average person" against whom Kierkegaard defined himself a century-and-a-half ago. Existential shock is the trauma of the self facing its existence and, as an essential fact of that existence, its mortality—the certainty of its eventual annihilation in death—without delusions and false transcendences. It encompasses Kierkegaard's dread, the anguish characterized by Heidegger and Sartre, and the pain inherent in Camus's absurd condition. This anxiety, Tillich wrote in *The Courage to Be*, "is existential in the sense that it belongs to existence as such and not to an abnormal state of mind as in neurotic (and psychotic) anxiety."[12] Anxiety (*Angst*) is to be distinguished from fear (*Furcht*) in that fear has a definite object which can be faced, analyzed, attacked, and endured, while anxiety has no definite object.* Paradoxically, its object is the negation of every object, i.e., Nothingness. Tillich describes the interrelatedness of the *fear* and the *anxiety* of dying:

Insofar as it is *fear* its object is the anticipated event of being killed by sickness or an accident and thereby suffering agony and the loss of everything. Insofar as it is *anxiety* its object is the absolute unknown "after death," the nonbeing which remains non-being

---

* Tillich's definition of anxiety is not consistent with current clinical theory. Fear always has an object, but there is also object-related anxiety, which must be differentiated from diffuse or free-floating anxiety that has no object.

even if it is filled with the images of our present experience. The dreams in Hamlet's soliloquy, "to be or not to be," which we may have after death and which make cowards of us all are frightful not because of their manifest content but because of their power to symbolize the threat of nothingness, in religious terms of "eternal death."[13]

Because anxiety has no object, it strives, Tillich says, to become fear, because fear, unlike anxiety, is concrete and can be dealt with. Furthermore, he says, if existential anxiety is not recognized and accepted as such, it can become pyschological anxiety and manifest itself as psychological fear. Although *The Courage to Be* was not published until 1952—at least a decade before the Death of God occurred for the "average person"—the following excerpt could have been a blueprint for what was to happen in the 1960s:

There is a moment in which the self-affirmation of the average man becomes neurotic: when changes of the reality to which he is adjusted threaten the fragmentary courage with which he has mastered the accustomed objects of fear. If this happens—as it often does in critical periods of history—the self-affirmation becomes pathological. The dangers connected with the change, the unknown character of things to come, the darkness of the future make the average man a fanatical defender of the established order. He defends it as compulsively as the neurotic defends the castle of his imaginary world. He loses his comparative openness to reality, he experiences an unknown depth of anxiety. But if he is not able to take this anxiety into his self-affirmation his anxiety turns into neurosis. *This is the explanation for the mass neuroses which usually appear at the end of an era. In such periods existential anxiety is mixed with neurotic anxiety to such a degree that historians and analysts are unable to draw the boundary lines sharply* [emphasis added].[14]

We have coined the term "existential shock" to commemorate what we have come to see as the forced metaphysical coming of age of contemporary man. About thirty years ago, Sartre said that existentialism was for "philosophers and specialists" exclusively. Although there will undoubtedly always be something "exclusive" about Sartre, so much has changed in our world since then that the major existential themes are fast becoming the concern of contemporary men—*whether they like it or not*—because their delusions and inauthentic transcendences no longer adequately mask their condition as existing human beings. Because there are no longer any viable absolutes, either transcendent *or* immanent, there are no longer any *paths* to absolutes along which the self may be drawn, absorbed, and, ultimately, lost. The "average person" of the present is now just beginning to feel the full weight of his existence, as the existentialists—the philosophers of existence—always have. Contemporary man, the "average person," has lost the *context* of his existence. He has become, in the words of Max Scheler, "problematic to himself." He no longer stands on terra firma, but is disoriented as if "shipwrecked" (a word used by Kierkegaard, Ortega, and Jaspers) at night in waters of indeterminate depth, with clouds obscuring the stars that had once made navigation straightforward.

Our problem now is, to coin another term, the problem of the "marginal self"*—*a self that is inadequate to the demands of its condition.* (By "condition" we mean what Sartre characterizes as the "human condition": ". . . the necessity for man to exist in the world, to be at work there, to be there in the midst of other people, and to be mortal there.") The marginal self is reeling from the effects of having just so recently lost its transcendences. Weaning it from sources that have given ontic life-support successfully for centuries will be difficult and painful, but the lack of satisfaction received from clinging to the vestiges of failed absolutes has itself become so painful that breaking the dependence seems to be the most salutary (as well as authentic) next step.

With a very different end in mind, Unamuno, a Christian existentialist who believed that consciousness would not cease with death, spoke in *Tragic Sense of Life* of "awakening the sleeper" to his existence, and of the pain that is inherent in this authentic existence:

---

* The terms "marginal self " and "existential shock" are typological ones and do not apply equally to everyone. Thus, some "selves" are less "marginal" than others, and it is possible for a person to experience existential shock even if the Death of God has no bearing on his life—as would be the case if he had never had faith, or had gotten over the need for transcendent affirmation—if, for example, his sense of the absolute has been repealed by some aspect of the Death of Reason (as immanent god). Existential shock follows from the absence of *any* viable absolute or transcendence. These terms characterize an ontic response *and* a cultural manifestation of that response. They are useful because, in helping to

The cure for suffering—which, as we have said, is the collision of consciousness with unconciousness—is not to be submerged in unconsciousness, but to be raised in consciousness and to suffer more. The evil suffering is cured by more suffering, by higher suffering. Do not take opium, but put salt and vinegar in the soul's wound, for when you sleep and no longer feel the suffering, you are not. And to be, that is imperative.[15]

To be—that is the imperative and the question. Where Unamuno called for a "higher suffering" through which men would open themselves to their *need* for immortality, Camus, an atheistic existentialist who denied the possibility of immortality, felt that we must become "superior to our fate," to the fate of the absurd (i.e., unrequited) longing of man for immortality and the absolute.

In *The Survivor* Terrence Des Pres has written about the fight for survival of the prisoners of Auschwitz and Buchenwald against a system of man-made horror on a scale that was not only unprecedented, but barely comprehensible. "When mythic structures collapse and symbolism fails," he wrote, "the choice is ourselves or nothing." He characterized the condition of self in the camps as "in extremity," and distinguished two stages in the prisoners' encounter with their condition:

The first encounter with extremity immersed prisoners in a world of pure terror, a world in which nothing made sense or promised hope. The impact was so sudden and overwhelming that the self floundered and began to disintegrate. In shock and disbelief, prisoners went about as if asleep, as if locked in a horrid dream, not responding intelligently, not looking out for themselves. The first phase of survival experience may thus be described as a period of *initial collapse*. Given time, however, breakdown was followed by a second stage, characterized by re-integration of selfhood and recovery of stability. Very much as if they were waking up, survivors went from withdrawal to engagement, from passivity to resistance. They

continuation

crystallize something that is illusive and amorphous in the present culture, they facilitate the analysis and, thus, the understanding of it.

emerged from their dream-state to face the hard reality, to see their predicament with relentless clarity.[16]

Existentially, we are all "in extremity" now. We are *metaphysical survivors*, survivors of failed philosophical and religious absolutes. Because at the present time the marginal self is inadequate to the demands of its condition, we are in what could be thought of, ontically, as a period of "initial collapse." The "second stage" will begin only after we are able to say as one survivor, a doctor, said of his experience: ". . . the horror turned into revolt [in the sense Camus uses the term] and this revolt shook me out of my lethargy and gave me a new incentive to live." We are now groping in the nihilistic miasma that Nietzsche said would come once the dead God began to putrefy. He described this collapse of belief in the meaning and value of life in *The Will to Power*:

> Extreme positions are not succeeded by moderate ones but by extreme positions of the opposite kind. Thus the belief in the absolute immorality of nature, in [aimlessness] and meaninglessness, is the psychologically necessary affect once the belief in God and an essentially moral order becomes untenable. Nihilism appears at that point, not that the displeasure at existence has become greater than before but because one has come to mistrust any "meaning" in suffering, indeed in existence. One interpretation has collapsed; but because it was considered *the* interpretation it now seems as if there were no meaning at all in existence, as if everything were in vain.[17]

Nietzsche felt that nihilism would be an unavoidable *stage* in the recovery of the self from the artificial worlds of Christianity and Reason, but that this stage would end once men developed the strength to accept the world as it was, to "deify becoming and the apparent world as the only world, and to call them good."

CAN MAN BE MAN?

The marginal self does not (yet) have, to use Tillich's phrase, the "courage to be *as oneself*," as contrasted with the "courage to be *as a part*." The historical "courage to be as a part"—i.e., as a part of something else, whether the Logos of Being and the divine power of reason (Stoic courage), the God of Theism (the courage of the Middle Ages), the collectivist god (the courage of the Communists and Nazis, for example), the courage of the "God above the God of Theism" (the God that issued from the Protestant Reformation), and so forth—is no longer viable because there is nothing now sufficiently viable to be a "part" of.

Our century appears to be an endpoint—and a starting point—in a kind of ontic evolution. This juncture represents, at once, a synthesis of every rational, aesthetic, cultural, and religious motif ever sounded, and a rejection of all that has been tried and found wanting. The Scholastics and the Greeks, confronting man's fragile condition, felt that their nostalgia had a goal, a destination. Even while Pascal was anguished because God was "hidden" from him, he felt he *had* to choose an absolute, i.e., believe. Camus *refuses* to believe because he *cannot*. His nostalgia remained unabated, but also undirected (hence the elegiac tone in much of his writing). The inability to choose—the *impossibility* of choosing—an absolute is, more than anything else, what characterizes contemporary man. This leaves open the question of man's ultimate meaning and gives rise to the anxiety of meaninglessness.

Tillich acknowledged that the closest man had come to being as oneself, i.e., without transcendent affirmation (but *not* without others), was the "creative courage" of the existentialists, the "courage of despair" that permits one to take the anxiety of meaninglessness into himself and, with that as the *starting point*, affirm a meaning for himself "in spite of" meaninglessness. This is the challenge to the marginal self if it is to "transcend" its marginality and become adequate to its condition.

The position of the existentialists rests on bedrock because all illusions are denied here, all transcendences other than the immanent transcendence of self are rejected. In *Temptations of Religion* Charles Davis characterized religion as "the drive toward transcendence, the thrust of man out and beyond himself, out of and beyond the limited order under which he lives, in an attempt to open himself to the totality of existence and reach unlimited reality and ultimate value." For the atheistic existentialist, transcendence toward an absolute (as in the quest for "unlimited reality and ultimate value"), whether attempted through the Christian God, the god of Reason, or some other external absolute, implies a loss of self, while the authentic, immanent transcendence of what is "transcendable" in *our condition* ("the limited order in which [we live]") results in the *creation* of self. As Camus said, it is necessary to become "superior to"—more than—our fate.

In contrast with Hegel's belief that reason would ultimately provide answers for all questions, it seems now, at least for the most important questions, that there *are* no answers, if by "answers" we mean prescriptions of thought and action spelled out by the individuals and institutions that fulfilled this function successfully in the past. The efforts to pursue objectivity—"to rise above the realm of Becoming and find a truth universal and eternal," as Jean Wahl expressed it—that underpinned the work of philosophers as diverse as Plato, Aquinas, Descartes, Spinoza, and Hegel, have proven, finally, to be unsatisfactory. This is the first time in history—it has taken this long—that so many men, standing in the wreckage of smashed religious and philosophical systems, are being forced to see themselves, as well as their relations with others and with this world, as Camus said, "without illusions and lights," and live in a "closed universe," "without appeal." Beckett must have sensed himself at this watershed when he wrote: "There is nothing to express, nothing with which to express, nothing from which to express, no power to express, no desire to express, together with an obligation to express . . ."[18] This would appear to be the ultimate cry, *de profundis*, of nihilism, the nihilism of which Camus said, "I have searched only for reasons to transcend it."

WHY TURN TO THE EXISTENTIALISTS?

For our consideration of the marginal self—and, through its unveiling, the authentic, integral self as well—we turn to the existentialists because the self has always been one of their chief concerns, in a sense, their province. The analytical philosophers (the philosophers of essence) are not much help here. Indeed, they have contributed their share to the fashioning of the marginal self, as we have already seen from the tribulations of Pirsig's fictional Phaedrus, and the delineation by Guthrie and Unamuno of what is intentionally omitted in this kind of philosophizing.

Existentialism, at least in this country, has had a bad press. It is understood by very few and superficially misunderstood by many. Part of the problem is that the existential revolt, at least that of the atheistic existentialists in all its implications, is on a scale equal to the introduction of Christianity into history. No discontinuity of this magnitude can be expected to occur smoothly. Christianity certainly did not! Then there is the forbidding and apocalyptic vocabulary of the existentialist, a vocabulary that reflects the weight of his themes: Nothingness, nihilation, anguish, dread, and so forth. Unfortunately—and incorrectly—these terms convey the impression that the thrust of existentialism is negative. (The titles of Sartre's novel *Nausea* and Camus's novel *The Plague* do nothing to assuage this suspicion.) Also, it must be admitted, there is a certain coldness and aridity in the writing of Sartre, who, wrongly, has come to epitomize the existential position for many people.

Tillich offers a somewhat different explanation for why so many have resisted the ideas of the existentialists:

> They are unable to understand what is happening in our period. They are unable to distinguish the genuine [i.e., existential] from the neurotic anxiety in Existentialism. They attack as a morbid longing for negativity what in reality is courageous acceptance of the negative. They call decay what is actually the creative expression of decay. They reject as meaningless the meaningful attempt to reveal the meaninglessness of our situation. It is not the ordinary difficulty of understanding those who break new ways in thinking and artistic expression which produces the widespread resistance to recent Existentialism but the desire to protect a self-limiting courage to be as a part.[19]

These people lack, to use Tillich's phrase, the "courage of despair." Their resistance is a symptom of neurotic character because in avoiding, among other realities, the idea and the implications of their own ineluctable confrontation with non-Being (Nothingness), they are distorting—and thus reducing—their Being. After all, as Tillich points out, "one does not feel spiritually threatened by something which is not an element of oneself."

There is a limit to what we can reasonably expect to learn about ourselves and our condition from the existentialists. The basic reason for this is the obvious, although often willfully overlooked, fact that our lives (our selves) are, finally, necessarily our own, and must be forged by each individual himself (although always in conjunction with others). The existential literature does not comprise an all-encompassing blueprint for living because there *is* no such thing. It endeavors to clear away religious and philosophical illusions that have accreted over centuries, diminishing man's ability to actualize himself. It does not so much provide answers to problems as delineate a starting point and *map the territory* for the pursuit of authentic existence. David E. Roberts has expressed this very nicely: "[Existentialism] calls men away from stifling abstractions and automatic conformity. It drives us back to the most basic, inner problems: what it means to be a self, how we ought to use our freedom, how we can find and keep the courage to face death. And even more important, it bids each individual thinker wrestle with these problems until he has grown into personal authenticity, instead of simply taking his answers from someone else."[20]

We are now approximately halfway through what Nietzsche, in *The Genealogy of Morals* (1887), called the "great hundred-act play reserved for the next two centuries of Europe" (see epigraph). At the moment, we do not seem to be doing very well. But, in a sense, it is still early. Our absurd condition has been "unmasked" for just a brief time now. If existential shock is to be coped with by the large segment of Western society now experiencing it—for it is irreversible and will not go away—this will be because we accept, finally, that trying to be God is, as Sartre said, a "useless passion," that the god of Reason has been interred alongside the Christian God, and that we must therefore become men. It will be because we achieve a viable dialectic between the possibilities of our freedom and the limitations of our condition. If there is an "existential imperative," it is that the subjective understanding of ourselves—*our selves*—must become more acute, and that we must feel our union with others and with the world more strongly than ever.

2

Self and the Existential Tradition (I):

Kierkegaard, Husserl, and Heidegger

Because the existential tradition is not widely understood, we are devoting this and the following chapter to a brief historical summary that covers five of the principal figures: Kierkegaard, Husserl, Heidegger, Sartre, and Camus. These are the "big guns" of existentialism because they played the most prominent parts in the "revolt" that the existential tradition is. Our summary is not intended to be comprehensive, either with respect to any one writer or to the tradition itself. But it should make clear what existentialism is and where it came from, as well as convey something of the ambience of the tradition. We will be referring to these five writers throughout the book, and to other existentialists, including Jaspers, Marcel, Ortega, and Buber.

Existentialism is not a philosophy in the usual sense, but a loose confederation of philosophical and literary ventures that have similar thematic elements. This is why we speak of the existential tradition, rather than, say, the existential system or movement. One cannot read a single existentialist and expect to get anything like the whole picture of the tradition. There are many facets, and there has been a great deal of intramural squabbling. In this century, just about everyone associated with the tradition—including Sartre—has declared at one time or another, "I am not an existentialist!"

Our summary focuses on two points: first, the emphasis that the existentialists, in their wrestling with the notion of self, have put on the concrete and the subjective, as contrasted with the abstract and the objective, the realm of the analytical philosophers; and second, the consequences of the fact that atheistic existentialism, in reversing the priority of essence over existence, generated a paradox that is the reverse of the Christian paradox. More concisely, this summary centers on the notion of self created in a world where the impact of the Incarnation has been neutralized.

KIERKEGAARD

There is more than a little irony in the fact that Sören Kierkegaard, the Danish thinker who lived between 1813 and 1855, has come to be known as the father of contemporary existentialism, a philosophical tradition that is today perceived largely as atheistic. In fact, Kierkegaard was a passionate, if not desperate (although certainly unorthodox) Christian for most of his life. He was not a philosopher in the usual sense. Rather, his motivation for writing was primarily religious, and he stated often that his ultimate goal was "to become a Christian."

Kierkegaard's argument was not with the existence of God or with what was required of a man to believe in him, but with what he saw as a corrupted Christianity. His anger was directed toward nineteenth-century Protestantism, which, he felt, was ignoring Christ's injunction that the individual create himself actively and passionately in relation to the Eternal, and was instead propagating rational abstractions in ethics and dogma. Kierkegaard's most virulent criticism of the theologians of his day was that they had become "systematic philosophers" in the spirit of Hegel. Kierkegaard attacked Hegel savagely for constructing a system that attempted to fit together the inner and the outer worlds in a way that he claimed was *rationally and historically necessary*. By being subordinated to the necessities of the total scheme, passions, desires, and anything else that characterizes the human and the individual are, in actuality, circumvented. The complexities and agonies of the self are explained away and subsumed in the categories. Kierkegaard felt that *any* philosophical system "fantastically dissipates the concept of existence." His reaction to reading Hegel was that "it is like reading out of a cookbook to a man who is hungry."*[1]

---

* In footnote 1, some idea is given of the provisions that Hegel (as well as Kant) made for

Kierkegaard's greatest achievement was to initiate a revolt against the prevailing tack of the analytical philosophers, that of abstraction and the ideal, and redirect attention to the individual, existing human being. The magnitude of this accomplishment can be appreciated only by realizing how radically his position went against the ethos of the time. Following Kierkegaard's lead, all the existential thinkers, Christian and atheistic, covering the spectrum from Heidegger to Tillich, emphasize the singleness and uniqueness of the individual, with subjectivity—in contrast with the objectivity of the analytical philosophers—as the starting point. Surprisingly, considering the compass of the tradition, Kierkegaard's voluminous work contains most of the seeds that came to fruition in the later generations of existentialists. For any reader who started with Sartre and Camus, reading Kierkegaard is like seeing for the first time the well-preserved face of the grandfather of a close acquaintance.

"Each age," Kierkegaard wrote, "has its own characteristic depravity. Ours is perhaps not pleasure or indulgence or sensuality, but rather a dissolute pantheistic contempt for the individual." Looking around him, he saw that his contemporaries, in their relations with both God and the world, had surrendered concreteness to abstraction, uniqueness to the mentality of the crowd. Ironically, the heritage of rationalism and progress from the Enlightenment, a movement that sought to place man at the center of things, had caused the center of man to be displaced from himself. Kierkegaard felt that the misfortune of his time was that it had "too much knowledge, that it [had] forgotten what it means to exist." He did nothing less than reopen the landscape of interiority and begin charting the contours of self. In *Repetition* he asks: "Who am I? How did I come into the world? Why was I not consulted? If I am compelled to take a part in it, where is the director? If there is no director, where shall I take my complaint? Am I guilty or not?"[2]

Kierkegaard saw the self as polar and split: man is human and finite, yet he clearly longs for something beyond the human and finite, namely, the Eternal. Augustine, perhaps the earliest existentialist forerunner, expressed the direction of this longing (for the Christian) in lapidary words: "Our hearts were made for Thee, O Lord, and are restless till they rest in Thine." On one hand, a man may have a good enough life if he works at it and is not overwhelmed by either the normal disappointments

continuation

"existence" in their systems. By implication, some idea is also given of what Kierkegaard and the other existentialists revolted against.

everyone encounters or by some prostrating tragedy handed out by fate. On the other hand, if he knows himself at all, this man will recognize at some point in his life that his existence is a contingent one, dependent upon the continuance of a mortal body. Now the self sees the possibility of its own annihilation in death and comes face to face with the prospect of Nothingness. Realizing that it will yield ineluctably to Nothingness, the self experiences dread, what Kierkegaard called "the sickness unto death." This is not the abstract knowledge of non-Being, or that of non-Being vis-à-vis others, but the concrete awareness that non-Being is part of one's own Being. As Tillich pointed out, dread (anxiety) is not psychological in origin—although if not confronted authentically it may lead to psychological anxiety—but existential, endemic, a part of existence itself.

Kierkegaard saw the authentic, unredeemed condition of man, conscious of the implications of his contingency and finitude, as despair. As a Christian, he felt that one does not have within himself the power to resolve this crisis: "For, humanly speaking, death is the last thing of all; and, humanly speaking, there is hope only so long as there is life. But Christianity understood death is by no means the last thing of all, hence it is only a little event within that which is all, an eternal life."[3] Only through a "leap" of faith, a leap that flies in the face of the Christian paradox, can the despair that comes with the apprehension of Nothingness be dealt with, and then, not once and for all, but as a continuing dynamic between despair and faith. The leap out of despair is "out of " in two senses: it is grounded in and based on despair, and it transcends this despair. One *is* not a Christian, Kierkegaard said, one *becomes* a Christian. Kierkegaard clearly understood the essential paradox of Christianity: that the guarantee of a mortal man's eternal life depended not only on an historical event, i.e., an event that had taken place in time, but that this event, the Incarnation of God as mortal man in Christ, defied every rule of human thought and experience, and thus comprehension. In believing, in making the "leap" of faith, a Christian undergoes what Jean Wahl called a "crucifixion of the understanding."

In *Concluding Unscientific Postscript* Kierkegaard wrote:

> Suppose Christianity never intended to be understood; suppose, that, in order to express this, and to prevent anyone from misguidedly entering upon the objective way [salvation attempted solely through the dogma and ethics of Christianity], it has declared

itself to be the paradox. Suppose it wished to have significance only for existing individuals in inwardness, in the inwardness of faith; which cannot be expressed more definitely than in the proposition that Christianity is the absurd, held fast in the passion of the infinite. Suppose it refuses to be understood, and that the maximum of understanding which could come in question is to understand that it cannot be understood . . . Suppose that the speculative philosopher is, not indeed the prodigal son, for so the anxious divinity would characterize only the offended individual whom he nevertheless continues to love, but is the naughty child who refuses to remain where existing individuals belong, namely, in the existential training school where one becomes mature only through inwardness in existing, but instead demands a place in the divine council chamber, constantly shouting that viewed eternally, divinely, theocentrically, there is no paradox. Suppose the speculative philosopher were the restless tenant, who though it is notorious that he is merely a tenant, in view of the abstract truth that all property is from the standpoint of the eternal and the divine, in common, insists on playing the owner . . .[4]

Kierkegaard maintained that faith could not "mend" the self, which remains polar and split, but only offer an authentic response to this condition. "The Christian heroism," he wrote in the Preface to *The Sickness unto Death*, "is to venture wholly to be oneself as an individual, this definitive man, alone before the face of God, alone in this tremendous exertion and this tremendous responsibility."[5]

Because Kierkegaard saw man's essence—what he is, what he is becoming, what he may yet become—as neither solely finite nor solely infinite, he insisted that the self could become itself only by living in both realms. For him, to become a self was to be a conscious synthesis of the finite and the infinite. Self cannot be chosen directly with respect to either the finite or the infinite, but only dialectically, i.e., by recognizing that while a choice is made in one realm, it is made by a Being who has at that moment an equal component (and thus an equal interest) in the opposite realm.

In the dialectical synthesis of self, the finite is the limiting factor and the infinite is the expanding factor. The dialectical creation of self occurs by moving *away* from oneself toward the infinite, and then *returning* to oneself in the finite. While self must be created from both realms, it may become lost in either. If in the flight toward the infinite the finite is rejected—if the flight "merely carries him away from himself and prevents him from returning to himself "—the self is lost because the dialectic has been short-circuited. A man who spends so much of his time in prayer that he seriously neglects his family and job has lost himself in the infinite. He has lost sight of the finite, and undergone what Kierkegaard calls "evaporation in the infinite." In his overture to the infinite, he has ceased to be a synthesis, ceased to be concrete.

Just as the self may be lost in the infinite, it may become lost at the opposite pole. To be lost in the finite is to capitulate to the world, to attribute, as Kierkegaard said, "infinite value to the indifferent." Self is lost in the finite when one will not "venture" belief in God, i.e., take the *risk* of the infinite. To find (create) himself with respect to the infinite, the Christian must, in a sense, lose himself with respect to the finite. Hence Wahl's phrase, the "crucifixion of the understanding":

> . . . the decisive affirmation comes only when a man is brought to the utmost extremity, so that humanly speaking no possibility exists. Then the question is whether he will believe that for God all things are possible—that is to say, whether he will *believe*. But this is completely the formula for losing one's mind or understanding; to believe is precisely to lose one's understanding in order to win God . . . This is the fight of *faith* . . .[6]

The "leap" of faith resolves the rational contradictions embodied in a self that is neither wholly finite nor wholly infinite. In a sense, a man must die to live, become pliant to become concrete. The "leap" is required for the choice of a concrete self, Kierkegaard insisted, because "if [a man] has no God, neither has he a self." He believed, very simply, that every man is born with one foot planted in this world and one in the next.

Self may also be lost in the finite if one fails to become an "individual"—a word that appears frequently in Kierkegaard's writing—but succumbs to the crowd instead:

> By seeing the multitude of men about it, by getting in all sorts of worldly affairs, by becoming wise about how things go in this world, such a man forgets himself, forgets what his name is . . . does not

dare to believe in himself, finds it too venturesome a thing to be himself, far easier and safer to be like the others, to become an imitation, a number, a cipher in the crowd . . . Such a man, precisely by losing his self in this way, has gained perfectibility in adjusting himself to business, yea, to making a success in the world. Here there is no hindrance, no difficulty, occasioned by his self and his infinitization, he is ground smooth as a pebble, *courant* as a well-used coin.[7]

This certainly has a modern ring, and could almost be an excerpt from David Riesman's *The Lonely Crowd* or William H. Whyte Jr.'s *The Organization Man.* Kierkegaard was probably the first writer to call attention to the large-scale capitulation of the individual to the pressures of society and history.

HUSSERL AND MERLEAU–PONTY (PHENOMENOLOGY)

Before turning to the atheistic existentialists—those thinkers who, like Kierkegaard, are concerned with existential themes such as the primacy of the individual, the limitations of reason, the authentic as contrasted with the inauthentic, the question of Nothingness (and the concomitant feeling of dread), freedom, and so on, but who do not believe in a transcendent divinity—something must be said about an area of philosophical inquiry that began independently of existentialism, but soon had a most important impact on it and eventually became wedded to it. This movement, known as phenomenology, was initiated by the German philosopher Edmund Husserl (1859–1938) and brought to full flower by Maurice Merleau-Ponty (1907–1961), a philosopher who was a professor of psychology at the Sorbonne and Sartre's collaborator on the existentialist journal *Les Temps Modernes.*

Phenomenology, as the name implies, is a study of essences. But, as Merleau-Ponty pointed out, it is a philosophy that "puts essences back into existence." The underlying phenomenological method derives as much from psychology as from philosophy.* For the phenomenologist,

---

* The phenomenological method is described in Chapter 4.

facticity, that of man and of the world, is the starting point. Husserl always kept in mind that man and the world were "already there" *before* the start of reflection and philosophizing. Husserl wanted to regain, through his work, a direct and primitive contact with the world that had been lost in the abstract theorizing of the analytical philosophers, for whom ideas were more real than the world itself. "The whole effort of phenomenology," Merleau-Ponty said, "is to recover this naïve contact with the world and give it, at last, a philosophical status."[8] If a single phrase may be said to signify the intention of the phenomenologist, it is one that was coined by Husserl and used by Merleau-Ponty in *Phenomenology of Perception*—"to return to things themselves"—by which was meant to the consciousness of things: "To return to things themselves is to return to that world which precedes knowledge, of which knowledge always *speaks*, and in relation to which every scientific schematization is an abstract and derivative sign language, as is geography in relation to the countryside in which we have just learnt beforehand what a forest, a prairie or a river is."[9]

Husserl gave the name "Life-World" (*Lebenswelt*) to the "world that precedes knowledge." The Life-World is pre-conceptual, i.e., it is there *before* we begin conceptualizing about it. Because it precedes conceptualization, the Life-World is pre-philosophical, pre-logical, pre-verbal, and pre-scientific. It is not the world of what "I think," as was Plato's cave world and that of all the other analytical philosophers, but the world of what "I live through." In the everyday lived world, we experience things and other people immediately, rather than through the mediation of ideas. The phenomenologists do not downgrade the act of cerebration, they merely insist that any intellectualizing activity be based on the world as *it is*, and not on some theoretical construct extrapolated from that world. Thought and language must never become detached from the reality they mirror. "There must," Marcel said, "be a *hold* on the real at the root of intelligence." In addition to rejecting the intellectualist and idealist approach to existence, the phenomenologists reject any view of man that makes him an "automatic machine," determined primarily by forces and events external to him. This is, of course, the position of the behaviorists.

Merleau-Ponty felt that the terrain of phenomenology was to be charted by what he called the "incarnated mind." He wanted to "make reflection emulate the unreflective life of consciousness." He wanted to break down the barriers of matter-mind, object-subject, causality-freedom, and reach an "interworld" (*intermonde*), a sphere within which these dialectics could interact syncretically and approach the whole. In this sphere of primary consciousness, Merleau-Ponty wrote, there would appear not only what words mean, but what *things* mean, "the core of primary meaning round which the naming and expression take shape."

Phenomenology emphasizes the pre-conceptual, "felt" dimension of our experience. William James, who is sometimes called the first American existentialist, distinguished between what he called "knowledge by acquaintance" and "knowledge about." "Knowledge by acquaintance" is the "felt knowledge" of the phenomenologists; "knowledge about" is the post-experiential, conceptual knowledge of thought. In *The Principles of Psychology* James expressed this distinction concretely in two brief sentences and at the same time showed the *interrelatedness* of the two kinds of knowledge: "Through feelings we become acquainted with things, but only by our thoughts do we know about them. Feelings are the germ and the starting point of cognition, thoughts the developed tree." The existential phenomenologist pursues both feelings *and* thoughts because he is interested in the "whole," i.e., in *meaning*. The unarticulated, felt dimension of our experience—the pre-conceptual, pre-symbolic, pre-verbal—is richer and more extensive than the thought, observation, speech, or action that emanate from it later. Thus, when we say that "we know more than we can tell" or "we mean more than we can say," it is of this ineffable, experiential reservoir that we are speaking. It is just this dimension of our existence that has been omitted from the philosophizing of the analytical philosophers.

During the soul-searching that accompanied the turmoil of the 1960s and 1970s, when everything that had seemed solid about the American way of life suddenly came unstuck, more than one sage said that we simply "lacked the vocabulary" to express what had been left out of lives that had previously seemed fulfilled. The recognition that there was some kind of meaning and value beyond the reach of reason and logic was undoubtedly the basis for the widespread interest in the occult, the mystical, even the magical and demonological, that occurred during the sixties and seventies. Neither academe nor the churches escaped this juggernaut. College professors donned bell-bottoms and wrote essays on rock music. Religious leaders, seeing that they had lost contact with their flocks, took a strong fundamentalist and Pentecostal turn, hoping to become "relevant." The surge of the "irrational" during the 1960s and 1970s was at bottom a floundering attempt to capture the ineffable sense of self that had so obviously been lost.

HEIDEGGER

If the "leap" of faith of Kierkegaard and the other Christian existentialists is paradoxical, then the leap, or whatever one chooses to call it, that gives meaning to life for the atheistic existentialist is just as much a paradox. Should not the recognition of his self-contingency and the dread of Nothingness (as Kierkegaard characterized it) that accompanies this recognition revoke any meaning of existence for one who has no faith? There is nothing inherent in the self that makes the thought of its self-contingency and eventual annihilation, the fact that it will cease to be following physiological death, anything but traumatic. A man on good terms with himself and this life does not want to die, to accede to Nothingness. Whereas the paradox for the Christian existentialist lies in believing, through the "leap" of faith, that the self is created by participation in the infinite in a way that defies human understanding, the paradox for the atheistic existentialist is that he believes the self is forged solely within the finite, while recognizing that man has a *desire* for the infinite that can never be satisfied.

Martin Heidegger was born in 1889 of Catholic peasant stock at Messkirch in the Black Forest of southern Germany. After a brief stint as a Jesuit novice, he studied philosophy and the theology of the Catholic Church at the University of Freiburg, where he wrote a probationary thesis on the Scholastic theologian Duns Scotus. When he became acquainted with Husserl's phenomenology at Freiburg, his interest shifted from theology to philosophy. In 1923 he was made a full professor at Marburg University, where he wrote his major work, *Being and Time* (*Sein und Zeit*), which was published in 1927. He succeeded Husserl at Freiburg in 1928, and served as rector from 1933 to 1934. After resigning as rector, he stayed at Freiburg to teach and write. He died in 1976 at the age of eighty-seven.

Heidegger's starting point for the analysis of human existence is consciousness: man is the only living being who is aware of himself and can reflect on himself, the only creature who *knows* that he exists. Heidegger chose the word *Dasein* which, in German, literally means Being-there or Being-in-the-world, to describe the situation of man existing consciously in the world. He characterized three modes of *Dasein*: facticity, existentiality, and forfeiture.*[10]

---

* These distinctions are intended to be formal, not actual. Existentially, the three modes of *Dasein* are inseparable.

Facticity (Being-in-the-world). My existence is first of all a fact. I am here and not not-here. My *appearance* in the world is not a matter of my choosing. I am cast into the world without my consent, without my permission. (Kierkegaard wanted to know why he had not been consulted.) Heidegger, therefore, speaks of our "thrownness" into the world (*Geworfenheit*). I am free, and yet I am not free, I find myself in a world not of my making. Nevertheless, within the undeniable limits of my contingency I am free to appropriate and assimilate much of what I encounter here.

Existentiality (Being-ahead-of-itself). My facticity—thereness—is not static, but dynamic. While I am "there" as long as I live, it is never the same "there" from one moment to the next. I interact continuously with the world outside me, from which I (my *Dasein*) am inseparable, and, therefore, my interior life changes constantly. Even if I deliberately withdraw from the world for a time (i.e., from everything that is offered by the physical world and by others), the *internal synthesis* of all I have experienced continues, relating and re-relating itself to itself. As we are changing physiologically every instant because of chemical synthesis and breakdown (the human body is said to completely renew itself approximately every seven years). we are changing ontically as well. My existence is an act of appropriation, of *making my world mine*. *Dasein* exists in advance of itself and has the power to transcend—to remake—itself by projecting itself into what is not yet. There are limits to this projection, the limits of the human condition as well as the limits of circumstance and fate, but *within* these limits we are free.

Forfeiture (Being-alongside). According to Heidegger, we may be "ahead-of-ourselves" (i.e., changing) either *authentically* or *inauthentically*. Inauthenticity is forfeiture of the self, the sacrifice of the "I" to the "they." It is the failure to become an "individual" (Heidegger read and was greatly influenced by Kierkegaard), a surrender to the pressures of what Heidegger called "everydayness," the loss of the "I" in the blur of the crowd (*das Man*). This is the "falling" from or forfeiture of authenticity (*Verfallen*). It is the turning away from and the loss of our Being, whose acquisition should be our main concern. Heidegger uses the word "falling" because he sees inauthenticity as necessarily diminishing our Being relative to our utmost potential, what might be thought of as a falling from ontic excellence. We cannot exist in isolation from others, but we must not let others call the shots for us. Heidegger maintains that the roots of nihilism (the denial of all meaning and value) are in the sacrifice of what he called Being for beings—the sacrifice of our selves for the approval of others, or to some absolute.

During a first reading, Heidegger's frequent neologistic use of hyphen-ated terms to characterize an ultimately ineffable Being may seem dis-agreeable, and appear to echo the pedantry of the systematic philosophers that the existentialists so despise. But Heidegger chose these terms delib-erately (rather than, say, "I" or "man") to emphasize the descriptive and dynamic aspects of our existence, our relatedness to others, and our relation to the only finally limiting factor of our existence, our death. By avoiding terms such as "I" and "man" in his philosophizing, he avoids the connotation, implicit in that terminology, that we are definite objects with fixed natures. In doing this, Heidegger was really reacting to Des-cartes, whose *Cogito ergo sum* ("I think, therefore I am") tended to isolate the "thinker" from the rest of his world.

Whereas Kierkegaard's motive for writing was religious and centered on the individual, Heidegger was a "formal" philosopher, whose avowed purpose was to explore the possibility of writing a new ontology, a new philosophy of Being. While Kierkegaard spoke for the individual (Kierke-gaard himself was an isolate and the notion of Being-in-the-world would undoubtedly have been foreign to him), Heidegger spoke for *all* individ-uals and defined Being (human existence) in general, as it is for all men. In so doing, he simultaneously sharpened and opposed Kierkegaard's focus on the individual.

Whereas Kierkegaard always remained *in* the existential, Heidegger set out to define the possibilities and the limitations—the perimeters—of existence itself. To a considerable degree, his systematic ontological excavation provided a structural framework for Kierkegaard's ontic un-earthing of the self.* Something is probably both gained and lost for our understanding of existence through Heidegger's systematic approach to Being. Jean Wahl remarked that Heidegger has "the profundity of what I would call the intuition of the feeling of Being [although] it is hidden by the ontological language." But that may be an inherent limitation of anyone's "ontological language," as well as a reminder that we cannot expect the "whole story" of existence from a single writer, or from a single tack.

In the Preface to *Being and Time*, Heidegger tells why he felt it was necessary to restate and reexamine the question of Being: "[This ques-

---

* The word "ontological" specifies a theoretical inquiry into the nature of Being or existence in general. "Ontic," on the other hand, denotes the concern of the individual with what is unique to *his* existence.

tion] is one which provided a stimulus for the researches of Plato and Aristotle, only to subside from then on *as a theme for actual investigation.* What these two men achieved was to persist through many alterations and 'retouchings' down to the 'logic' of Hegel. And what they wrested with the utmost intellectual effort from the phenomena, fragmentary and incipient though it was, has long since been trivialized."[11] Initially, there was an existential element in the philosophizing of Plato and Aristotle, but this was overridden when they came to regard the intellect as the highest faculty of man's existence. Like Kant, Heidegger knew that Being was not an "entity" or "category" and was not subject to definition and the rigors of logic. But where Kant, recognizing this, turned his back on the question of existence, Heidegger (like Kierkegaard) met it head-on. "The indefinability of Being," he wrote, "does not eliminate the question of its meaning. It demands that we look the question in the face."[12] The very *asking* of the question What is Being? becomes a *mode* of Being for the inquirer. Heidegger insists that the question of existence never gets straightened out "except through existing itself."

It is not difficult to see that Heidegger's characterization of *Dasein* was based on Husserl's Life-World, although Heidegger greatly extended and systematized this notion. Indeed, Paul Ricoeur has noted that existential phenomenology "makes the transition between transcendental phenomenology, born of the reduction of everything to its appearing to me, and ontology, which restores the question of the sense of Being for all that is said to 'exist'."[13] Being-in-the-world is what it means to exist in Husserl's Life-World. What most distinguishes Heidegger's thought from that of the other existentialists is his analysis of the consequences of man's mortality, his Being-towards-death.

"Death," Heidegger says, "is the possibility of the absolute impossibility of *Dasein*." A moment will come when there will be no more possibilities, when there will be no more "ahead of us." Because death is certain, it is "*distinctively* impending." Heidegger distinguishes two meanings of the word "impending." A storm or the anticipated arrival of a friend, for example, may be said to be impending in the sense that their effects will be limited, since life will continue more or less as before after these events have taken place. In contrast, death is impending in the sense that *Dasein* is *at every moment* characterized and determined by this future event, which cannot be "outstripped." This means that death is not merely a future event, but is embedded in living. My death may not only come at *any* moment; my dying is occurring at *this* moment. Being-towards-death is *contained* in Being-in-the-world. In "The Wreck of the

Deutschland," Gerard Manley Hopkins uses a striking space-time image for "impending" death: "I am soft sift in an hourglass." The judgment of whether any particular day was a "good" day or a "bad" day must give way, finally, to the recognition that it was one *less* day. On any given day it may be said that we live a little and that we die a little. At the moment of birth, we begin a losing race with time. We are not *in* time, Heidegger says, we *are* time. We are all "downhill racers," and it was this recognition that led Camus to remark that there is nothing so tragic as a happy man. Death be not proud? O yes. Death stand tall!

There are, according to Heidegger, two ways in which one may face the imminence of his death. The most common way is that of escape or forfeiture—"fleeing in the face of death"—the inauthentic way: In the end I will die too, but right now this has nothing to do with me. The "they" (*das Man*) see death as an event only, and therefore deny its force as a process. "Everydayness" concedes, in a general way, that death is certain—as a *future event*—only to keep it at arm's length by denying the *process* of dying, what Heidegger calls our "thrownness" into death.

Is it possible, Heidegger asks, to emerge from forfeiture? Can the self (*Dasein*), in flight from itself, turn back to itself and face its own Being directly, without the masks and props that are often required to survive in the everyday world—in our work, our relations with others, in love, and especially vis-à-vis death? For Heidegger, this is equivalent to asking if, even momentarily, one's self can be grasped as a whole, rather than experienced in fragments, as is the case in "everydayness." He maintains that such a unifying intuition can come only through what he calls the "key-mood of dread," the dread that comes with the recognition of the inescapable annihilation of all that I can imagine as myself in death. Death is the only event in my life that is uniquely "my own" (*eigen*), for which I am not, in some way, dependent on others. Death being "my own," I cannot, while aware of what this means, become lost through some relation with another person, through some surrender to the "they" (*Verfallen*). Only by realizing the consequences of my perpetual dying can I see things in true perspective—i.e., accord the highest value to my Being (self) rather than my accomplishments and disappointments, important as they seem and are—and thus face life with what Heidegger calls a "freedom towards death." Through dread, I am recalled from self-betrayal to self-knowledge. Because dread has no *object*—its "object" being Nothingness, the negation of all objects—I am, while in its grip (in a moment of isolation), wholly coincident with myself. Dread is the bridge from forfeiture to authenticity.

As Tillich pointed out, dread (anxiety) does not originate from any neurotic disorder, although, if not faced squarely (i.e., authentically), dread may precipitate neurosis subsequently. It must not be confused with what is thought of as "depression," but is inherent in the awakened, authentic condition of *Dasein*, or self. Dread is not psychological in origin, but ontological. Dread is pre-conceptual and pre-logical, and is in the domain of Husserl's Life-World. It is an element of the experiential dimension that is left out of the philosophizing of the analytical philosophers. Dread, Heidegger says, reveals Nothing (the Void): "We ourselves confirm that dread reveals Nothing—when we have got over our dread. In the lucid vision which supervenes while yet the experience is fresh in memory we must needs say that what we were afraid of was 'actually' Nothing. And indeed, Nothing itself, Nothing as such, was there."

In D. H. Lawrence's *Women in Love*, Gerald Crich experiences dread as his father nears death, following a long illness. Gerald feels that he is "caving in":

> . . . life was a hollow shell all round him, roaring and clattering like the sound of the sea, a noise in which he participated externally, and inside this hollow shell was all the darkness and fearful space of death. He knew he would have to find reinforcements, otherwise he would collapse inwards upon the great dark void which circled at the center of his soul. His will held his outer life, his outer mind, his outer being unbroken and unchanged. But the pressure was too great. He would have to find something to make good the equilibrium. Something must come with him into the hollow void of death in his soul, fill it up, and so equalise the pressure within to the pressure without. For day by day he felt more like a bubble filled with darkness, round which whirled the iridescence of his consciousness, and upon which the pressure of the outer world, the outer life, roared vastly.[14]

Gerald has experienced what Sartre called the "hole of Being at the heart of Being."

Dread occurs only in rare moments. Most of the time, *Dasein* represses dread, masking it in everydayness. An experience with a serious illness or the death of another may reveal the Void, but this is not always the case.

Camus recognized his finitude after a brush with death at seventeen from tuberculosis. Gerald Crich recognizes his after seeing life drained slowly from his father. Dread is an unveiling of something that was lurking there, unseen, all along. Gerald tells Gudrun Brangwen: "It's something you don't reckon with, you know, till it is there. And then you realise that it was there all the time—it was always there—you understand what I mean?—the possibility of this incurable illness, this slow death." Most people, according to Heidegger, *never* experience dread.

Only after I have grasped the meaning of my finitude—my communion with non-Being—can I make the most of my potential for Being as a "freedom towards death." William Barrett has expressed the subtleties of this notion very nicely: "We tend to think of finitude principally in connection with physical objects: objects are finite because they are contained within definite spatial boundaries. They extend so far and no farther. The essential finitude of man, however, is experienced not at his boundaries but, so to speak, at the very center of his Being. He is finite because his Being is penetrated by non-Being."[15]

> Human finitude is the presence of the *not* in the being of man. That mode of thought which cannot understand negative existence cannot fully understand human finitude. Finitude is a matter of human limitations, and limitations involve what we can*not* do or can*not* be. Our finitude, however, is not the mere sum of our limitations; rather, the fact of human finitude brings us to the center of man, where positive and negative existence coincide and interpenetrate to such an extent that a man's strength coincides with his pathos, his vision with his blindness, his truth with his untruth, his being with his non-being. And if human finitude is not understood, neither is the nature of man.[16]

We are now in a position to see even more clearly why Heidegger uses terms such as *Dasein*, Being-ahead-of-itself, and Being-alongside—terms that express an ontic dynamism. To create itself and to transcend itself, *Dasein* is constantly pushing into Nothing.* It is the essence of *Dasein* to go

---

* With Heidegger, the classical metaphysical *ex nihilo nihil fit* (nothing comes from

beyond itself, to be, as Marcel said, "on the way." But while *Dasein*, always in flux, is "ahead-of-itself" (authentically), it is, at the same time, "alongside" or "falling" (inauthentically). It is impossible to be authentic all the time. There are pressures from all sides, some of which cannot be avoided no matter how good our intentions or how strongly we feel our Being. Through what Heidegger calls "conscience," our care as conscious human Beings (*Sorge*) calls us out of the distractions of "everydayness" toward a higher state of fulfillment, what he called our "destiny." But while destiny pulls us forward, the pressures of the moment, as well as our "facticity" (what we "are" in our situation at any given time), pull us backward. We can never escape completely the tension between the call to destiny and the inevitable claim of forfeiture. This is why Heidegger elected a terminology that made provision for the dynamism of our Being, why he used the dynamic and relational *Dasein*, rather than the static and solipsistic "man."

Heidegger's ontology finishes on a positive note. There is a progression from the consciousness of death, to dread, to the experience of Nothing, to care, to self, and then beyond a momentary state of self, through transcendence. Our *Dasein* is a series of sequential selves created, through transcendence, from the nihilation of Nothing. With Heidegger, the direction of the transcendence of Christianity (toward God) has been reversed. Transcendence has lost its religious character and become, paradoxically, a transcendence of immanence. This is the other side of the coin of Kierkegaard's "leap" of faith to the divine—and a paradox that is just as strong.

But how does all this relate to Heidegger's original stated intention to "interrogate" Being and reestablish Being as the ground for our existence? According to Heidegger, our quest for Being—our true vocation—has been short-circuited because, since the time of Plato and Aristotle, men have deliberately avoided the real issue—*themselves*. "The courage to be as oneself" was forsaken for "the courage to be as a part," to recall Tillich's

continuation

---

nothing) has been stood on its head so that now *ex nihilo omne ens qua ens fit* (every Being, so far as it is a Being, is made out of Nothing). "Nothing," Heidegger says, "not merely provides the conceptual opposite of what-is but is also an original part of essence. *It is in the Being of what-is that the nihilation of Nothing occurs.*" To nihilate means to "make nothing." But to nihilate Nothing is to *create something*, namely ourselves. Thus by "nihilate," which in every other usage implies an ultimately negative act, Heidegger, as well as the other existentialists who use the term, specifies something that is not only positive, but the foundation of all we are and may become.

phrases (although not his position), of something "larger" than man, whether the God of Christianity or some aspect of the immanent god of Reason (rationality). According to Heidegger, a life lived with "the courage to be as a part" amounts to a forfeiture of self to the "crowd," to becoming a part of the "they" instead of an "I." The principal agents to which self has been relinquished are Christianity and rationality. This loss of self has caused what Heidegger calls the "darkening of the world." Even more important, it has caused us to become alienated from that darkened world.

To be alienated is to feel separated from the world as we experience it daily, from the "center" of ourselves, and from others who are having the same problem. Alienation is what a man feels when he has lost his sense of belonging to the world, what the pre-Socratic philosophers Heraclitus and Parmenides felt as their *presence* in it.

PRESENCE: STANDING IN THE CLEARING OF BEING

In the *Letter on Humanism*, Heidegger recalled a story about Heraclitus that Aristotle told in *De Partibus Animalium*:

> An anecdote tells of an explanation that Heraclitus is said to have given strangers who wanted to approach him. Upon approaching they found him warming himself at a stove. They stopped surprised and all the more so because as they hesitated he encouraged them and bade them come in with the words: "For here too there are Gods present . . ."[17]

The unknown visitors had come to see the Great Man at his work, undoubtedly hoping to catch him during a moment of profound meditation. What will they tell their friends of this encounter with the philosopher? He wasn't *doing* anything, and, to all outward appearances, he wasn't even *thinking* about anything. He was merely standing by the stove, trying to get warm. Heraclitus sensed their disappointment, and encouraged them to come closer—"*For here too there are Gods present.*"

What Heraclitus means by this becomes clear when we consider two fragments of his writing that Heidegger cites in the *Letter on Humanism*. The first fragment: "A man's character is the open space in which man dwells." This "open space" is not just where a man makes his home, but anywhere he happens to be. According to Heraclitus, a man approaches his essence in the "open space" and, through the acquisition of this essence, is united with the world. He is at home. He is *present* in the world. The second fragment: "Man, in so far as he is man, dwells in the nearness of God." For Heraclitus, a man experiences God when his essence becomes one with the world, and that union constitutes his divinity, his holiness. Thus, he could assure his visitors that the Gods were present even there, while he was warming his hands at the stove.

Heraclitus lived and thought in a world that had not yet experienced the division between mind and matter that was to be initiated shortly by Plato and Aristotle. Thought was still tied to Being, and the process of thinking was still in the service of bringing truth out of the dark into the "open space." At this point, the Greeks did not have a word for "truth." For them, the "truth" was that which was not hidden, but open, evident, manifest, *present*. The word they used to designate the truth—*aletheia*— stood for the conquering or wrenching from darkness of what was hidden (*letheia*). The truth was to be found in one's everyday mode of existence, in one's home, *anywhere* in the world. It is precisely this sense of presence that was lost when truth became, for Plato, Aristotle, and the long line of analytical and idealist philosophers that continues into our own time, something to be demonstrated *in the mind* through propositions and proofs, rather than sought *in the world*.

The task of the existential philosopher is nothing less than that of leading the way toward restoring man's sense of presence in a world without absolutes. Husserl felt that the ultimate goal of the philosopher vis-à-vis the self was not to "postulate" or to "interpret" but to "bring to light." Heidegger uses the term "Being" to specify a process of "lighting" or "clearing" an area—what he called *Spielraum*—within which the self (*Dasein*) may actualize itself. This "standing in the clearing of Being" is what he called "ex-sistence," which means literally to "stand out." Here Heidegger is, of course, looking over his shoulder at Heraclitus.

In existential philosophy it is both implicit and explicit that the words "Being," "existence," "self"—even Heidegger's more encompassing and dynamic *Dasein*—are limited in how far they can bring us toward the desired goal of presence. "If man," Heidegger wrote, "is once again to find himself in the nearness of Being, he must first learn to exist in the nameless." But the problem is not merely one of returning to the "open space" of Heraclitus. Some twenty-five hundred years of philosophy and history—and nearly two thousand years of Christianity—separate us from

Heraclitus's presence there. In the hope of being able to stand there once again, Heidegger felt he had to construct an ontology that would neutralize the deleterious effects of an erroneous ontology that had been built up since Plato and Aristotle. He wanted to restate and reexamine the question of Being, to "interrogate" Being. The return to the "nameless" would have to be made by way of thought and language. The revolt could occur in no other way.

In the *Letter on Humanism*, Heidegger sets down his view of the relation between thought, language, and the essence of man (which, for the existentialist, is his existence):

> . . . thought brings to fulfillment the relation of Being to the essence of man, it does not make or produce this relation. Thought merely offers it to Being as that which has been delivered to itself by Being. This offering consists in this: that in thought Being is taken up in language. Language is the house of Being. In its home man dwells. Whoever thinks or creates in words is a guardian of this dwelling. As guardian, he brings to fulfillment the unhiddenness of Being insofar as he, by his speaking, takes up this unhiddenness in language and preserves it in language.[18]

The "house of Being" is constructed with thought and language, and it was for its construction that Heidegger wrote *Being and Time*.* But the "house of Being" is not complete until "in its home man dwells." Dwelling in that home, man re-achieves his presence in the world. Clear thinking is not the enemy of genuine feeling. But it should be pointed out that this presence is a limited one, a presence achieved through the mind—the *thinker's* presence—which may be as close as any ontology can bring us. In Chapter 5, we will see how Mersault, in Camus's novel *A Happy Death*, achieves a presence that is *corporal* as well as cerebral.

Heidegger felt it was time "to get rid of the habit of overestimating philosophy and thereby asking too much of it," that there should be less philosophy and more attention to thought. "Thought," he said, "gathers

---

* In *Being and Time* Heidegger tried to "push" ontology as far as it could go. For a discussion of what he did and did not achieve, see William Barrett's *Irrational Man*, pp. 235–38.

language in simple speech. Language is thus the language of Being . . ."
Although he was not aware of it, Heidegger was giving here an excellent
description of the literary style of Beckett and Hemingway, who are as
concerned with homelessness, dread, and the Void (and, equally, with the
converses of presence, joy, and the world) as any philosopher. They pared
down their sentences, eliminating everything but the essential—*to get at the
essence*. Theirs is truly the language of Being, even if they frequently
approach Being from the negative side.

3

Self and the Existential Tradition (II):

Sartre and Camus

In addition to distinguishing existentialists as either Christian or atheistic, there is an historical progression within the tradition, one in which three "generations" of existentialists may be discerned. The first generation (nineteenth century) was made up of Kierkegaard and Nietzsche—the founding fathers—who, between them, experienced and wrote about most of the things now thought of as constituting a philosophy of existence rather than essence. Heidegger and Jaspers are the principal figures of the second generation (early twentieth century), which translated the reflections and intuitions of Kierkegaard and Nietzsche into more formal and systematic terms, thus, in a sense, universalizing them. The major figures of the third generation of existentialists (from, say, the 1930s to the present) are Sartre and Camus. Coming to maturity between two world wars that left much of Europe physically and spiritually in ruins, they appeared in a world deprived of the philosophical, political, and social certitudes that had underpinned Western culture for hundreds of years. As philosophers and literary artists, Sartre and Camus wrote about existential man in a landscape of devastation, emphasizing the necessity for commitment and action in the face of this condition. Their success was due in part to the readiness of their audience for the questions, explicit and implicit, posed in their writing, as well as to an eagerness for some kind of answer. It is through the third generation descendants that existentialism has become known to (but not necessarily understood by) a wide audience.

SARTRE

Sartre was first called an "existentialist" by Gabriel Marcel in his review of *Being and Nothingness* (*L'Être et le Néant*), published in 1943. The roots of the existential tradition had been set down a century earlier, but it is with the name of Jean-Paul Sartre that existentialism has become most widely associated. Sartre became a literal personification of existentialism by insisting in his writing and in his life that what was implied by the tradition in principle must find its ultimate validation through action.

Sartre was born in Paris in 1905 of a French father and a German mother. Raised nominally as a Catholic, he was also exposed to the Calvinism of his maternal grandfather, with whom he and his mother went to live following the death of Sartre's father when the boy was two. His formal education was principally in philosophy, and he received the *aggrégation de philosophy* in 1929. He became a professor at the *lycée* in Le Havre, but took a leave of absence in 1933 to study modern German philosophy at the French Institute in Berlin. It was here that Sartre first read Husserl and Heidegger, the two thinkers who were to become so influential in his own philosophical development.

All the existentialists have emphasized the existential over the essential and the subjective over the objective. But there is an important distinction to be made between what this meant to Kierkegaard as a Christian and what it meant to Heidegger, Sartre, and the other atheistic existentialists. For a Christian who believes that man was created by God, there is the inference that human nature is derivative of divine nature. Thus, essence may be said to precede existence because one is born into this world to fulfill a destiny, to be reunited with God. A Christian is a child of God and heir to heaven—"Our hearts were made for Thee, O Lord . . .," Augustine said. Kierkegaard emphasized the existential in the sense that he insisted that the individual and his subjective relation to God were primary. But in spite of all he wrote about the subjective choice of self (through "venturing")—and about the *difficulty* of that choice—he never questioned the Christian notion that a man's existence had to be worked out in accordance with a nature that was rooted in both the finite and the infinite.

If, on the other hand, one rejects the idea of God, as Heidegger and Sartre do, then one cannot claim that human nature (man's essence) is, even in the broadest outline, externally predetermined. In other words, if there is no God (and therefore no divine nature), then there is no inherent or predetermined human nature, and the Christian priority of essence over existence is reversed: now, *existence precedes essence*. Tillich, a Christian existentialist, called this proposition "a flash of light which illuminates the whole Existentialist scene. One could call it the most despairing and the most courageous sentence in all Existentialist literature."[1] According to this new priority, man comes into the world without a nature and creates his own essence (what he is) through his existence or, more precisely, through his *existing*—i.e., his choices, actions, and so forth. "Man," Sartre says, "is nothing more than he makes of himself." In a limited sense (historically and socially), Heidegger held to the priority of existence over essence. But for him there was another proposition even more basic than this: namely, that *Being precedes existence*. Unlike Sartre, Heidegger does not feel that man is radically separated from others and from nature, but rather that man (*Dasein*) has his roots in what he called the "ground of Being." At one point Heidegger declared, "I am not an existentialist," to distinguish his position from the Sartrean school. He felt that Sartre's thinking on this point remained restricted to the human subject, like that of Descartes.[2] It is only with Sartre, then, that all the implications of the reversed priority of existence over essence come into play.

Although Sartre rejects the idea of any kind of universal essence that could be called human nature, he does recognize a universal "human condition." By the human condition, Sartre means the a priori limits that characterize man's fundamental situation in the world. Although, as he says, historical situations vary—a man may be born a slave in a pagan society, a feudal lord, or a proletarian—"what does not vary is the necessity for him to exist in the world, to be at work there, to be there in the midst of other people, and to be mortal there."[3]

According to Heidegger and Sartre, consciousness leads a man to the recognition of his self-contingency. For Heidegger, contingency is that of mortal flesh, a contingency where death is not merely a future event but is "built into" life. In contrast, Sartre sees death as something external, not chosen, and therefore something, in a sense, to be taken for granted. Unlike Heidegger, Sartre's mortality does not seem to weigh heavily on his shoulders; death seems to hold no particular terror for him. For Heidegger, anguish is rooted in the consequences of the necessity of our dying. For Sartre, anguish is rooted in the consequences of the necessity that, as free men, we must act. If there is no God, Sartre maintains, we are "condemned to freedom": "Everything is permissible if God does not exist, and as a result man is forlorn, because neither within him nor without does he find anything to cling to. He can't start making excuses for himself. If existence really does precede essence, then there is no explaining things away by a fixed and given [or fallen] human nature. In other words, there is no determinism, man is free, man is freedom."[4] In the sense that a "quest for Being" propelled Heidegger's philosophizing, Sartre's raison d'être as a philosopher (and as a man) is centered on the question of the use of man's freedom.

What distinguishes atheistic existentialism from any number of other philosophical traditions that deny the existence of God is that the atheistic existentialists have attempted to set down *all* the consequences of what it means to live in a world without God. This is particularly true of Sartre, who has tried to work out the implications of the freedom implied by the recognition of man's self-contingency. Sartre asks: How is a man to live? What considerations are to govern what he does? If the Decalogue no longer has any meaning, then what are the rules? Sartre is, in the final analysis, an atheistic moralist. He, along with Nietzsche, is the closest embodiment yet of the promised Antichrist. And because Sartre has taken an "ultimate" position on a paradoxical theme (as Christ did), his philosophizing embraces contradictions, as did the teachings of Christ.

In *The Flies* Zeus, Sartre's stand-in for the Christian God, tries to persuade Orestes to acknowledge that his murder of Clytemnestra and Aegistheus in retribution for their murder of his father, Agememnon, requires expiation. Orestes replies that he is responsible only to himself for what he did. Zeus warns him that his refusal to admit guilt would bring anathema from the citizens of Argos, and even exile. But Orestes maintains that his freedom is absolute and tells Zeus why he is destined to follow no law other than his own: "Suddenly, out of the blue, freedom crashed down on me and swept me off my feet. Nature sprang back, my youth went to the wind, and I knew myself alone, utterly alone in the midst of this well-meaning universe of yours. I was like a man who's lost his shadow. And there was nothing left in heaven, no right or wrong, nor anyone to give me orders."[5]

There is something in both the substance and the tone of Orestes's proclamation of freedom that is reminiscent of certain descriptions of religious conversion. He has undergone an anti-conversion to become, vis-à-vis Zeus, the Antichrist. Zeus recognizes the challenge for what it is, saying: "In the fullness of time a man was to come, to announce my decline. And you are that man, it seems." In Euripides' *Electra*, the tragic drama on which Sartre based *The Flies*, Orestes accepts the verdict of the gods and is resigned to their disapproval. But in Sartre's play, Orestes refuses to acknowledge the judgment of Zeus and chooses exile rather than compromise his autonomy. Recalling Tillich's phrase, he acts with "the courage to be as himself." When Electra asks where they will go now, Orestes replies: "I don't know. Towards ourselves. Beyond the rivers and mountains are an Orestes and an Electra waiting for us, and we must make our patient way towards them."

As we have seen with Heidegger, the atheistic existentialist reverses the direction of Christian transcendence—transcendence now becomes immanent, i.e., to self—so that the "human condition" becomes, in many important respects, the mirror image of the Christian's "human nature." Ralph Harper has pointed out in his book *Existentialism* that "existentialism is but an outcropping of [the] distinctively Christian concern for persons." No religion other than Christianity, or philosophy other than existentialism, Christian or atheistic, has valued man so highly. For the Christian, anguish is overcome (not quenched, but dealt with) by a paradoxical leap of faith that mitigates man's self-contingency by identification with the non-contingency of God, this identification having been made possible through the Incarnation. Sartre claims that this is man's attempt to escape his self-contingency—"to flee anguish in bad faith"—by trying to become his own non-contingent foundation or cause, an *Ens causa sui* (man's concept of God). "Thus the passion of man is the reverse of that of Christ, for man loses himself as man in order that God may be born. But the idea of God is contradictory [Sartre means false] and we lose ourselves in vain. Man is a useless passion."[6] Sartre, the Antichrist, rejects the Christian transcendence because through it, he says, "we lose ourselves," and thus all that we have. The reversal of the priorities of essence and existence is a statement, in ontological terms, that the effect of the Incarnation on human history has been neutralized.

If we are free to choose ourselves, this means that we are concomitantly choosing mankind as well. A person who understands the implications of his freedom must admit not only that he is the author of his own actions but also that they invite, and to some degree determine, the response of others. A man must therefore accept the consequences of his actions. "For every man," Sartre says, "everything happens as if all mankind had his eyes fixed on him and were guiding himself by what he does." For the existentialist, subjectivity is the starting point, and intersubjectivity— where "man decides what he is and what others are"—is the natural condition of the self. Being an individual and being part of a society are not inherent opposites, but are complementary. Each is part of the single process of existing. According to Sartre, "Every one of our acts has, as its stake, the meaning of the world and the place of man in the universe. Through each of them, whether we wish it or not, we set up a scale of values which is universal." Again, the atheistic existentialist reflects the Christian concern: we *are* our brother's keeper.

Sartre makes very clear what he means by the anguish that is brought on by recognizing the consequences of our freedom:

> What do we mean by anguish? The existentialist frankly states that man is in anguish. His meaning is as follows—When a man commits himself to anything, fully realizing that he is not only choosing what he will be, but is thereby at the same time a legislator deciding for the whole of mankind—in such a moment a man cannot escape from the sense of complete and profound responsibility. There are many indeed, who show no such anxiety. But we affirm that they are merely disguising their anguish or are in flight from it. Certainly, many people think that in what they are doing they commit no one but themselves to anything: and if you ask them, "What would happen if everyone did so?" they shrug their shoulders and reply, "Everyone does not do so," but in truth, one ought always to ask oneself what would happen if everyone did as one is doing; nor can one escape from that disturbing thought except by a kind of self-deception. The man who lies in self-excuse by saying "Everyone will not do it" must be ill at ease in his conscience, for the act of lying implies the universal value which it denies. By its very disguise his anguish reveals itself.[7]

Sartre goes on to describe the anguish of a military leader who knows that a certain decision will be a life-or-death one for his men. Here anguish does not prevent action, but is the very condition of action:

> It is anguish pure and simple, of the kind well known to all those who have borne responsibilities. When, for instance, a military leader takes upon himself the responsibility for an attack and sends a number of men to their death, he chooses to do it and at bottom he alone chooses. No doubt he acts under a higher command, but its orders, which are more general, require interpretation by him and upon that interpretation depends the life of ten, fourteen or twenty men. In making the decision, he cannot but feel a certain anguish. All leaders know that anguish. It does not prevent their acting, on

the contrary it is the very condition of their action, for the action presupposes that there is a plurality of possibilities, and in choosing one of these, they realize that it has value only because it is chosen. Now it is anguish of that kind which existentialism describes, and moreover, as we shall see, makes explicit through direct responsibility towards other men who are concerned. Far from being a screen which could separate us from action, it is a condition of action itself.[8]

The anxiety that comes with the recognition of our having to choose, whether for the Christian or the atheist, must not be confused with a lack of human courage or with undue pessimism, although it frequently is. This anxiety, Tillich wrote in *The Courage to Be*, "is existential in the sense that it belongs to existence as such and not to an abnormal state of mind as in neurotic (and psychotic) anxiety."[9] Sartre often writes about dark situations, but the emphasis is always on the possibilities for meaningful and constructive action as an authentic response to the burden that self-contingency places on men. The Danish critic Oleg Koefoed has called Sartre's outlook "the most rashly optimistic humanism which our generation has produced." When Sartre writes that "man is a useless passion," he is saying that the inauthentic attempt of men to claim the heritage of a divine nature is "useless" (i.e., futile) because this heritage simply does not exist.

In all Sartre's writing on philosophy, literature, and politics, and, even more important, in his unceasing (although often muddled and discursive) work on behalf of government in France and other countries, he is insisting that this world is *our* world, a necessary consequence of the condition that "man is nothing more than he makes of himself." One of Sartre's most singular traits is that, in spite of disappointment and disillusionment, he has not abandoned the struggle for a better world. (Sartre supported the French Communist Party vigorously for many years, and the disillusion with Russia that came after the bloody repression of the Hungarian revolution in November 1956 must have been devastating to him.) The scale and duration of his involvement in political causes is probably unprecedented for someone whose primary vocation is philosophy. Sartre's pronouncements can be cloying—he is, at times, a bit of a bore, and he is frequently bitchy—but he is in no sense passive or cynical in the face of the "dark situations" he portrays in his writing or experienced in the course of his political activity. Nor does he seem bitter.

In an interview he gave when he was seventy, Sartre, in spite of the fact that he was almost blind and was unable to read or write, had, to all appearances, the serenity of a retired Archbishop of Canterbury—*before* the Death of God.[10]

Whereas Heidegger distinguished three modes of *Dasein* (Being-in-the-world)—its facticity, its existing, and its forfeiture—Sartre's primary ontological distinction is between what he calls Being-in-itself (*L'être en soi*)—the world of objects outside man that are predetermined, passive, and silent—and Being-for-itself (*L'être pour soi*), man himself, who does not have a predetermined nature or essence. The In-itself is the self-contained being of a thing; a stone is just that, no more and no less. There is nothing about a stone that makes it want to transcend itself. Its being is static and always coincides with itself. In contrast, the For-itself, because it is consciousness, is perpetually beyond itself. We have desires and make plans. Through our imagination, we construct images of what we would like to become. Sometimes we fulfill the vision, sometimes we do not. I can never be wholly myself (like the stone) because my Being always stretches beyond itself, exceeds itself. In order to become myself I must first *postulate* myself, i.e., assume roles. If I fill the role in such a way that I do not misrepresent my activity (what Sartre calls my "project") either to myself or to others, then I am acting authentically. If, on the other hand, I try to deceive myself or others regarding my project, I am acting in "bad faith" and am inauthentic.

The For-itself, Sartre says, is a Being who "is not what it is and is what it is not." I am, simultaneously, more than I am and less than I might be. For Sartre it is this self-contingency, this lack of being externally determined, defined, and limited, that causes man's most basic anxiety: he wants to be secure, to have his Being rooted in some "ground." He wants his existence to have the self-contained Being of a thing, an In-itself. On one level, this drives man toward God, since God is the uncaused cause (*Ens causa sui*), an In-itself as well as a For-itself. This, according to Sartre, is our attempt to escape from self-contingency, our "useless passion." On another level, Sartre says, man tries to escape his self-contingency—i.e., the burden of becoming himself—by refusing to take his freedom into his own hands, to be authentic, *to act*. In effect, he strives to become an In-itself and thus not human, but a thing (like the stone).

Having just made the point about Sartre's optimism, this may not be the most propitious place to begin a discussion of a book with a title like *Nausea* (*La Nausée*), his first novel, published in 1938. The protagonist of *Nausea* is Antoine Roquentin, a French writer of about thirty, living in

Bouville, a small town several hours by train from Paris. After traveling through Central Europe, North Africa, and the Far East, Roquentin has settled in Bouville to finish his book on the Marquis de Rollebon, an obscure French nobleman whose life spanned the late-eighteenth and early-nineteenth centuries. He has been there about three years, living in a hotel near the library, when he starts a diary. (The novel is written in this form.) The initial entry (Monday, 29 January 1932) begins: "Something has happened to me, I can't doubt it any more." His malaise has the symptoms of Nausea. He feels sick.

For years, Roquentin has occupied himself with the book on Rollebon to the extent that the project has become a substitute self:

> M. de Rollebon was my partner; he needed me in order to exist and I needed him so as not to feel my existence. I furnished the raw material, the material I had to re-sell, which I didn't know what to do with: existence, *my* existence. His part was to have an imposing appearance. He stood in front of me, took up my life to *lay bare* his own to me. I did not take notice that I existed any more, I no longer existed in myself, but in him; I ate for him, breathed for him, each of my movements had its sense outside, there, just in front of me, in him; I no longer saw my hand writing letters on the paper, not even the sentence I had written—but behind, beyond the paper, I saw the Marquis who had claimed the gesture as his own, the gesture which prolonged, consolidated his existence. I was only a means of making him alive, he was my reason for living, he had delivered me from myself.[11]

Roquentin has lost himself, lost his freedom ("I am no longer free, I can no longer do what I will"), become an object. In fact, he tells us, objects *touched him*. In Sartre's terminology, Roquentin had become an In-itself. Finally, the Nausea becomes so paralyzing that he is forced to stop work on the book. Then, quite suddenly, Roquentin has the first intuition of his existence, i.e., that *he exists*:

> *I exist*, I am the one who keeps it up. I. The body lives by itself once it has begun. But thought—*I* am the one who continues it, unrolls it.

. . . My thought is *me*: that's why I can't stop. I exist because I
think . . . and I can't stop myself from thinking . . . *I am the one* who
pulls myself from the nothingness to which I aspire . . .[12]

Roquentin is now becoming what Sartre calls a For-itself, pulling
himself, as he says, from the Nothingness to which he at the same time
aspires. He feels the saliva in his mouth, the warmth of his body, his
weight on the floor. And his diary entry for the next day reads, simply:

Tuesday:
Nothing. Existed.

The fact that Roquentin is able to do, as he says, nothing but "exist" on
that day means that, at least momentarily, he has his existence in his
hands and does not require any kind of transcendence or escape to define
and orient himself.

But what of the Nausea? It persists; it comes and goes in waves. In the
climactic scene of the novel, Roquentin, while sitting on a bench in the
park looking down at the large, protruding root of a chestnut tree,
suddenly realizes that the Nausea is not "out there" as he had thought,
but *within him*. It is the taste of existence itself:

This moment was extraordinary. I was there, motionless and icy,
plunged in a horrible ecstasy. But something fresh had just appeared
in the very heart of this ecstasy; I understood the Nausea, I possessed it . . . The essential thing is contingency. I mean that one
cannot define existence as necessary. To exist is simply *to be there* . . .
I believe there are people who have understood this. Only they tried
to overcome this contingency by inventing a necessary, causal being.
But no necessary being can explain existence: contingency is not a
delusion, a probability which can be dissipated; it is the absolute,
consequently, the perfect free gift . . . here is Nausea; here there is
what those bastards—the ones on the Coteau Vert and others—try
to hide from themselves with their idea of their rights. But what a
poor lie: no one has any rights; they are entirely free . . .[13]

Roquentin stares at the root of the chestnut tree and becomes mesmerized: objects lose their shape and identity, and become detached from the words used to name them. As Roquentin has previously had an intuition of existence (the For-itself), he was now having an intuition of the In-itself: objects—silent, noncommunicative, "in the way," "superfluous," "*de trop*." But people who didn't "exist" were like that too. "Those bastards—the ones on the Coteau Vert" (the bourgeoisie)—did not feel the Nausea because they did not "exist," but "[hid] from themselves" instead. Roquentin's Nausea is precisely what separates him from them, from the human In-itself.

The Nausea that overtakes Roquentin as soon as he begins to get the feel of his existence is derivative of the anguish, described by Sartre in *Being and Nothingness*, that comes with the recognition of one's self-contingency and the inescapable burden (the necessity of acting) imposed by this self-contingency on the existing self. The condition of Nausea as the "feel" of authentic existence (existential pain expressed through a physiological symptom) is a device used by Sartre to shock the reader out of his complacency and the comfort of "everydayness." It is an exaggeration, a trick—a hype. As in Alcoholics Anonymous, the first step of the cure is the recognition and admission of the problem: "I am John Doe, and I am an alcoholic." Roquentin's real sickness (but not the reason for his Nausea) is inauthenticity. He is, initially, unconscious of his condition as a self-contingent, existing human being. But during the course of the novel, he faces up to this and says, in effect: "I am Antoine Roquentin, and I EXIST!" In *Nausea* Sartre, the Antichrist, accomplishes the creation of Antoine Roquentin, literally drawing him painfully from the womb of Nothingness.

Sartre does not leave Roquentin groveling in his Nausea. Roquentin is more a victor than a victim. At the start of the novel, he is not "existing" and, by his own admission, not free. At the end of the novel, he *is* "existing" and free, although he does not (yet?) know what to *do* with this freedom. For Roquentin, this newly found existence is both a joy and a burden. At times he longs *to be* (an In-itself) rather than *to exist* (as a For-itself) because it is easier and more comfortable to be.

CAMUS

Much has been made of the differences—philosophical, political, and personal—between Sartre and his contemporary Albert Camus. Like

Sartre, Camus belonged to the French Resistance. After the war, the two men shared the spotlight and the fire that came with being the principals of European existentialism. They were close friends until 1952, when a vitriolic review of Camus's *The Rebel* by Francis Jeanson appeared in Sartre's journal *Les Temps Modernes.*[14]

The names of Camus and Sartre have become inextricably linked. Each was influenced by the other, and each defined himself against the other, to their mutual benefit and chagrin, on significant questions. Camus denied that he was an existentialist, and Sartre once told an interviewer that the label did not suit Camus. But whatever their differences, it appears that Sartre and Camus inhabited very similar Life-Worlds: the pre-conscious, pre-philosophical, "gut" reaction of each to the conditions of his existence was similar. They were very much brothers in "that world which precedes knowledge, of which knowledge *speaks*," as Merleau-Ponty characterized it. This is seen poignantly in the eulogy Sartre wrote following Camus's sudden death: "We had quarreled, he and I. A quarrel is nothing—even should you never see each other again—only another way of living together and not losing sight of each other in the narrow little world which is given us. That did not prevent me from thinking of him, from feeling his gaze upon the page of the book, upon the paper he was reading, and from asking myself: 'What is he saying about it? What is he saying about it *at this moment?*'"[15] The tone here is more Camus's than Sartre's.

Like Sartre, Camus was only half French. His father, a laborer, emigrated from Alsace to Algeria. His mother was Spanish and also of humble origin. Camus was born in Mondovi, Algeria, in 1913, and approximately a year later his father was killed in the battle of the Marne. He was raised by his mother in what would, at best, be considered poverty. He, his brother, and his mother lived in a two-room apartment with a grandmother who was dying from liver cancer and an uncle who was paralyzed. As a boy, Camus came to know the sun and the beaches of Algiers, and this bond with nature became a counterpoint and antidote to the squalor of his life at home. Camus never became bitter about this situation. In fact, he considered himself fortunate. In an early essay he wrote: "Poverty never was for me a misfortune. It was always counterbalanced by the riches of light. Poverty kept me from judging that all was well in the world and in history. The sun taught me that history was not everything . . . Fear or discouragement, I may have known; bitterness, never."

And in the same vein:

There is a solitude in poverty, but a solitude that grants each thing its true price. At a certain stage of wealth, the sky itself and a night studded with stars may seem like a natural gift. But at the bottom of the ladder, one finds the sky regaining its full significance: that of a priceless boon of grace. Summer nights, mysteries amid the crackling of the stars. Behind the child that I was, there stretched a stinking corridor; his broken little chair collapsed under him. But once he raised his eyes, he drank from the purity of the stars.[16]

It is in his early essays (many are included in the collection entitled *Lyrical and Critical Essays*) that Camus's most haunting writing can be found—his celebration of sea, sky, and sun. The "invincible sun" illuminated everything he wrote. It was this passion for nature, an intense interest in the life and culture of the Hellenic Greeks, and a rejection of the notion of original sin ("I have never," he said, "been able to understand the meaning of certain words, sin for example") that earned him the citation of "pagan" by some critics.

In 1930, when he was seventeen, Camus was diagnosed as tubercular and had a close brush with death. Hoping to pursue an academic career, he studied philosophy at the University of Algiers from 1932 to 1936 and wrote a dissertation examining the relationship between the work of Augustine and that of the Greek philosopher Plotinus. During this time, he had various jobs—in the weather bureau, in an automobile accessory firm, in a shipping company—to help pay the tuition, and was also involved in the theatre, writing, directing, and appearing in avant-garde plays. His hope for an academic career was thwarted when another attack of tuberculosis made it impossible for him to pass the medical examination required for the *aggrégation* degree. At this point, Camus turned to journalism. He went to Paris during the early part of World War II and became the editor of *Combat*, an underground newspaper of the French Resistance. For his philosophical essays, plays, and novels, Camus was awarded the Nobel Prize for literature in 1957. He was killed in an automobile accident while driving from Loumarin to Paris on 4 January 1960 at the age of forty-six.*

---

* Occasionally, one hears that Camus committed suicide. The facts are these. Camus was about to return by train to Paris from a midwinter vacation in the South of France when he met, by chance, his friend and publisher, Gallimard. Gallimard convinced Camus to make

Most of Camus's writing is concerned with what he saw as the distance that separates what men want from what they are able to have. Camus felt that this gap was inherent in the human condition and gave rise to a situation he called the "absurd." Men long for meaning, familiarity, clarity, unity, cohesion, and the absolute, but these longings are largely snubbed, ignored, and rebuffed by other men and by the world. The absurdity of man's situation does not originate with his nostalgia for a home (a center, a metaphysical focus), or from the coldness and indifference of the world, but from the relation of, and the *tension* between, the two. The poles of what is asked for and what is given are, as the expression has it, poles apart.

The word "absurd" is derived from the Latin *absurditas*, which denotes a discordance, a disharmony, a gap. This is the meaning Camus intends, rather than what "absurd" connotes to us in English, namely, something ridiculous, farcical, and vaguely corrupt. Camus uses the word "absurd" in two senses. First, there is the absurd condition, and then there is the absurd man who is aware of this condition and draws the inevitable conclusions. For most people, the absurd—and thus the response to it—is masked by what Heidegger called the posture of "everydayness." "The feeling of the absurd," Camus wrote with a nod to the phenomenologists, "is not the same as the *idea* of the absurd. The idea is grounded in the feeling, that is all. It does not exhaust it." Sartre has pointed out that Camus, in his novel *The Stranger*, gives us the *feeling* of the absurd, while in *The Myth of Sisyphus* he gives us the *idea* of it.[17]

Camus first spelled out his "idea" of the absurd in a collection of essays entitled *The Myth of Sisyphus* (*Le Mythe de Sisyphe*), published in 1942, shortly after the appearance of *The Stranger*. These essays were written around 1940, while France was being buffeted by World War II. The war "widened" the gap of the absurd, and the dislocations it caused are felt throughout the book. "A world," Camus wrote, "that can be explained even with bad reasons is a familiar world. But on the other hand, in a universe suddenly divested of illusions and lights, man feels an alien, a stranger. His exile is without remedy since he is deprived of the memory of a lost home or the hope of a promised land. This divorce between man and

continuation

---

the trip by car with him instead. On the way, it started to rain. The car, with Gallimard at the wheel, skidded, spun off the road, and crashed. The driver was shaken up; Camus was killed instantly. An unused train ticket for Paris was found in Camus's pocket (see William Barrett, *Time of Need* [New York: Harper & Row, 1972], pp. 27–28).

his life [his 'self,' others, and the world], the actor and his setting, is properly the feeling of absurdity."

In *The Myth of Sisyphus* Camus distinguished three ways in which a man may confront the absurdity of his existence:

1. He may commit suicide and thus end *his* involvement with the absurd. Camus rejects suicide as a response because it is an admission of a man's failure in the face of the absurd. It is a negation of one-half of the absurd condition and an admission, very plainly, that life is not worth it.

2. He can "ignore" his absurd condition, live around it, or "leap" over it. This is what Camus would say that Kierkegaard (whom he had read thoroughly and been influenced by) had done through his "leap" of faith. For Camus, faith in a transcendent Being and the hope of a better life beyond this one amount to an inauthentic response to the absurd and a loss of self through intellectual suicide—what he called a "humiliation of the intellect." Camus would have had nothing but scorn for the note on which Tillich concludes *The Courage to Be*: "The courage to be is rooted in the God who appears when God has disappeared in the anxiety of doubt."

3. He may accept his fate and straddle the poles of the absurd. Camus holds that only in this way can a man be true to himself and live without illusions. The authentic response to the absurd condition is *revolt*, not what is commonly thought of as revolution or anarchy, but a struggle that recognizes the tension and insecurity inherent in our absurd condition and places the responsibility for living a just life with the individual himself. Living, for Camus, is keeping the absurd *alive*. "The absurd is [man's] extreme tension, which he maintains constantly by solitary effort, for he knows that in that consciousness and in that day-to-day revolt he gives proof of his only truth, which is defiance."

The freedom implied by the absurd condition is the antithesis of the freedom achieved by one who hopes for resolution of the absurd through a transcendent divinity (or any transcendence other than that of self). Absurd freedom is freedom *to* as contrasted with freedom *from*, the freedom of not being responsible. The mystics, Camus said, found freedom in giving themselves: "By losing themselves in their God, by accepting his rules, they became secretly free. In spontaneously accepted slavery they recover a deeper independence."

Camus's absurd man must be distinguished from Nietzsche's Superman. Nietzsche, like Dostoevski, felt that for man to dispense with the notion of a transcendent God he had to become a god himself, through some kind of Dionysian assertion. Rather than a Dionysian transcendence of self, Camus felt the absurd required a response similar to the *aretê* of the

Greeks. Sisyphus is closer to the model than Prometheus. "Like those buffoons in Dostoevski," Camus wrote, "who boast of everything, ascend to the stars and end up by displaying their shame in any given public place, we lack the pride in man which is fidelity to one's limits, clear-sighted love of one's condition."

Camus wanted to find out if he could live, as he said, "without appeal": "I do not know whether this world has a meaning that is beyond me. But I do know that I am unaware of this meaning and that, for the time being, it is impossible for me to know it. What can a meaning beyond my condition mean to me? I can understand only in human terms. I under-stand the things I touch, things that offer me resistance." Camus refuses to "leap" out of the paradox of his absurd existence. The word "hope," i.e., the hope of external justification or salvation, has no place in Camus's vocabulary because, to him, this is the first step in taking a "leap," and amounts to resignation in the face of the absurd. He would say that to live is the opposite of being resigned. He would scorn Job for his resignation—literally, his resignation as an absurd man—to his fate.

Writing in *Combat*, the newspaper he edited, Camus castigated the Vatican (i.e., Pius XI and Pius XII) for turning its back on the atrocities of Franco's regime in Spain and Hitler's establishment of concentration camps in Germany. In the Introduction to *Actuelles* (1950), a collection of essays, he accused the Christians of what Sartre would call "bad faith" for their readiness to accept the evil of the moment. The Christian, after all, sees this life as just temporary, a mere preparation, in the "hope" of some eventual mitigation and the promise of his own immunity from harm. Camus turned back the accusations of pessimism and despair leveled at the existentialists and directed them at the Christians themselves. "True despair," he wrote, "does not arise in the presence of obstinate misfortune or of exhaustion in an unequal fight. It comes from one's not knowing one's reasons for struggling, or even whether, precisely, one must take up arms."

In addition to the influences of Kierkegaard, Nietzsche, and Heidegger, Camus has roots that go back to the French moralists, Montaigne and Diderot, among others. Camus is more an anti-theist than an atheist. His writing asserts, both explicitly and implicitly, that if God were eliminated, man would have a better chance of coming into his own through revolt, and of establishing an ethics higher (more authentic) than the Christian ethics. In an incisive essay, Henri Peyre described him as an "anti-Christian moralist."[18] Camus would have agreed with Alfred de Vigny who said in his *Journal d'un poète* in 1834 that "Christ's religion is one of despair, since He despairs of life and hopes only in eternity." With Camus, this order is essentially reversed: he said that he was "a pessimist where man's destiny was concerned [even if everything else in his life is satisfactory, man's desire to be immortal is denied], an optimist where man is concerned." Camus saw Christianity as an attempt to transfer responsibility and feelings of guilt from individuals to a power beyond man. Religion was, he said, a "huge laundering venture." In *The Fall* (*La Chute*) Clamence tells one of the customers at the Mexico City bar not to wait for the Last Judgment because "it takes place every day." Citing the Vatican's eagerness to sign a pact with Mussolini and the cooperation of the German and Austrian hierarchies with Hitler, Camus wrote in an article in *Combat* (8 September 1944) that "Christianity in its essence is a doctrine of injustice. It is founded upon the sacrifice of the innocent and the acceptance of that sacrifice . . ." Like Sartre, he felt that man's best chance lay in expunging from his mind and heart the notion of the Incarnation, which, he thought, was as responsible as any other factor for masking the truth of his absurd condition. Whereas Kierkegaard advocated a "leap" of faith that found its victory in the paradox of God's grace, Camus felt that victory for the absurd man came through a revolt whose paradox lay in the recognition that the absurd could be dealt with, but not outstripped.

It is ironic that Camus should have elicited such sympathetic interest, even what might be called admiration tinged with envy, not just from Christians but from Christian clergymen. Writing in the *Nouvelle Revue Française* (March 1960), Father R. -L. Bruckberger said that Camus "was engaged in an anti-Christian undertaking . . . trying to find a substitute body for Christianity." In the same issue of this magazine, Jean-Louis Barrault described Camus as a "secular monk, all steaming with a God whom he dared not name." And the Jesuit Henri de Lubac said in *The Drama of Atheistic Humanism* (1949) that those who deny the Incarnation are "more Christian at times than those who fight against them; often they also prove more clear-sighted interpreters of history." In other words, the anti-theist often comes closer to the mark set by Christ than the Christian. "Man eliminates God," de Lubac wrote, "in order to recover human greatness which he sees as unfairly taken over by another being." This theme was also sounded by Walker Percy, himself a Catholic (and an existentialist), in his novel *Love in the Ruins*. Dr. Thomas More is speaking here: "No one ever expects the English to be rascals (compare Greeks, Turks, Lebanese, Chinese). No, the English, who have no use for God, are the most decent people on earth. Why? Because they got rid of God. They got rid of God two hundred years ago and became extraordinarily decent to prove they didn't need him. Compare Merrie England of the fifteenth and sixteenth centuries. A nation of rowdies."*

Nowhere in Camus's writing is the "superiority" of the nonbeliever seen and felt more strongly than in his novel *The Plague* (*La Peste*), published in 1947. Oran, a city in Algeria, has been sealed off because of an epidemic of bubonic plague. The story turns on the dilemma posed by the plague. The Jesuit, Father Paneloux, tells his parishioners, recalling the Slaughter of the Innocents, that this misfortune is the will of God and has to be met with a (Kierkegaardian) "leap" of acceptance: "One must either believe all or deny all. Who among you would dare deny all?" Here, the absurdity of the tragedy is negated, and the injustice is seen as originating from, and given meaning by, an order higher than man. But Dr. Rieux, the physician who takes charge of the medical effort to contain and subdue the epidemic, will not see this human tragedy resolved (negated) by hurling it into the lap of God. Rieux is speaking for Camus. He will not allow that the epidemic has any transcendent meaning and will defy and struggle against it. He will keep the absurd alive and not neutralize it with any divine panacea. That, according to Camus, would be to render to God what is not God's. The struggle will be more authentic if God is thrown out.

At the end of the novel, when the plague has subsided (but only after great suffering and many deaths), Rieux is able to affirm that "there are more things to admire in men than to despise." He has had the cooperation and friendship of Rambert and Tarrou. In the struggle against the plague, he had, as Camus said of himself, been both "solitary" and "solidary." Revolt in the face of the plague had made him what he was as a man and, at the same time, joined him with other men. Rieux understood the fragility of the victory—that it was not final—because *no* victory is final. Whether one reads *The Plague* as a pure allegory of the absurd or infers a reference to the Vichy government of occupied France during World War II, it is clear that Camus sees the absurd condition as existentially endemic, and its symptoms, whether manifested in physical illness or political oppression, certain to reappear. The absurd cannot be vanquished, but only repeatedly and continuously opposed through re-

*For a corroboration of this point see Lionel Trilling's *Sincerity and Authenticity* (Cambridge, Mass.: Harvard University Press, 1972), pp. 115–18.

volt. Man can "win" only by becoming "superior to his fate." *The Plague*
concludes:

> None the less, he knew that the tale he had to tell could not be one
> of final victory. It could be only the record of what had had to be
> done, and what assuredly would have to be done again in the never
> ending fight against terror and its relentless onslaughts, despite their
> personal afflictions, by all who, while unable to be saints by refusing
> to bow down to pestilences, strive their utmost to be healers.
>
> And, indeed, as he listened to the cries of joy rising from the town,
> Rieux remembered that such joy is always imperiled. He knew what
> those jubilant crowds did not know but could have learned from
> books: that the plague bacillus never dies or disappears for good;
> that it can lie dormant for years and years in furniture and linen-
> chests; that it bides its time in bedrooms, cellars, trunks, and
> bookshelves; and that perhaps the day would come when, for the
> bane and the enlightening of men, it would rouse up its rats again
> and send them forth to die in a happy city.[19]

Rieux (like Camus) would not "bow down to pestilences." If he could
not be a "saint," then he would be a "healer" and serve absurd man. (For
the anti-Christian moralist, perhaps that is the equivalent of being a
secular saint.) One reviewer of *The Rebel*, Camus's essay on revolt, said that
its author had spoken with "the voice of a man of unshakable decency."
In the eulogy cited previously, Sartre said that Camus's life and work
amounted to an "unshakable affirmation."

Camus and Sartre, indeed all the existentialists, have been charged as
nihilists. In the sense that nihilism exalts non-Being over Being, anarchy
over government, and denies the validity of any value, nothing could be
further from the truth. What is true is that the existentialists have
confronted Nothingness, given it its due, and loudly affirmed the value of
man created from it. "In the lower depths of nihilism," Camus wrote in
the *Atlantic Monthly* (June 1953), "I have searched only for reasons to
transcend it."

Camus felt that nostalgia (the desire for unity, clarity, and so forth) was
the mark of the man, not the silence of the world or the condition of the
absurd. In an important essay on *The Stranger*, Sartre remarked that
Camus was "very much at peace within disorder,"[20] i.e., the absurd. It is

unfortunate that Camus's readers have associated him more closely with
The Stranger—of all his books, the one that dwells most on what might be
called the negative aspects of nihilism—than with *The Plague*. Camus is
not Mersault, but Rieux. He never took his eye from the Life-World and
never ceased loving what was human and mortal. In *The Myth of Sisyphus*
he wrote:

> And here are the trees and I know their gnarled surface, water
> and I feel its taste. These scents of grass and stars at night, certain
> evenings when the heart relaxes—how shall I negate this world
> whose power and strength I feel? Yet all the knowledge on earth will
> give me nothing to assure me that this world is mine. You describe it
> to me and you teach me to classify it. You enumerate its laws and in
> my thirst for knowledge I admit that they are true. You take apart
> its mechanism and my hope increases. At the final stage you teach
> me that this wondrous and multicolored universe can be reduced to
> the atom and that the atom itself can be reduced to the electron. All
> this is good and I wait for you to continue. But you tell me of an
> invisible planetary system in which electrons gravitate around a
> nucleus. You explain this world to me with an image. I realize then
> that you have been reduced to poetry: I shall never know. Have I the
> time to become indignant? You have already changed theories. So
> that science that was to teach me everything ends up in a hypothesis,
> that lucidity founders in metaphor, that uncertainty is resolved in a
> work of art. What need had I of so many efforts? The soft lines of
> these hills and the hand of evening on this troubled heart teach me
> much more. I have returned to my beginning. I realize that if
> through science I can seize phenomena and enumerate them, I
> cannot, for all that, apprehend the world. Were I to trace its entire
> relief with my finger, I should not know any more.[21]

In the quiet of the hills on an Algerian evening, Camus has returned to
his "beginning." But this beginning is not "home" (although Camus was
born in Algeria and felt an intense union with this country) because, for
Camus, man was, by nature, homeless. The beginning of which he speaks
here is his nostalgia, the *desire* for presence in a world that is indifferent to
this desire. For Kierkegaard and Sartre, the starting point was despair.
For Husserl and Merleau-Ponty, it was a "return to things themselves."

For Heidegger, it was the dread-filled consciousness of one's mortality that led to a recognition of the preciousness of Being, and hence of the Time in which that Being had to be won. Each of these men was concerned with a facet of the same jewel—the self—the self they were trying to refashion from the debris of Western civilization. The existentialists revolted against a loss of self that was brought on when man sundered the connection between his intellect and everything else that made him human, and set the highest value on the fruits of this intellect. In *An Introduction to Metaphysics* (1953) Heidegger showed that the prevailing dichotomy of Being and Thought did not always exist in the West, but was generated sometime between Parmenides and Aristotle.* Marjorie Grene has summarized Heidegger's conclusions on this point:

> For Parmenides, *einai* (Being) and *noein* (Thought), which Heidegger calls *Vernehmen* (in a very general sense, "awareness"), were one. Human existence, according to Heidegger, was rooted in this oneness. Man was deep in Being and drew his life from the appearance of Being—which was truly appearance, not illusion—as well as from the becoming of Being, which again was at one with Being, not the mere flux which the misinterpretation of Heraclitus has led us to think it was. Logos, which is the same as Being, held man, rooted and at home. But by the time of Aristotle, man had broken loose from this first great anchorage and floated out upon that tide of nihilism on which we are still adrift. Man had become "a rational animal," the animal that "*has* logos," can calculate, knows its way about—the most successful animal, but the animal, torn from its ground in Being, whose very being is *unheimlich*, uncanny, literally "unhomely," "not-at-home." Heidegger's theory of truth tells the same story. For the pre-Socratics truth was *aletheia*, the unhiddenness of being. By the time of Aristotle truth had become a property of propositions—their "correspondence" with "facts." And this loosening of truth from Being led directly to nihilism and to Nietzsche's dictum that Being is a "haze."[22]

---

*Recall the epiphanic unveiling of *aretê* to Robert M. Pirsig's Phaedrus in *Zen and the Art of Motorcycle Maintenance*. We may only speculate whether Phaedrus could have been spared some of the agony of his search—going down the blind alleys of analytical analysis—had he read Kierkegaard and Heidegger rather than Plato, Aristotle, Hegel, et al.

Thus, the "fall from Being" that began with Plato and Aristotle became the secular original sin of the Occident, a haunting parallel to the Christians' fall of Adam in the Garden of Eden. So, Heidegger tells us, we should not be surprised to find ourselves in the mess we are in now. It *had* to happen this way. We betrayed ourselves by falling out of Being. We destroyed ourselves for abstractions. We became marginal selves.

4

Self, Other, and World:

A Phenomenological Description

> The Self must be conceived, not theoretically as subject, but
> practically, as agent . . . Human behaviour is comprehensible only in
> terms of a dynamic social reference; the isolated, purely individual
> self is a fiction.
>
> —John Macmurray, *The Self as Agent*

> Theory provides the empty and abstract frames into which each
> can put his own autobiography.
>
> —Ortega y Gasset, *Man and People*

Before proceeding further with our inquiry into the notion of self,
something more should be said about the phenomenological
method that was described in broad terms in Chapter 2. This
method—approach would be a better word—was initiated by Husserl and
adopted implicitly by all the existentialists, and explicitly by Heidegger,
Sartre, Merleau-Ponty, Ortega, and Marcel, among others.

THE PHENOMENOLOGICAL METHOD

In practice, the phenomenological method is an antidote to the dualistic
mind-matter split that has permeated Western thought since Plato and
Aristotle. As we have pointed out many times before, the great fault of the
analytical philosophers was (and is) that they lost sight of the fact that the

world—objects, events, persons, etc.—is there *before* (and after)the thinker initiates his analysis of it. Descartes's *Cogito* is perhaps the fullest expression of this failure. For Descartes and the other philosophical idealists, existence found its fullest expression in what the mind formulated following its experience of the world. In place of an "account" of the world, Merleau-Ponty wrote in *Phenomenology of Perception*, they offer a "reconstruction." There is an element of irony in the method of the phenomenologist: by constantly reminding himself of the distinction between the world and what can be thought and said of that world following his experience of it, by being constantly on guard that this distinction is not blurred during his philosophizing activity, he avoids severing his mental activity from the object of its consideration.

We are not merely conscious, we are conscious *of* something. Husserl called this aspect of consciousness *intentionality*.* Consciousness is *directed toward* whatever it encounters. What we see is *there for us*, i.e., our perception of an object or an occurrence is not simply the object or occurrence abstracted in its entirety into our mind, but is colored by our prior experience (through prior perception) of that object or occurrence, as well as by everything else in our experience that is related to it and impinges upon it. What we perceive something to be depends in part on our *perspective*, i.e., the perspective we bring to it.

The phenomenologist works through what Husserl called the "phenomenological reduction." Any phenomenon that the philosopher wishes to investigate—some aspect of Being in general, or of the self, or of the relation of self to other—is a part of, or, shall we say, is caught up in, the world, the "temporal flux" (Merleau-Ponty). To seize hold of it, he carries out what Husserl called an *epoché*, or forced halt. This amounts to "putting it in brackets," shutting it out from the phenomenological field of the world as it exists and delivering it to the world of consciousness, the world in which it is perceived, remembered, judged, thought, valued, etc. In the phenomenological reduction, persons and events (I, you, and our interaction with each other) are replaced by their respective meanings *in consciousness*. It is important to see clearly how the phenomenological

---

*Intentionality was "discovered" by the German philosopher, Franz Brentano (1838–1917), a teacher and friend of Husserl's. To say that human consciousness has intentionality is to say that it is a *going out to the world*, in contrast with Descartes's *Cogito*, which isolates consciousness (the thinker) from the world. Intentionality is the foundation upon which the phenomenologist hopes to rebuild the bridge between the mind and the world.

method differs from the method of philosophical idealism: in the former, some phenomenon is taken from the world into consciousness through the *epoché*, analyzed, and then related back to the world from which it was perceived; in the latter, phenomena are *abstracted* into consciousness, analyzed, and the results of that analysis declared more significant (a higher reality) than the world in which the phenomena occurred.

To see how the phenomenological method works, let us consider the following analogy. Let us say that the daily, weekly, monthly, and yearly events that make up our lives—what Husserl called the Life-World—could be represented as a continuous series of images projected on a screen, as in a motion picture film. It is self-evident that certain days, hours, minutes, and seconds, because of what occurs during these intervals, have greater significance to our lives than others, just as there are episodes and key scenes in a film. The philosopher, therefore, wishes to examine these intervals closely. For his analysis, the phenomenologist would stop the "moving picture" (*epoché*) and photograph the sequences of images of special interest from the screen. Next, he would develop the photographs and enlarge and crop them, in order to examine details of the important scenes ("putting it in brackets"). With the information he gathered from a careful examination of the photographs in hand, he would then rerun the "film," relating what he had learned from them back to the "moving picture" as he sees it projected again on the screen. Because he now has a better understanding of the important scenes, his understanding of the "whole story" will be enhanced. In this analogy, the "moving picture" represents life as it is lived. The still photographs that are taken from the screen and examined in detail represent a part of our *conscious effort* to come to grips with and understand that life. When the "moving picture" is viewed again in its entirety, there is a fuller appreciation because details and perspectives are now seen that would have been overlooked during a "continuous showing" only (i.e., without the "bracketing" of the *epoché*).*

We can see now even more clearly how the approach of the phenomenologist differs from that of the analytical and idealist philosopher. The

---

*All through this book, there is a kind of "mixed discourse" between the existential and the phenomenological, between lived experience and what can be learned about it by interrogating certain essences. Repeatedly, essences are uncovered to illuminate the phenomenon of "marginal" existence. Inevitably, in going from existential experience to the phenomenological reduction and back again, a dissimilitude and tension are created between the poles of what is lived and what is known.

latter would not bother to rerun the film. He would forget that the photographs he took came from a screen that had projected a "moving picture" ("whole story"). He would continue to pore over the photographs, delighting in the details, contrasts, shadows, gradations, textures, etc. He would hang them on the wall of his study and think, "What marvelous enlargements!"

In *Man and People* the Spanish philosopher Ortega y Gasset (1883–1955) uses another analogy to describe the *epoché* of the phenomenological method:

> . . . confronted with a good tapestry *we do not see the threads, precisely because the tapestry is made up of them*, because they are its elements or components. What we are accustomed to is things, but not to the ingredients of which they are made up. *To see the ingredients we have to stop seeing their combination*, which is the thing—just as, to see the pores in the stones of which a cathedral is built, we have to stop seeing the cathedral. In practical daily life, what concerns us is manipulating already finished and compounded things; hence it is their shape that is familiar to us, that we know and understand. Inversely, *to become aware of their elements or components we have to go counter to our mental habits* and in imagination, that is, intellectually, break things down, cut up the world so that we can see what is inside it, its ingredients [emphasis added].[1]

When we look at the tapestry, we see it as a whole—all at once—while the details of the complex network of threads that are its components remain unnoticed. And so it is with the world we live in and through, the world that is the setting for self and other. To see what the structure of this world is, what Ortega called its "anatomy," the phenomenologist carries out a series of *epochés* ("forced halts") that permit close examination of something previously overlooked, either because it was inherently recondite, or because it was simply taken for granted. To do this, it is necessary to suspend what Husserl calls the "natural attitude," the unreflective way we normally look at the world that presents itself to us in our everyday experience.

In *Man and People* Ortega set out to uncover the "structure" inherent in the self, the other, and the world in which we meet and live. Later in this chapter, we will quote extensively from his book, so as to lay bare the beams and girders of his thought. There are places where a paraphrase or summary would diminish the rigor of his analysis by what would amount to a surfacing of his analytical structure with wire lath and plaster. His language, illustrations, and allusions are so rich that we decline to let this occur. Ortega's Mediterranean outlook offers a warmth that is frequently lacking in the writing of Husserl, Heidegger, and Sartre, whose work he knew and absorbed. He is, in every sense, their heir.

THE "STRUCTURE OF THE WORLD"

Husserl distinguished between what is immediately accessible to the eye at the instant of "seeing" (what is *present*), and what is undeniably there but hidden from the eye (what he specified as *compresent*). Making use of this distinction, Ortega begins his structural analysis with the example of an apple—specifically, the apple that Eve convinces Adam to eat in the Garden of Eden.

Eve offers the apple to Adam. He reaches out to accept it. Now we must ask whether the apple that is moving away from Eve and toward Adam is one and the same apple. Is it the same apple for Eve as it is for Adam? That the apple being transferred is the same *object* cannot be denied. But is the apple the same to the *consciousness* of both Eve and Adam? Recalling Husserl's characterization of intentionality—that consciousness is always consciousness *of* something—we realize that only *half* of the apple is visible either to the giver or to the receiver. For Eve the apple is the side that faces her as she passes it to Adam; for Adam the apple is the side that faces him as he receives it. They are each *conscious of* different halves of the apple. The half that faces Eve is *present* to her, but *compresent* to Adam. The half that faces Adam is *present* to him, but *compresent* to Eve. Similarly, every corporal body has (at least) two faces, only one of which is present to us during any instant of perception. Strictly speaking, we never *see* the apple (or any other object), but rather we mentally add the second half of it to the half we perceive at any particular instant. In our mind we add compresence to presence.* It is this composite apple I mean when I say "apple." The apple in its totality is never entirely present to me; it does

_____

*Obviously, this epistemological presence is different from the existential presence we have been considering here.

not exist for me. To be able to say "apple," I must have first added the compresent apple to the present one.

What we perceive are not actually objects, but perspectives of *properties* of objects. *To us*, objects are really "sense objects," i.e., objects as they appear to us through our senses. Shapes, forms, colors, sounds, smells, resistances that are hard and soft, rough and smooth, exist for us because our bodies have organs that permit us to sense them. We know the objects of our environment less as *essences* than as *signals*.

SELF AND OTHER

Try, Ortega asks, to imagine community with a stone: "the stone *is* a stone *to me*, but to the stone I absolutely *am not*."[2] Because I have consciousness, I can recognize the stone. Because the stone lacks consciousness, it cannot respond to me. There is no possibility of my having any communication or community with it. The stone is totally other, and I cannot *feel* anything for it. The animal is another story: ". . . it not only *is to me*, but I also *am to it*, that is, to it I am another animal."[3] Ortega tries to imagine what takes place in the donkey when the driver strikes its back with a stick to goad it on: "What a brute! this animal, in the world of fable where even we donkeys talk, we call 'man'! How different from that other animal that comes into the stable and licks me and I call him 'dog'!"[4]

Saying that "we—the animal and I—are" has some degree of meaning, whereas saying "we—the stone and I—are" has no meaning whatever. The "we" arises because we mutually are *to each other*. Certain actions of mine will cause the animal to respond to me. "We"—the dog and I—can sit by the fire together or take a walk together. There is between us what Ortega calls mutuality or reciprocity. The dog exists for me and I exist for the dog. This kind of relationship is impossible with the stone, as it is with the tree, no matter how splendidly its form strikes me, or how the play of the wind in its leaves thrills me. But I must recognize the limitations of the animal's response and, therefore, of the mutuality and reciprocity that I can have with it.

> I can train or tame the animal and then imagine that it corresponds to a larger number of my gestures and other acts; but I soon observe that in the tamed state the animal does not respond [for the most part, anyway] from itself, from its spontaneous center, but

becomes a pure mechanism, that it is a machine into which I have put a few discs, like the phonographic answers that the parrot grinds out, always the same, according to program.[5]

The animal *responds*, but it cannot *cor-respond*. The stone, the tree, and the dog are part of my environment, but they do not offer me community *on my own level*, i.e., *co*-existence. "Co-existence," Ortega says, "is an intertwining of existences, is two beings inter-existing, not simply 'being there' without having anything to do with each other.'"[6] The only "other" with whom co-existence is possible is the other who is another person.

What can we say of this other?

As a sensible presence, all that I have of him is a body, a body that displays its peculiar form, that moves, that manipulates things in my spirit, in other words exhibits external or visible "behavior" . . . But the surprising thing, the strange and finally mysterious thing, is that, though there are present to us only a figure and some bodily movements, in or through this presence we see something that is essentially invisible, something that is pure inwardness, something that each of us knows directly only of himself—his thinking, feeling, desiring, operations that, by themselves, cannot be presences to other men, that are non-external and that cannot be exteriorized directly because they do not occupy space or possess sensible qualities, so that, over against all the externality of the world, they are pure inwardness.[7]

It is this inwardness that makes co-existence with the other possible. The extent of co-existence will depend upon the extent to which two inwardnesses become *felt* to each other. The animal possesses only a very slight degree of inwardness, the faculty that makes "humanness" possible. We can now see the structural basis for the charge that is often made against someone who is behaving in a particularly execrable way: "You are acting like an animal!"

I am known to the other and the other is known to me through a *body*. This body is the interface between my interior and exterior worlds. As Marcel pointed out, we simultaneously *are* a body and *have* a body. My existence is one of both *Being* and *Having*. My body signals my inwardness, i.e., what is within me, to the other, as the sky signals fair weather or the time of day. The eyes—Ortega calls them the "windows of the soul"—are perhaps the most expressive part of our bodies. They manifest more of our interior and reveal more of the interior of the other than any other part of the body. As the eyes of the other look out from within, we can tell from what depth the body is looking.

The "within" we have been speaking of is never completely present, but is compresent, like the side of the apple we do not see. Most of what we experience of the other is compresent, just as much of what we experience in our immediate environment and all that we experience in the world beyond that environment is compresent. But there is an inherent difference between the compresence of the apple and the compresence of the other: ". . . in the case of the apple the part of it that is hidden at any moment has been present to me at other times, but the inwardness that the other man *is* has never made itself, nor can ever make itself, present to me. Yet, I find it there—whenever I find a human body."[8]

The other is different from me and separated from me precisely because he is *other* than me. Only the body of the other is radical and unquestionable reality to me. It is only his body that I can see and touch. I know that he possesses an inwardness, that this inwardness is in some ways like my own, that he is a "quasi-I." But no matter how long and how hard I try, I can never grasp his inwardness at its roots. I can never be certain of the motives behind what he says and does. Betrayal, as Marcel observed, is possible at any moment and "seems pressed upon us by the very shape of our world."[9]

Not only am I separated from the radical reality of the other, I am separated to a very considerable degree from the primary reality of myself. Even though I am closer to myself than I may become to another (or he to me), there are many realities in my life that are not patent and radical, but presumptions, although I live *as if* they were radical realities:

> . . . *I am not aware of my genuine life*, of what it is in its radical solitude and truth, but instead, *I presumptively live presumed things*, I live among interpretations of reality which my social environment and human tradition have been inventing and accumulating [emphasis added].[10]

Most of what we live is not only presumptive, but illusory. Without analysis, we accept *as our own truth* things that we have heard named, defined, evaluated, and justified by other persons and by institutions. Most of the time we live "second hand" lives, i.e., we live out of touch with life as radical reality. Ortega's characterization of the alienating potential of society here is very much like Heidegger's description of "everydayness," the loss of self that results, inevitably, from giving in to the pressures of the crowd. "In solitude," Ortega maintains, "man is his truth; in society, he tends to be his mere conventionality and falsification."

> The genuine reality of human living includes the duty of frequent withdrawal to the solitary depths of oneself. This withdrawal, in which we demand that the mere seeming probabilities, if not sheer enchantments and illusions, in which we live shall show us their credentials of genuine reality, is known by the manneristic, absurd, and confusing name of *philosophy*. Philosophy is withdrawing, *anabasis*, settling accounts with oneself, in the fearsome nakedness of oneself before oneself.[11]

Ortega is saying here that philosophy is truth, "things laid open," the *aletheia* we have spoken of previously. The existential philosopher tries, through the *epoché*, to get to the root of the presumed realities that we live by daily—to "radical reality":

> ... ⌐we summon before this judgment-seat of the reality of the genuine human life all the things that are commonly called "social," in order that we may see what they are in their truth—that is, we proceed by constantly resorting from our conventional, habitual, daily life and its constituent perspective to our primary reality and its unwonted, difficult, and severe perspective. This is what we have done step by step, from our most elementary observation concerning the apple. Hailed before this judgment-seat, the apple that we believed we saw turned out to be slightly fraudulent; it has a half that is never present to us at the same time as the other half, and hence the apple as patent, present, seen reality does not exist, it is not such a reality. Then we observe that the greater part of our

sensible world is not present to us, but rather that the part of it that is at each moment present to us hides the rest and leaves it only compresent, as the room in which we are conceals the city from us, yet we live in the room as being in the city, and the city in the country, and the country in the World, and so on and so on.[12]

SOCIALITY AND THE APPEARANCE OF THE "I"

At our center we are *radical solitude*. We must concede that we are born in our own time and that we die in our own time. I am closer to myself than anyone else may become, and there are things about me that no other person can ever know. But each "I"—each inwardness—is *incomplete*. We therefore attempt to *de-solitudinize* ourselves (Ortega's term) by "showing ourselves to the other human being, desiring to give him our life and to receive his."[13]

I am not only a self or an "I" to myself, but, necessarily, an "other" to everyone I encounter:

> . . . being the other does not represent an accident or adventure that may or may not befall Man, but is his original attribute. I, in my solitude, could not call myself by a generic name like "man." The reality represented by this name appears to me only when there is another being who responds or reciprocates to me. Husserl says very well: "The meaning of the term 'man' implies a reciprocal existence of one to the other, hence *a community of men*, a *society*." And conversely: "It is equally clear that men cannot be apprehended unless there are (really or potentially) other men around them." . . . to speak of man outside of and apart from a society is to say something that is self-contradictory and meaningless . . . Man does not *appear* in solitude—although his ultimate truth is solitude; man appears in sociality as the Other . . .[14]

When an "I" opens his inwardness to the other, and the other cor-responds and reciprocates, a *we are* is created. When I cor-respond and reciprocate with another, the other becomes a *You*. This is the first time the word "you" appears in Ortega's analysis. This *You* is not simply a man or an "other," but a unique, unmistakable man (or woman) who

participates in my inwardness as I participate in his (or hers). There can
be no *we are* with the stone. With the animal there is just a limited
reciprocity. Only with another man (or woman) can I *de-solitudinize*
myself. (Discussion of Buber's *I-Thou* is delayed until Chapter 8.)

My inwardness is shared not with one, but with many *You*'s. The degree
of sharing determines the degree of intimacy.

> . . . I find the human World appearing to me as a horizon of men
> whose nearest circle to me is full of You's; that is, of those individ-
> uals who for me are unique. Beyond them lie circular zones occu-
> pied by men of whom I know less, and so on to the horizon-line of
> my human environment, the place of the individuals who to me are
> indeterminate, interchangeable. Thus the human world opens be-
> fore me as a perspective of greater or less intimacy, of greater or less
> individuality or uniqueness, in short, a perspective of close and
> distant humanity.[15]

At this point, Ortega asks us to pause and take note that we have made
a dramatic discovery: in our systematic effort to define the structures of
self-other-world, we began with "world" and ended with "self," the order
precisely opposite to what we would have anticipated naïvely, without the
rigor of the phenomenological method. It is only through the world and
the other as a *You*, in his varying degrees of cor-respondence with me, that
I am able to discover myself, i.e., *my self*.

> . . . the concrete and unique I that each one of us feels himself to
> be is not something that we possess and know from the outset but
> something that gradually appears to us exactly as other things do,
> that is, step by step . . . we discover that we are *I* after and by virtue
> of having first known the *you*'s, our *you*'s, in our collision with them,
> in the strife that we called social relation.[16]

> . . . in this strife and collision with the *you*'s, I gradually discover
> my limits and my concrete figure as a man, as *I*; my *I* continues
> slowly becoming apparent to me all through my life, as a vaporous
> reduction and contraction of that immense, diffuse, unlimited thing
> that it was before and still was in my childhood. My knowledge of

the *you's* keeps pruning and paring down this vague and abstract *I*
which yet, in the abstract, believed that it was everything. Your
mathematical talent shows me that I have none. Your graceful
speech shows me that I am without it. Your strong will shows me
that I am a milksop. Obviously, the reverse is also true; your faults
reveal my virtues to my own eyes. Thus, it is in the world of the *you's*,
and by virtue of them, that the thing that I am, my *I*, gradually takes
shape for me. I discover myself, then, as one of the countless *you's*,
but as different from them all, with gifts and defects of my own, with
a unique character and conduct, that together draw my genuine and
concrete profile for me . . .[17]

There is a great paradox running in and through Ortega's structural
framework: while it is only through the other (as a *You*) and through the
world that I can know and create myself, this same other and this same
world are a constant threat to my authenticity, ceaselessly calling me
away from the radical reality of my self.

5

"Action" and "Contemplation":

A Dialectic of Self

> ... men go abroad to admire the heights of the mountains, the
> mighty billows of the sea, the broad tides of rivers, the compass of the
> ocean, and the circuits of the stars, and pass themselves by ...
>
> —Augustine, *The Confessions*

What does it mean to be an *I*, an integral self? Just what does the word "self" specify? As a beginning, we could say that self is the content and configuration of my Being, or, more precisely using Heidegger's terminology, my Being-in-the-world. It is the mode of existence I choose from the many possibilities that are open to me.

"ACTION" AND "CONTEMPLATION"

Unlike the animal which lives almost totally in response to what is outside it, a man has an interior world as well as an exterior world. Neither world is complete, but a half-world instead. Neither world is reality itself, but each world contributes to reality. A man becomes himself —creates himself—by incorporating into his life elements from both half-worlds through a kind of ontic synthesis. If either the interior world or the exterior world is neglected or overstressed vis-à-vis the other, the synthesis falters and the self suffers, i.e., becomes less than it might have

become. The post-Socratic Greek philosophers got our Western civilization off to a bad start when they all but severed the connection between
the intellect and the exterior world, and then placed the highest value on
the harvest of this isolated intellect. When the link between the two worlds
was broken, the way was opened for the self to be lost in *both* worlds.

In *Man and People* Ortega rigorously probes the interior and the exterior
half-worlds. He describes their functions as *ensimismamiento* and *alteración**
respectively. We will call them *contemplation* and *action* here. Self is lost in
contemplation, through what Ortega called the "intellectualist aberration,"
when ideas are separated from the exterior world and become autonomous. Ortega knew that "every idea is dangerous" because he knew that
every idea is capable of being abused. In Chapter 1 we saw the agony that
Pirsig's Phaedrus (*Zen and the Art of Motorcycle Maintenance*) went through
when he tried, unsuccessfully, to fit his life to the curves of analytical
philosophy. To sever the interior world from the exterior world, mind
from matter, thought from life, is to live as if *thought lies outside life*, instead
of being a necessary and integral part of it. The following excerpt from *The
Way of Chuang Tzu* is another illustration of the intellectualist aberration:

> The wise man, then, when he must govern, knows how to do
> nothing. Letting things alone, he rests in his original nature. He who
> will govern will respect the governed no more than he respects
> himself. If he loves his own person enough to let it rest in its original
> truth, he will govern others without hurting them. Let him keep the
> deep drives in his own guts from going into action. Let him keep
> still, not looking, not hearing. Let him sit like a corpse, with the
> dragon power alive all around him. In complete silence, his voice
> will be like thunder. His movements will be invisible, like those of a
> spirit, but the powers of heaven will go with them. Unconcerned,
> doing nothing, he will see all things grow ripe around him. Where
> will he find time to govern?[1]

---

*The literal meanings of the Spanish words are "within-oneself-ness" and "otheration."
This distinction is, of course, a fiction. In fact, a man's inner world cannot be separated from
his outer world. As we pointed out earlier in our analogy describing the phenomenological
method, we work with the unreal *part* (the photograph) to illuminate the real *whole* (the
moving picture).

Chuang Tzu evokes here the sense of a ruler in consonance with himself and the world. There are times, during a crisis, when the wisest thing is to sit tight and wait for the storm to pass. (To do nothing can be a conscious decision "to do no thing.") But there are times when the passivity Chuang Tzu idealizes here would be self-destructive, even suicidal. The ruler seems to be completely unaware of any danger from the outside. He is locked within himself, and lives solely in the world of *contemplation*. He does not even consider the possibility of action as a response to the crisis. He assumes that "the powers of heaven" are with him, but does not seem to be aware of the admonition that "heaven helps those who help themselves," a warning which, although it appeals to a transcendent divinity, at least acknowledges an outer world and the necessity for *action*.

Just as self may be lost through the intellectualist aberration, it may be lost at the other extreme, through what Ortega calls the "voluntarist aberration." Here, *contemplation* is thrown overboard, and *action* is deified. The interior world is denied, and "life" is lived solely in the exterior world. The synthesis of self ceases. To characterize the voluntarist aberration, i.e., pure *action*, Ortega summons the monkey as an illustration. In the preceding chapter, we saw that the donkey and the dog have a degree of inwardness that makes some cor-respondence and sharing with a man possible. But the monkey seems to have no inwardness whatever.

The monkey in its cage at the zoo is ceaselessly concerned with what is happening around it. While awake, it cannot relinquish its attention, even momentarily, to its fellow monkeys or to the people outside its cage who come to see it. The monkey is perpetually uneasy and perpetually alert to what is going on around it. It is in constant fear of its world and in constant hunger for the things of this world. It does not rule its life or live for itself, but lives in constant reaction to what is happening outside it. "To say that the animal lives not for *itself* but from what is *other* than itself, pulled and pushed and tyrannized over by that *other*, is equivalent to saying that the animal is always estranged from itself, beside itself, that its life is essential *alteración*—possession by all that is *other*."[2] The monkey lives from the outside in. It lacks the capacity for being its self, and is constantly beside itself. It functions as pure *action*.

But men can be this way too. Western history offers many examples of the voluntarist aberration, of *action* cut off from *contemplation*. The chapter in *Man and People* where Ortega characterizes the intellectualist and voluntarist aberrations was read as a lecture in Argentina in 1939. The political reverberations go back to the Spanish Civil War and ahead to the world war that was about to begin:

The demagogues, impresarios of *alteración*, who have already caused the death of several civilizations, harass men so that they shall not reflect, see to it that they are kept herded together in crowds so that they cannot reconstruct their individuality in the one place where it can be reconstructed, which is in solitude. They cry down service to truth, and in its stead offer us: *myths*. And by all these means they succeed in throwing men into a passion, in putting them, between ardors and terrors, *beside*, that is, *outside of*, *themselves*. And clearly, since man is the animal that has succeeded in putting himself *inside himself*, when man is *beside himself* his aspiration is to descend and he falls back into animality.[3]

Like Ortega's monkey!

Western civilization could be summed up by saying that the philosophers suborned the intellect in *contemplation*, while the dictators and the generals suborned the will in *action*. From the very beginning, Plato's severing abstraction sabotaged his own ideal of the philosopher-king.

In the summer and fall of 1940, after the fall of France, Simone Weil wrote an analysis of Homer's *Iliad* which she called *The Iliad, or The Poem of Force*. Her theme was that the true subject of Homer's epic was force—its use and abuse, and how, invariably, those who abused force were in turn crushed by it. She defined force as "that x that turns anybody who is subjected to it into a *thing*. Exercised to the limit, it turns man into a thing in the most literal sense: it makes a corpse out of him." The Greeks, she argued, from the Pythagoreans to Socrates and Plato, understood that force always rebounded on its perpetrators, "that those who have force on loan from fate count on it too much and are destroyed." The ancient Greeks abused force, but they at least knew enough to expect retribution from fate. The West, she wrote, has now lost that understanding: "Conceptions of limit, measure, equilibrium, which ought to determine the conduct of life are, in the West, restricted to a servile function in the vocabulary of technics. We are only geometricians of matter; the Greeks were, first of all, geometricians in their apprenticeship to virtue."[4]

In Anouilh's *Antigone*, Creon tries to convince Antigone that the political crisis he inherited required him to use force without thought of its consequences, that, in effect, *action had* to be severed from any interior consideration. The ship of state was sinking, and so, he maintains, someone had to take the wheel:

Was that a time for a man to be weighing the pros and cons, wondering if he isn't going to pay too dearly later on; if he wasn't going to lose his life, or his family, or his touch with other men? You grab the wheel, you right the ship in the face of a mountain of water. You shout an order, and if one man refuses to obey, you shoot straight into the mob. Into the mob, I say! The beast is as nameless as the wave that crashes down upon your deck; as nameless as the whipping wind. The thing that drops when you shoot may be someone who poured you a drink the night before; but it has no name. And you, braced at the wheel, you have no name, either. Nothing has a name—except the ship, and the storm.[5]

Creon has lost all reference to anything that could be considered human. His self-synthesis has ceased because his exterior world lacks any interior dimension. *Contemplation* has been thrown overboard to "save" the ship of state. He has become a "beast," and he treats the men under his command as beasts.

In a similar vein, in Sartre's play *The Condemned of Altona*, Gerlach, a captain of German industry, tells his diffident son, Werner: "If you want to command, think of yourself as someone else."[6] If carried out, Gerlach's suggestion would amount to the temporary closing off of a man's interior world so that he would literally *become another person* through a persona of "otherness." Creon and Gerlach come as close to embodying Ortega's voluntarist aberration as any man can. With their interior worlds shut down, they act solely in response to what is outside them. They are pushed, pulled, and tyrannized by external forces so that they are beside themselves, estranged from themselves, really, no selves at all. They are pure *alteración*. Like Ortega's monkey! Like the beast! In Sartre's play Franz, Gerlach's older son (and a stand-in for Sartre), has the final word: "The century might have been a good one had not man been watched from time immemorial by the cruel enemy who had sworn to destroy him, that hairless, evil, flesh-eating beast—man himself . . . The beast was hiding, and suddenly we surprised his look deep in the eyes of our neighbors. So we struck. Legitimate self-defense. I surprised the beast. I struck. A man fell, and in his dying eyes I saw the beast still living—myself."[7]

Unlike the monkey or stone, a man does not have a predetermined essence or nature (recall Sartre's distinction between the In-itself and the For-itself). "While the tiger cannot stop being a tiger, cannot be de-tigered," Ortega declared, "man lives in perpetual danger of being dehumanized."[8] Because his Being (self) is constantly in flux, subjected as it is to every kind of call from himself, others, and his situation, a man is always at the point of not becoming himself, of losing himself.

A DIALECTICAL SYNTHESIS OF SELF

We have characterized the extremes of *action* and *contemplation*, and seen how ignoring elements from one sphere leads to the crushing of the self at the other, to a self literally in extremity. If the self can be characterized, at least in part, by a phenomenological analysis of the extremes that lead to the loss of self, then our principal goal is not the specification of the extremes themselves, but rather a description of the self that is created through what might be thought of as a *dialectical synthesis* of elements from both spheres. We would like to describe the self as coming about through a dialectical interaction of *action* and *contemplation*, i.e., by considering self as the synthesis term of an *action* (thesis)-*contemplation* (antithesis) dialectic.* To pursue this idea, we will use illustrations from three novels— André Malraux's *The Temptation of the West*, E. M. Forster's *Howards End*, and Albert Camus's *A Happy Death*—novels whose major characters "personify" the integration of elements from the spheres of *contemplation* and *action*. These characters become fictional presences created within the field of self, other, and world.**

---

* While the dialectic we are considering here is similar in form to Hegel's dialectic, the similarity ends there. Hegel felt that omnipotent reason could create existence out of itself, that thought generated existence. In contrast, our dialectic is *existential*, and generates a *concrete self* (see footnote 1 in Chapter 2).

** In the effort to characterize the possibilities of self, the novelist is a natural ally of the philosopher. The artist works toward the real with the unreal, toward what eventually can be seen through what is initially unseen. About the problem of apprehending an unseen foe, the thriller writer, Adam Hall, wrote in *The Striker Portfolio*: "We don't know anything. We don't know who they are or how many or where they are or what they're doing or why. We have to find them by letting them find us first." There are things about ourselves that we do not know and want to find out. The novelist finds out by creating fictional characters (unreal people) from his experience and imagination, forcing them to face complex situations with other characters under circumstances of his choosing, and then *letting them find him*. In the course of several hundred pages, these characters go through what would, in many cases, take a lifetime (or a significant fraction of a lifetime) for a person living in the real world. They succeed or fail to varying degrees, but when the novel ends, the novelist has their "whole story." If he has succeeded, i.e., written a good novel, he knows something more

MALRAUX'S *THE TEMPTATION OF THE WEST*

Malraux's first novel, *The Temptation of the West*, published in 1926, is a series of letters written and exchanged by two fictional characters. A. D., who is French and has some knowledge of Oriental art, goes to China with the hope of finding in its culture a complement to what he feels is missing in his own. Ling, who is Chinese and is also aware of a certain one-sidedness to his life in the Orient, visits France with a similar intention. Both men are in their early twenties, impressionable, serious, and anguished by the limitations of their own lives.

In one of Ling's first letters, written from Paris after visiting the Louvre, he notes that all the heroes portrayed in Western art are engaged in some sort of action—action that, he judges from the faces in the paintings, seems to have brought not joy, but sadness. He contrasts this observation with his own experiences in China:

> Every civilization shapes a sensibility. The great man in the Orient is neither the painter nor the writer, but rather the man who is capable of carrying this sensibility to its perfection. Refining in themselves the sensibility of their race, and, in expressing it, moving constantly toward a higher pleasure—that is the life of those among us whom you would call "masters." Greatness, whether yours, that of armed men, or ours, that of perfection, arises from the intensity of emotion a feeling wakes in men. For you, it is the sentiment of sacrifice: *admiration is reserved for action* [emphasis added]. For us, it is but the awareness that we exist in accord with the most beautiful mode. The forms of art which you have been accustomed to call sublime express an *action* rather than a *state*. This state, of which we know nothing except that it gives, to those who attain it, a sense of purity, of the separateness of the soul in the heart of the eternal light, has never been sought by Occidentals, although the languor offered

---

continuation

about himself than before he started writing. Enter the reader. During several hours or days, he becomes involved with the characters, their situations, and their fictional ending. They fire his imagination and enter his consciousness. Once there, the reader makes analogies and connections, on different levels and through different mechanisms, between these (unreal) characters and their (unreal) situations, and his own (real) experience. Because *they* found *him*, he will find out something about himself.[9]

by certain stretches of the Mediterranean affords them the opportunity to seek it. Thence springs the sole sublime expression of art
and of man; it is called serenity.[10]

There is a strong correspondence between what Malraux calls *action*
(the characteristic tenor of the West) and *state* (the characteristic tenor of
the East), and Ortega's delineation of *action* and *contemplation*, the dialectical elements that he saw as constituting the self. For a Western man to be
considered a success, his contemplative experience must, at some point,
be projected into the outer world and culminate in an achievement. The
"masters" of the West *stand out*. In contrast, an Oriental "master" is a
man who *blends into* his world and attains a *state* of harmony with it. He
moves "constantly toward a higher pleasure"—from within. "We," Ling
writes to A. D., "do not wish to be conscious of ourselves as individuals.
The work of our mind is to experience lucidly our fragmentary nature and
to draw from that feeling a sense of the universe, not as your pedants
reconstruct prehistoric animals with a few bones, but rather as we, merely
by reading a name on a post card, evoke unknown countrysides striped by
giant vines; for the supreme beauty of a cultured civilization is to be found
in the careful avoidance of nurturing the 'I.' "[11] In another letter, Ling
tells A. D. that the idea of individual existence was so alien to the Chinese
that, until the Revolution, parents were punished along with their children for crimes which the children committed without their parents'
knowledge.

The Being or existence of the Oriental occurs almost totally within the
sphere of what Ortega called *ensimismamiento* ("within-oneself-ness"), as
was the case with the ruler in the excerpt from *The Way of Chuang Tzu*,
cited earlier. But this interiority is not the same as the isolation from the
world that occurs when the Occidental man "reconstructs" the world in
his mind through thought (as in Descartes's *Cogito*), severing his ties with
it. Ling called this "that strange European illness . . . overdevelopment of
the intellect . . ."[12] The Oriental comes to the world passively, through
feeling. The Occidental man thrusts himself upon the world through
action and achievement. Ling tells A. D.: "Experiencing the universe is
not the same as systematizing it . . . You analyze what you have already
felt; we think in order to feel."[13]

The concept of self is a Western concept. As Ling says, the Oriental
does not wish to be conscious of himself as an "individual," and carefully
avoids "nurturing the 'I.'" Selfless, the Oriental seeks the "serenity" that

comes with the awareness that he exists "in accord with the most beautiful mode." In the context of Ortega's dialectic of the self, the Oriental, never having had what we think of as a self (an "I"), cannot lose it. That is our Western prerogative. Ling sees this clearly: "You are completely carried away by the goals toward which you are incessantly aiming . . . We Chinese try to grasp only the entirety of life. Not that we are able to do this. Still, we know that this entirety is, and must be, greater than any one of our individual acts."[14] Ling's use of the expression "carried away" is trenchant. To be carried away in aiming at a goal is to be lost as self, to displace Ortega's dialectic toward *action.*

Malraux's novel closes with Ling conceding to A. D. that the young Chinese were beginning to be influenced by elements of European culture. The products of technological civilization—cinema, electricity, mirrors, phonographs—had found their way to China and had, according to Ling, "seduced us like new breeds of domestic animals." A new, young, educated elite was emerging, and this worried Ling because he felt this imitation of the West, this *Temptation* of the West, would lead to the loss of much that the Chinese valued in their lives and saw lacking in the lives of Europeans. In *Irrational Man* William Barrett pointed out that it was Plato's differentiation of rational consciousness as a separate psychic entity (the mind-matter split) that made it possible for Western civilization to develop science and technology: "The Greeks' discovery [of rationality, later to become the god of Reason] represents an immense and necessary step forward by mankind, but also a loss, for the pristine wholeness of man's being is thereby sundered or at least pushed into the background."[15] Until early in the twentieth century, this Greek influence had not been felt in the Orient. But once it arrived, via Europe, it began taking the same toll on the Chinese as it had taken on the Europeans. Once the genie of reason and technology was out of the bottle, and a path to the outer world was opened up, the "serenity" that came with existing "in accord with the most perfect mode" did not stand a chance. The "temptation" could not be withstood.

FORSTER'S *HOWARDS END*

Forster's novel *Howards End* is set in England, just before the start of World War I. The protagonists, the Schlegels and the Wilcoxes, are two very different kinds of families and, even more significantly, lead very different kinds of lives.

Following their parents' death, Helen and Margaret Schlegel inherit a
large house and receive an annual income that makes them financially
independent. The sisters belong to the upper-middle class of London
society and spend most of their time traveling, reading novels, and
attending concerts and art exhibitions. The Schlegel sisters are two rather
cerebral young women: they are interested in Beethoven, Nietzsche, and
England's colonial policy. They embody Forster's idea of the inner life,
the life of introspection and personal relationships.

Henry Wilcox is a London businessman whose wife inherited Howards
End, a country house for which the novel is titled. They have two sons and
a daughter. The Wilcoxes live in the business world and have the business
mentality. Theirs is the outer life, the world of "telegrams and anger."
The Schlegel sisters and the Wilcoxes meet during a holiday on the
Continent. Shortly after returning to England, Helen is invited by the
younger Wilcox son, Paul, to spend a weekend at Howards End. Helen is
captivated by the Wilcoxes and their way of life. Living, for them, is
perpetual motion: cars, cricket, tennis, orders shouted to the servants.
They seem "to have their hands on the ropes."

One evening, under a darkening summer sky, Helen and Paul experience what each at the moment feels is love, and marriage is proposed. But
the next morning, Paul, in a state of agitation, tells Helen that he cannot
accept the responsibility of marriage and must leave England to begin his
career in Africa. Helen is momentarily stunned, but then quickly regains
her balance when she realizes that she had not fallen in love with an
individual, but with the way of life of a family, with an *idea*. In the busy,
external life of the Wilcoxes, she saw a complement to her own life. Paul
Wilcox had momentarily opened to her the life of the outer world and the
life of the body.

Not long after the sudden death of his wife, Mr. Wilcox asks Margaret
Schlegel, the older sister, to marry him, and she accepts. It is an unlikely
union, considering how differently the two families approach life. But
Margaret feels that, through love, she can help Mr. Wilcox bridge the gap
between the inner and the outer worlds: "Mature as he was, she might yet
help him to the building of the rainbow bridge that should connect the
prose in us with the passion. Without it we are meaningless fragments,
half monks, half beasts, unconnected arches that have never joined into a
man."[16] Both the Schlegels and the Wilcoxes live in "fragments." Margaret and Helen understand the social and political currents that run
through the complex modern world, and desperately *want* things to come
out right. But they do not *function* well in the world. They can't even

manage to find a new house to move into when theirs is threatened by the wrecker's ball. They live almost exclusively in what Forster calls the world of *passion*. The Wilcoxes, on the other hand, shun ideas and "culture," but participate and compete successfully in the world. They live almost exclusively in what Forster calls the world of *prose*. At times, they remind us of Ortega's monkey.

Margaret sees the problem as one of "connecting," i.e., of integrating elements of the interior and exterior worlds, the *passion* and the *prose*: "Only connect the prose and the passion, and both will be exalted, and human love will be seen at its height. Live in fragments no longer. Only connect, and the beast and the monk, robbed of the isolation that is life to either, will die." What Margaret is aiming at is very much like the Greek ideal of proportion: "The business man who assumes that this life is everything, and the mystic who asserts that it is nothing, fail, on this side and on that, to hit the truth."[17] But how does one "connect"? The Schlegels' Aunt Juley suggests that perhaps the truth is "halfway between" the *prose* and the *passion*. "No," Forster replies. "Truth, being alive, [is] not halfway between anything. It [is] only to be found by continuous excursions into either realm, and though proportion is the final secret, to espouse it at the outset is to insure sterility."[18]

Margaret is not successful in getting Mr. Wilcox to "connect." The habits of a lifetime are not easily changed. She had not realized the extent of his "obtuseness"—that "he simply did not notice things." Caught up in the whirl of the Wilcox's exterior world, there are times when Margaret herself feels that life is flattening out, that she is losing herself. But she is determined to keep the synthesis alive. After a particularly difficult period with her husband in London, she visits Howards End, the country house that Forster means to stand for the life of personal relationships and ties with the land, and quickly regains her sense of presence: "Her evening was pleasant. The sense of flux which had haunted her all the year disappeared for a time. She forgot the luggage and the motor-cars, and the hurrying men who know so much and connect so little. She recaptured the sense of space, which is the basis of all earthly beauty, and, starting from Howards End, she attempted to realize England."[19] Margaret is learning to connect the *prose* and the *passion*, to integrate the exterior and the interior worlds.

There is a structural similarity between Forster's notion of how one is to "connect" and John Ciardi's description of how a poem "means" in his book, *How Does a Poem Mean?*[20] Ciardi uses Robert Frost's brief poem "The Span of Life" to illustrate an aspect of the dynamics of poetic form:

The old dog barks backward without getting up.
I can remember when he was a pup.

The poem *means*, Ciardi says, by setting "one part against another
across a silence." First, the reader receives the image of an old dog, so frail
that it does not get up to acknowledge its master. Then we are told that
the poet recalls the dog as a puppy. We are given images of two temporal
extremes in the dog's life. By allowing these images to become juxtaposed
in our mind, the poet makes it possible for our imagination to integrate
them, and thus grasp the *span* of the animal's life (and, by extension,
something of the span of our own lives as well). Similarly, in *Howards End*
Forster characterizes the *prose* and the *passion* in the persons of the
Wilcoxes and the Schlegels. It is then left to the reader to stand astride the
poles, bridge the silence, and "connect."

In his novel Forster, like Malraux, asks the question, What is the fullest
possible life we can have? Malraux poses the question abstractly, even
metaphysically, while Forster works concretely by introducing the
Schlegels and the Wilcoxes to each other. Ling and A. D. travel to other
continents, hoping to find in another culture something that will make
their lives more complete. Margaret and Helen Schlegel look for completion by pursuing relationships with men from a different class. (When it
comes to fusing elements from the cultures of the East and the West on
one hand, and "connecting" elements from the intellectual and the
business worlds on the other, the differences—and the distances—seem to
be as great.) Ortega, Malraux, and Forster all seem to agree that what is
most important in life must be *sought* at the extremes, but *acquired* somewhere in between. It is the *synthesis* that counts, the synthesis from
Ortega's dialectic of *action* and *contemplation*, Malraux's modes of *action* and
state, the *prose* and the *passion* of Forster.

Howards End is a prophetic novel. Forster wrote it on the eve of World
War I, when it was becoming obvious that whatever had held Europe
together for the preceding century could no longer be counted on to do so.
Forster saw the Wilcoxes as an example of a "new breed" that was
appearing in Europe, people who lacked the interior dimension and
functioned without any center (Ortega's *alteración*). To all appearances
decent Englishmen, the Wilcoxes were the vanguard of a new nihilism.
Helen Schlegel says to Leonard Bast:

I believe in personal responsibility. Don't you? And in personal everything. I hate—I suppose I oughtn't to say that—but the Wilcoxes are on the wrong tack surely. Or perhaps it isn't their fault. Perhaps the little thing that says "I" is missing out of the middle of their heads, and then it's a waste of time to blame them. There's a nightmare of a theory that says a special race is being born which will rule the rest of us in the future just because it lacks the little thing that says "I."

. . . there are two kinds of people—our kind, who live straight from the middle of their heads, and the other kind who can't, because their heads have no middle. They can't say "I." They *aren't* in fact, and so they're supermen.* Pierpont Morgan has never said "I" in his life.[21]

The Wilcoxes are caught up in the Hegelian juggernaut of Progress toward the Absolute. "Our civilization is molded by great impersonal forces," Mr. Wilcox tells Margaret, " . . . and you can't deny that, in spite of all, the tendency of civilization has on the whole been upward." Henry Wilcox was one of those men who had reconciled science with religion— "You grab the dollars. God does the rest."

Forster seems to have anticipated not only the war that was impending, but the one that would follow a quarter of a century later ("Life's going to be melted down, all over the world"). If there is any hope of understanding what made the atrocities of this century possible, the analysis will first have to come to terms with those people whose "heads have no middle," who can't say "I." They seem to be the inevitable result of what Heidegger called "the fall from Being." They are the root of the new nihilism.

CAMUS'S *A HAPPY DEATH*

In the first letter we quoted earlier from Malraux's *The Temptation of the West*, Ling tells A. D. that although the serenity that is the goal of the Oriental had never been sought as an end in itself by Occidentals, the Mediterranean offered an ideal setting for its pursuit. The coast of Algeria

---

* This is the exact opposite of what Nietzsche meant by the Superman (*Übermensch*).

is very much like the Mediterranean coast, and, in the abiding presence of the sea, the sky, and the sun, Camus realized, in his life and in his writing, something very much like the serenity Ling describes. In *A Happy Death*—a novel written between 1936 and 1939, when he was in his early twenties, but not published until 1972—Camus achieves a dialectical synthesis similar to those adumbrated by Malraux, Forster, and Ortega. The novel is about cultivating "a will to happiness," i.e., the possibility of creating happiness in oneself.

As an impoverished, disoriented, and bored young office worker, Patrice Mersault makes the acquaintance of Ronald Zagreus, an older man who has a great deal of money. Before losing both legs in an accident, Zagreus had used his wealth to pursue happiness directly as an end in itself, rather than, let us say, indirectly, through work and marriage, as most people do. Zagreus is drawn to Mersault because of the latter's youth and vigor, and, no doubt, because Mersault's mistress at the time of their meeting had been Zagreus's lover before his accident. Zagreus tells Mersault that he has been "made for happiness," just as he, Zagreus, had been. He counsels him to become rich, since money can buy the time that is needed to pursue happiness. Seeing the chance to commit a perfect crime and obtain instantly the money necessary to begin a new life, Mersault kills Zagreus with the man's own revolver. (Zagreus had prepared a suicide note so as to be reminded constantly of the other option to life, and Mersault uses the note, successfully, to cover the murder.) Mersault takes Zagreus's money and leaves Algiers to travel through eastern Europe. Not finding contentment in this, he returns to Algiers and lives, for a short time, in a villa high above the city with several girls who are old acquaintances. He begins to be happy here, giving himself over to the sun and the sky, becoming one with the world. He buys a house near a village on the Chenoua coast, and goes there *to live*.

While getting the house ready, Mersault stays at the hotel in the village. Although the solitude oppresses him at times, he begins to feel close to the land and the sea, and achieves a degree of peace. But then, for a period of several days, he becomes so absorbed by his work that this peace slips away, and he becomes fretful:

> He had to set up his house, organize his life. The first days passed quickly. He whitewashed the walls, bought hangings in Algiers, began to install electricity; and as he went about his work, interrupted by the meals he took at the village café and by his dips in the

sea, he forgot why he had come here and lost himself in his body's fatigue, loins aching and legs stiff, fretting over the shortage of paint or the defective installation of a light fixture in the hallway.[22]

Mersault loses himself momentarily because he forgets momentarily what he has come here for. He ceases to cultivate "a will to happiness." He becomes lost in, his self becoming absorbed and engulfed by, his work. The balance of the dialectic between *action* and *state* shifts so far in the direction of *action* that Mersault loses touch with himself. For a time, Mersault's self-synthesis falters. But when the house is completed and he moves his things into it, he recovers his strength and reopens himself to life.

But Mersault still has not realized serenity. He eats and sleeps fitfully and is unable to read. He sleeps late, does not shave or comb his hair, chain-smokes cigarettes, and feels phlegmatic. He writes to Lucienne, his estranged wife, and asks her to visit. She comes from Algiers, and her company gives Mersault some relief from his solitude. They walk on the beach and spend the night together. Lucienne asks if they could live together, but Mersault does not love her, and says no. She leaves the next day, and Mersault, still at loose ends, goes back to Algiers to his old neighborhood. He walks around, talks with some friends, and ends up spending the night at Lucienne's apartment.

The next evening, while driving back to the Chenoua along the steep hillside above the waves, Mersault experiences an epiphany:

Rounding one curve after the next, Mersault steeped himself in this humiliating yet priceless truth: the conditions of the singular happiness he sought were getting up early every morning, taking a regular swim—a conscious hygiene. He drove very fast, resolved to take advantage of his discovery in order to establish himself in a routine that would henceforth require no further effort, to harmonize his own breathing with the deepest rhythm of time, of life itself.

The next morning he got up early and walked down to the sea. The sky was already brilliant and the morning full of rustling wings and crying birds. But the sun was only touching the horizon's curve, and when Mersault stepped into the still-lusterless water, he seemed to be swimming in an indeterminate darkness until, as the sun climbed higher, he thrust his arms into streaks of icy red and gold.

Then he swam back to land and walked up to his house. His body
felt alert and ready for whatever the day might bring. Every morning, now, he came downstairs just before sunrise, and this first
action controlled the rest of the day. Moreover, these swims exhausted him, but at the same time, because of the fatigue and the
energy they afforded, they gave his entire day a flavor of abandonment and joyful lassitude. Yet the hours still seemed long to
him—he had not yet detached time from a carcass of habits that still
punctuated the past. He had nothing to do, and his time stretched
out, measureless, before him. Each minute recovered its miraculous
value, but he did not yet recognize it for what it was. Just as the days
of a journey seem interminable whereas in an office the trajectory
from Monday occurs in a flash, so Mersault, stripped of all his
props, still tried to locate them in a life that had nothing but itself to
consider. Sometimes he picked up his watch and stared as the
minute hand shifted from one number to the next, marveling that
five minutes should seem so interminable. Doubtless that watch
opened the way—a painful and tormenting way—that leads to the
supreme art of doing nothing. He learned to walk; sometimes in the
afternoon he would walk along the beach as far as the ruins of
Tipasa; then he would lie down among the wormwood bushes, and
with his hands on the warm stone would open his eyes and his heart
to the intolerable grandeur of that seething sky. He matched the
pounding of his blood with the violent pulsation of the sun at two
o'clock, and deep in the fierce fragrance, deafened by the invisible
insects, he watched the sky turn from white to deep-blue, then pale
to green, pouring down its sweetness upon the still-warm ruins. He
would walk home early then, and go to bed. In this passage from sun
to sun, his days were organized according to a rhythm whose
deliberation and strangeness became as necessary to him as had
been his office, his restaurant, and his sleep in his mother's room. In
both cases, he was virtually unconscious of it. But now, in his hours
of lucidity, he felt that time was his own, that in the brief interval
that finds the sea red and leaves it green, something eternal was
represented for him in each second. Beyond the curve of the days he
glimpsed neither superhuman happiness nor eternity—happiness
was human, eternity ordinary. What mattered was to humble himself, to organize his heart to match the rhythm of the days instead of
submitting their rhythm to the curve of human hopes.

Just as there is a moment when the artist must stop, when the sculpture must be left as it is, the painting untouched—just as a determination *not to know* serves the maker more than all the resources of clairvoyance—so there must be a minimum of ignorance in order to perfect a life in happiness. Those who lack such a thing must set about acquiring it: unintelligence must be earned.[23]

Now Mersault has his synthesis, a synthesis of what Malraux's Ling saw as the epitomic traits of the West (*action*) and the Orient (*state*). The contentment and happiness that Mersault finally achieves come about through a delicate balance of this dialectic. During the time that he was refurbishing his house, when he "lost himself in his body's fatigue," the balance was displaced toward *action*, in this case the action of physical labor. When he first moved into the house, when he had no planned daily routine and everything that he did was desultory, the balance was displaced in the opposite direction, toward a *state* of lethargy. Then, Mersault learned what Forster's Margaret Schlegel knew: that the truth—or serenity—was not "halfway between" the *prose* and the *passion*, but was realized by continuous forays into both extremes. Or, to put it in Ortega's terms, for a man to be truly human, his life must encompass the spheres of both *action* and *contemplation*, and these spheres must be *integrated*.

The *action* of the daily swimming that "exhausted" Mersault also made possible a *state* that "gave his entire day a flavor of abandonment and joyful lassitude." He began to understand the meaning of time, so that "each minute recovered its miraculous value." And he learned to walk, to "open his eyes and his heart to the intolerable grandeur of that seething sky." On the Chenoua, Mersault had all he needed or wanted: "stripped of all his props," he could live "a life that had nothing to consider but itself." In the terminology of Jung, every trace of persona was forsaken, and a self was created based solely on a "will to happiness."

Mersault was not alone. Lucienne would come from Algiers, stay a few days, and then leave. He became friends with Bernard, the village doctor, and accompanied him on his rounds. He came to know Perez, an old fisherman who supplied fish to the hotel where Mersault had stayed while getting his house ready. On Sundays he played pool with Perez, and, occasionally during the week, he would accompany the fisherman out to sea.

Mersault needed others—which is to say that he took from and gave to others—but not as a *condition* of his happiness. The nucleus for this, he felt,

was within himself: "What matters—all that matters, really—is the will to
happiness, a kind of enormous, ever-present consciousness. The rest—
women, art, success—is nothing but excuses. A canvas waiting for our
embroideries."[24] Mersault was now, as Camus liked to say of himself,
"solitary" but "solidary." He was a separate self, but at the same time a
part of the lives of others, although in a limited way. His body was truly
his own, as the interface between his interior and exterior worlds, and
between himself, others, and the world. He had reversed his alienation
from the world by becoming present *to* it. This presence was at once a
"judge and a justification," and he saw the world as a "personage." This
is what Heidegger means by ex-sistence, literally, to "stand out . . . in the
clearing of Being." We could easily imagine Mersault saying, with Heraclitus, that there are gods present here.

> Day after day, Mersault let himself sink into his life as if he were
> sliding into water. And just as the swimmer advances by the
> complicity of his arms and the water that bears him up, helps him
> on, it was enough to make a few essential gestures—to rest one hand
> on a tree trunk, to take a run on the beach—in order to keep himself
> intact and conscious. Thus he became one with a life in its pure
> state, he rediscovered a paradise given only to the most private or
> the most intelligent animals. At the point where the mind denies the
> mind, he touched his truth and with it his extreme glory, his extreme
> love.[25]

When Camus says that "there must be a minimum of ignorance in
order to perfect a life of happiness," he is talking about bridging the gap
between what the mind has to come to know of the world through
abstraction, and the world itself. Mersault "touched his truth and with it
his extreme glory . . . *at the point where the mind denies the mind*" (emphasis
added). For someone who has always lived in an ambience of
abstraction—and thus alienation—this is not easy. "Unintelligence,"
Camus realizes, "must be earned."

HOW SELF IS LOST

Our efforts so far have been directed toward making palpable the notion
of self, what the self is, how self is acquired, and how it is lost. We would

now like to distinguish two mechanisms through which self may be lost, two paths through which the marginal self may come into being.

THE DEFAULT OF SELF

Self may not be developed simply because one fails to do what is necessary to create it. We have already seen that when life is lived disproportionately in either the realms of *contemplation* or *action* the self fails to become itself, i.e., is diminished relative to what it might have become. Self may also be relinquished through an inadequate response to what Jaspers called a "boundary situation." As concrete, embodied persons living in the world, we are confronted with certain limits that cannot be gotten around, reduced, or explained. They are simply *there*, either as an unavoidable part of our situation, or as something inherent in the human condition. These limiting situations include intractable conflicts, the consequences of personal failure, suffering (physical and mental), the loss of someone close to us (through, say, frustrated love or death), and the anxiety that comes with the recognition of one's own "impending" death. At the "boundary," one cannot go forward (i.e., remove the obstacle), but one cannot go backward either (i.e., deny that the obstacle is there). There is tension here, and one has a choice of response. He can either, as Jaspers says, "sink through the vacuum into the absolutely groundless" or he can "hold [himself] open for the encounter with Being."[26] In the former choice, the boundary situation is treated as a dead end, and the self withers. In the latter choice, the boundary situation becomes a frontier where transcendence is achieved, where self is created.*

Many people go through their entire lives "backing off" from the boundary situations they encounter, so that they never generate a center or core of self. Instead, they respond mechanically to exterior influences and pressures, very much like Ortega's monkey. We can think of them as selves who never were. Their failure is the failure to become. They are marginal selves by virtue of *default*.

---

* Jaspers's notion of transcendence is similar to Camus's exhortation that we become superior to our absurd fate through *revolt*. In *The Plague* Rieux confronts the boundaries of isolation, suffering, and death. He will not deny the human tragedy of what is happening in Oran by attributing it to some divine purpose, as Father Paneloux urges his parishoners to do. As a physician, Rieux does as much as he can to curb the spread of the plague and cure those infected by it. He achieves transcendence—authentic selfhood—through *revolt*, a response that, to use Jaspers's phrase, opens him to the "encounter with Being."

THE EROSION OF SELF THROUGH SCHIZOID SPLITTING

The second principal mechanism through which self may be lost is the erosion of self brought about through schizoid splitting. Splitting was first identified by Bleuler, and was characterized further by Jung, R. D. Laing, and others. Erosion of self occurs through splitting when a false self (persona) is created along with a real self so that the real self is cut off from the world and from others. Lacking the sustenance that it requires from the world, the real self withers. Laing called this scission of the psyche into two parts the *divided self*. A person becomes a divided self through an inauthentic choice of self (the persona), which may or may not be recognized by him as such.* There is an authentic component to the divided self, but this real self is in constant conflict with the false self, in addition to being estranged from the world. When psychic splitting occurs on the level of neurosis, it leads to a diminution of self, to a marginal self. When splitting occurs on the level of psychosis, the result is more devastating.

In the next chapter, we will explain the theory behind the notion of the divided self, and then show how a number of characters from fiction are diminished by schizoid erosion. In Chapter 7 and Chapter 8, we will see how self is acquired and lost (by default and through schizoid erosion) in the work we do and in love. In Chapter 9, we will hold up for scrutiny a man—Richard Nixon—who we feel is a paradigm of the marginal self. In Chapter 10, we will say something about how the marginal self can be superseded.

---

* Psychic splitting may also be induced organically, through some chemical imbalance in the brain, but we will not consider this here.

6

Masks, Splitting, and the Schizoid Erosion of Self

All the world's a stage,
And all the men and women merely
  players:
They have their exits and their
  entrances;
And one man in his time
  plays many parts . . .

—William Shakespeare, *As You Like It*

Born Originals, how comes it to
pass that we die Copies?

—Edward Young

We have been told that we live in an alienating culture so many times and from so many sources that we have become desensitized to the charge. The accusation is true, but it is made so broadly and indiscriminately that we learn nothing from it. The culture we live in is alienating, i.e., literally capable of making us strangers to ourselves, because it offers so many easy paths through which the self may be lost. We are eager to relinquish ourselves because it is a difficult and painful matter to become a self, and because we long for the rewards that our culture is only too ready to give us in exchange for that self. The catch is that once these rewards have become ours, the self that was neglected to acquire them—what has become a marginal self—is inadequate to *enjoy* them. We would like to consider now, in detail, the self that splits itself to reap the rewards of accommodation, and see why it must pay such a high price for this accommodation. But first we must say something more about the self that is integral and unsplit.

THE DYNAMIC, INTEGRAL SELF

"It is true," Merleau-Ponty said, "neither that my existence is in full possession of itself, nor that it is entirely estranged from itself, because it is action or doing, and because action is, by definition, the violent transition from what I have to what I aim to have, from what I am to what I intend to be."[1] Heidegger coined the term Being-ahead-of-itself to characterize the dynamic state of man's Being. Because men, alone among creatures, have consciousness, i.e., the *awareness* that they exist, only men have the power to make or create themselves, to *choose* themselves, as Kierkegaard said.

Because we are perpetually "ahead of" ourselves, we never fully *coincide* with ourselves, we never fully *are* ourselves.* Men are open possibilities, living in a present that is not a true present, but which is always being encroached upon by the future, as well as by the past. As we have already seen, the stone can never be anything but a stone (Sartre's In-itself), and the donkey can never be anything but a donkey (Ortega). Neither the stone nor the donkey can betray itself, so as to become less than itself. Of everything that may be said to "exist," only men have this capability. Thus, a man may be born an "original" and end up a "copy." He may at some point in his life be authentic, only to later become inauthentic. He may at one time be "normal," only to later become neurotic or psychotic. When we say that the self is never wholly itself, we are really describing an ontological property of the self, i.e., how it is for *all* men.

In an attempt to find some verbal correspondence to the dynamic but *concrete* self that he felt had to be chosen continuously between the poles of the finite and the infinite, Kierkegaard used the metaphor of a "spot" to describe the relation between what one is at a given moment (the necessary) and what one is not but may become (the possible). Kierkegaard

---

* Heidegger maintains that the self is fully coincident with itself only in those rare moments when it experiences dread, the mood that arises when one glimpses the end of one's mortal existence (see Chapter 2). What we might call the near coincidence of self with itself occurs during moments of presence. Recall Camus's Mersault from *A Happy Death*.

challenged the long-standing philosophical tenet that necessity is the unity of possibility and actuality, and insisted, rather, that *actuality is the unity of possibility and necessity*.[2]* Kierkegaard's "spot" represents the concrete self that has *actuality*. To become concrete and actual, he said, one must move from the core of the existing self (the "spot") to what has not yet been actualized, i.e., to what is still a possibility. Creation of self is the addition of possibility to necessity, the addition of what is not to what already is. It is "movement from the spot," but, if it is to result in an authentic increment to the self (and not fall back on the despair of inauthenticity that is non-self), it must also be "movement *at* the spot,"[3] so that what formerly was not can be joined to what is—as with a solid crystal growing in a solution of its own substance.

Because the Being of man is dynamic, the "spot" which is the self is always changing, always becoming more or less than it was. Unamuno remarked that "there is nothing that remains the same for two successive moments of its existence."[4] While the self may change, and even change radically, it may not, without becoming psychotic, become totally discontinuous with its past, as Faulkner understood so clearly.** Unamuno felt that the basis of individual personality was memory.[5] Partly because of the memory of what one has been, the "spot" retains its integrity and continuity throughout the changes that the self undergoes while its choices propel it to actuality. "It appears to me to be indisputable," Unamuno said, "that he who I am today derives, by a continuous series of states of consciousness, from him who was in my body twenty years ago."[6] The self that is *actual* may be thought of as coming into being through a dialectic between continuity and change, between necessity and possibility.

---

* This is another way of saying, as all the existentialists do either explicitly or implicitly, that existence precedes essence (see Chapter 2).

** "My ambition," Faulkner said, "is to put everything into one sentence. Not only the present but the whole past on which it depends and which keeps overtaking the present, second by second." According to Malcolm Cowley, Faulkner wrote his prodigious sentences "to convey a sense of simultaneity, not only giving what happened in the shifting instant, but everything that went before and made the quality of that instant" (excerpted from *The Faulkner-Cowley File*, ed. Malcolm Cowley [New York: Viking Press, 1966] in *Harper's*, June 1966).

THE DIVIDED SELF

In *The Divided Self*,[7] a classic study of the causes and manifestations of schizophrenia, R. D. Laing begins his analysis of psychic splitting by distinguishing between the self that is "ontologically secure" and the self that is "ontologically insecure."* Despite the uncertainties and dangers that are inherent in a dynamic self, a man may come to feel his presence in the world, and successfully give to and take from others. The ontologically secure person is, according to Laing, "a real, alive, whole, and, in a temporal sense, a continuous person. As such, he can live out into the world and meet others: a world and others experienced as equally real, alive, whole, and continuous."[8] In Sartre's terminology, the ontologically secure person is one who is able to use his freedom to realize his "project."

In his notebooks, Gerard Manley Hopkins gives what seems to be an almost definitive description of ontological security: "I find myself both as man and as myself something most determined and distinctive, at pitch, more distinctive and higher pitched than anything else I see; I find myself with my pleasures and pains, my powers and my experiences, my deserts and my guilt, my shame and sense of beauty, my dangers, hopes, fears, and all my fate, more important to myself than anything I see."[9] And in *The Existential Experience*, Ralph Harper gives this penetrating statement of the intuition of self: " . . . I understood when I was quite young what lay beneath the passion of a lover or the ruthlessness of an artist. Nothing must be allowed to get in the way of this chance to be and become oneself, least of all the safe rules and abstractions of those who have never learned that the first aspect of existence (*Existenz*) is that it is *mine*."[10]

We have here two ringing expressions of what it means to be an ontologically secure person in full command of his powers, and on top of things. But no person, no matter how strongly he feels himself or how securely he is tied to Being (a Heideggerian notion), can maintain his existence at this pitch all the time. At certain points in his life, the expectations raised by a commitment to existence on this level are bound to be dashed, so that the sense of solidity of the self with the world and with others—one's sense of presence—will temporarily evaporate. Ionesco

---

* As Laing points out, he uses the word "ontological" here as an adverbial derivative of "Being," and not as we have used it previously, following Heidegger and Sartre, to denote the general *structure* of Being.

gives this account of what it is like to have one's sense of reality and presence wrenched away suddenly:

> Sometimes it seems to me that the forms of life are suddenly emptied of their contents, reality is unreal, words are nothing but sounds bereft of sense, these houses and this sky are no longer anything but facades concealing nothing, people appear to be moving about automatically and without reason; everything seems to melt into thin air, everything is threatened—myself included—by a silent and imminent collapse into I know not what abyss, where there is no more night or day. What magic power still holds it all together? And what does it all mean, this appearance of movement, this appearance of light, these sorts of objects, this sort of world? And yet there I am, surrounded by the halo of creation, unable to embrace these insubstantial shades, lost to understanding, out of my element, cut off from something undefinable without which everything spells deprivation. I examine myself and see myself invaded by inconceivable distress, by nameless regrets and inexplicable remorse, by a kind of love, by a kind of hate, by a semblance of joy, by a strange pity (for what? for whom?); I see myself torn apart by blind forces rising from my innermost self and clashing in some desperate unresolved conflict; and it seems I can identify myself with one or other of these, although I know quite well I am not entirely this one or that (what do they want from me?), for it is clear I can never know who I am, or why I am.[11]

Ionesco is describing here an encounter with the Void, of Being being penetrated by non-Being—what Sartre called the "hole of Being at the heart of Being." His description reminds us of the experiences of certain characters in Beckett's literature of absence. This feeling is not in itself neurotic, but existential, i.e., a part of existence itself. It may come as the result of a disappointment in one's work or in love, or through any other serious assault on what underpins one's sense of self. (There are times, when things are going well, that virtually everything seems within one's grasp; and there are times, when things are going badly, that *nothing* seems possible.) But the person who is ontologically secure can withstand such an assault, and rebound to become represented to the world that has, for a time, slipped through his fingers.

The person who is ontologically secure comes to feel his autonomy, which is to say that even with others he is *separate*. Laing gives this description of the autonomous self:

> The capacity to experience oneself as autonomous means that one has really come to realize that one is a separate person from everyone else. No matter how deeply I am committed in joy or suffering to someone else, he is not me, and I am not him. However lonely or sad one may be, one can exist alone. The fact that the other person in his own actuality is not me, is set against the equally real fact that my attachment to him is a part of me. If he dies or goes away, he is gone, but my attachment to him persists. But in the last resort I cannot die another person's death for him, nor can he die my death . . . In short, he cannot be me, and I cannot be him.[12]

There are, however, some people who never attain a sense of solidity about themselves. They do not become "integral," "real," "alive," and "concrete." These people may be said to be ontologically insecure and to lack ontological autonomy. The ontologically autonomous person who is capable of a separate existence may become related and attached to another person through a genuine mutuality. But someone without autonomy, someone who is in a position of ontological dependence, *depends on the other for his very Being*. "Utter detachment and isolation," Laing says, "are regarded as the only alternative to a clam- or vampire-like attachment in which the other person's life-blood is necessary for one's survival, and yet is a threat to one's survival. Therefore, the polarity is between complete isolation or complete merging of identity rather than between separateness and relatedness. The individual oscillates perpetually between two extremes, each equally unfeasible."[13] Dick Diver, from F. Scott Fitzgerald's *Tender Is the Night*, is a particularly poignant example of an ontologically insecure person. After marrying Nicole Warren and becoming part of an American expatriate "jet set" in post–World War I Europe, he loses the autonomy he had previously:

> His love for Rosemary and Nicole, his friendship with Abe North, with Tommy Barban in the broken universe of the war's ending—in such contacts the personalities had seemed to press up so close to

him that he became the personality itself—there seemed some necessity of taking everything or nothing; it was as if for the remainder of his life he was condemned to carry with him the egos of certain people, early met and early loved, and to be only as complete as they were complete themselves.[14]

At the end of the novel, Dr. Richard Diver is merely a composite self of those he knew and loved. Everything that had made him unique as a man and as a psychiatrist had been drained from him.

Laing characterizes three forms or degrees of anxiety experienced by the person who lacks ontological autonomy: engulfment, implosion, and petrification.

The ontologically insecure person has such a tenuous hold on himself that he fears *any* contact with the other. Every relationship threatens this individual with the loss of his precarious identity. He experiences every human contact as a drain and a threat because he fears the loss of his Being by absorption into the other. This is the anxiety of engulfment. Because he has no autonomy—really, no self—he will *desire* as well as *fear* this absorption as a means of shoring up his precarious Being. But his contacts with others amount only to a further escape from and loss of self, because there is no possibility of an authentic merging with the other when there is nothing with which to merge.*

When a person reaches a certain state of ontological insecurity, he may become more attuned to Nothingness than to Being. He is empty, a vacuum. And because the slight sense that he has of himself is felt as a vacuum (a negation), he fears that any contact with another person would, in effect, occupy this vacuum and destroy his only hold on reality. While he longs for the emptiness that is himself to be filled, he sees anything external to him that threatens to rush in and fill it as annihilating the little that he is. This is what Laing means by the anxiety of implosion.

The anxieties of engulfment and implosion may lead, eventually, to what Laing calls petrification. The term is an apt one since it describes not only the state of hardening that the "imploding" self may reach—literally,

---

* In Chapter 8, we will see how Johan and Marianne in Bergman's film, *Scenes from a Marriage*, come to realize that the collapse of their marriage is due primarily to their lack of autonomy as separate selves.

to petrify is to turn to stone—but also the feeling of terror that one experiences while undergoing this process. The petrified self is a self under siege, a self turned into an object. In Sartre's terminology, the For-itself becomes an In-itself. And in "self-defense," the petrified self turns others to stone as well, so that no mutuality is possible. In this state, there can be no genuine giving to or taking from others. The petrified self may be either totally isolated from others or totally dependent on others, or even both simultaneously. There is no possibility of a "between" with the other.

THE EROSION OF SELF THROUGH SCHIZOID SPLITTING

In the preceding chapter, we distinguished two mechanisms through which the self may be lost, two paths through which the marginal self may come into being. The ontologically insecure person, the person who lacks ontological autonomy, is one who *fails to become*. He fails to create a self that is "real," "alive," "integral," and "concrete." He can neither maintain a satisfactory relationship with the world nor draw nourishment from it. Such a person repeatedly loses himself not only at the brink of what Jaspers called "boundary situations"—incidents that make special demands on us—but by failing to respond adequately to lesser situations as well. We are calling this the default of self.

The person who is ontologically insecure may live out his life as a diminished self, nakedly under siege. But there is another possibility. Rather than continue to submit to the assaults of the world outside it, an ontologically insecure person may assume, for cover, what Laing calls a "false self," or persona,* that acts *as if* it were coping with the requirements and demands of the world. The diminished self, for all its inadequacy, may at least be authentic because it makes no pretense of being other than it is. The false self, on the other hand, is inauthentic because it is a pose and an accommodation to external pressures. Creation of a false self requires the scission or *splitting* of the self into two parts. The false self is a facade constructed to protect the besieged and terrified real self. It is a ploy to save a self so precarious that it cannot face the world on its own. In its most extreme degree, splitting may lead to a psychosis that the Swiss

---

* In Latin, the word originally meant the mask worn by an actor signifying the role he played.

psychiatrist Bleuler called schizophrenia, a word that literally means broken (*schiz*) soul (*phrenos*).*

To see how a person with a "shaky ontological foundation"[15] may undergo splitting in an effort to preserve his precarious self, we will quote here, at length, the case of David, which Laing presents in *The Divided Self*. Laing first saw David when he was eighteen. His mother had died when he was ten, and he lived with his father until he went to the university to study philosophy. David was referred to Laing by his tutor, who was concerned about the boy because of his odd behavior: he attended lectures in a cloak that he wore over his shoulders and arms; he carried a cane, although there was no obvious reason to do so; his entire manner was artificial; his speech consisted largely of quotations.

> The boy was a most fantastic-looking character—an adolescent Kierkegaard played by Danny Kaye. The hair was too long, the collar too large, the trousers too short, the shoes too big, and withall, his second-hand theatre cloak and cane! He was not simply eccentric: I could not escape the impression that this young man was *playing* at being eccentric. The whole effect was mannered and contrived. But why should anyone wish to contrive such an effect?
>
> He was indeed quite a practised actor, for he had been playing one part or other at least since his mother's death. Before that, he said, "I had simply been what she wanted." Of her death he said, "As far as I can remember I was rather pleased. Perhaps I felt some sorrow; I would like to think so anyway." Until his mother's death he had simply been what she wanted him to be. After her death it was no easier for him to be himself. He had grown up taking entirely for granted that what he called his "self" and his "personality" were two quite separate things. He had never seriously imagined any

---

* The psychic splitting that leads to a divided self must not be confused with multiple personality. In the former, one consciousness becomes separated into two parts, the real self and the false self, neither of which is complete. In the latter, there may be two or even three different consciousnesses—i. e., two or three *different persons*—inhabiting the same body, each of which may be psychically whole, although in competition with the others for possession of the body. In the film *The Three Faces of Eve*, a young woman who exhibits inconsistent and erratic behavior is found to be three different women, each with a personality radically different from the other two. Near the end of the film, her psychiatrist is able to bring out each of the three women in turn. Eve's cure is brought about when the two weaker (and less desirable) persons are "subdued" by the dominant person.

other possibility and he took it equally for granted that everyone else was constructed along similar lines. His view of human nature in general, based on his own experience of himself, was that everyone was an actor. It is important to realize that this was a settled conviction or assumption about human beings which governed his life. This made it very easy for him to be anything his mother wanted, because all his actions simply belonged to some part or other he was playing. If they could be said to belong to his self at all, they belonged only to a "false self", a self that acted according to *her* will, not his.

His self was never directly revealed in and through his actions. It seemed to be the case that he had emerged from his infancy with his *"own self"* on the one hand, and "what his mother wanted him to be", his "personality", on the other; he had started from there and made it his aim and ideal to make the split between his own self (which only he knew) and what other people could see of him, as complete as possible. He was further impelled to this course by the fact that despite himself he had always felt shy, self-conscious and vulnerable. By always playing a part he found he could in some measure overcome his shyness, self-consciousness, and vulnerability. He found reassurance in the consideration that whatever he was doing he was not being himself. Thus, he used that same form of defence which has been already mentioned; in an effort to mitigate anxiety he aggravated the conditions that were occasioning it.

The important point he always kept in mind was that he was playing a part. Usually, in his mind, he was playing the part of someone else, but sometimes he played the part of himself (his own self): that is, he was not simply and spontaneously himself, but he *played* at being himself. His ideal was, *never to give himself away to others.* Consequently he practised the most tortuous equivocation towards others in the parts he played. Towards himself, however, his ideal was to be as utterly frank and honest as possible.

The whole organization of his being rested on the disjunction of his inner "self" and his outer "personality". It is remarkable that this state of affairs had existed for years without his "personality", i.e., his way of behaving with others, appearing unusual.[16]

Laing considered David a "borderline case," which is to say that he is highly schizoid, but not psychotic. It seems almost unnecessary to point out that David has become diminished (relative to the person he might have become) because he chose to deal with his insecurity by adopting a false self. He is an excellent example of someone who has undergone, to an extreme degree, the schizoid erosion of self.

We saw in the preceding chapter that the body is the *interface* between one's interior and exterior worlds, and that we can learn about another's interior world only by what is made manifest through his body. When the self is essentially whole it is felt as being centered in the body. Laing calls this the "embodied" self. Mersault, from Camus's *A Happy Death*, is, once he achieves his dialectical synthesis of *action* and *state*, an excellent example of an ontologically secure, embodied self. But when splitting occurs— i.e., when a false self is created to deal with the world which the real self cannot handle—the self, in a sense, becomes separated from the body. One's interior world "withdraws" from the body, so that the self becomes literally disembodied. The body, displaced from the center of itself, presents a false self (persona) to the world. This body ceases to be the true interface between the interior and exterior worlds, so that no *authentic* interaction between the self and the other is possible.

We are reproducing below two drawings from Laing's *The Divided Self* that give a schematic description of the self-other relation.[17] The embodied self may make direct contact with the other and enter into a real relationship with him (figure 1).

Figure 1

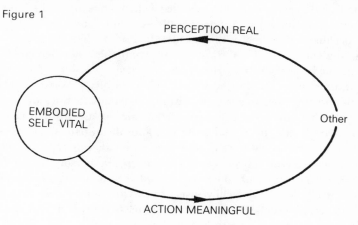

PERCEPTION REAL

EMBODIED
SELF VITAL

Other

ACTION MEANINGFUL

There is a link between the embodied self and the other that makes action vis-à-vis the other meaningful. This link also makes it possible for the other to perceive the embodied self as real and vital.

But in the disembodied self, the true or "inner" self is cut off from that part of the psyche that makes contact with others—the false self (figure 2).

Figure 2

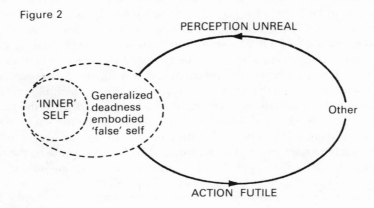

The false self, or persona, has no life or animating principle. It is a sham and is dead. There can be no mutuality with the other because there is no way to link that part of the disembodied self which is alive (the "inner" or real self) with the other. Action is futile—it does not sustain the "inner" self—because any action of the disembodied self is directed solely toward sustaining the false self. And, of course, what the other perceives of the disembodied self is not real either, only a mask.

As Laing says, "If the individual delegates all transactions between himself and the other to a system within his being which is not 'him' [the personal], then the world is experienced as unreal, and all that belongs to this system is felt to be false, futile, and meaningless."[18] Thus, the behavior of David, whose case we have just cited, was eccentric because it was the behavior of a *literally eccentric self*, a person whose actions emanated from a disembodied self—a self that is off-center—a self that was not itself. An ontologically insecure David adopted this stance (persona) toward his experience to spare himself the effort and pain that would have been required to become an autonomous self. Tillich could have had David in mind when he wrote about this mode of avoiding the self in *The Courage to Be*:

He who does not succeed in taking his anxiety courageously upon himself can succeed in avoiding the extreme situation of despair by escaping into neurosis. He still affirms himself but on a limited scale. *Neurosis is the way of avoiding nonbeing by avoiding being.* In the neurotic state self-affirmation is not lacking; it can indeed be very strong and emphasized. But the self which is affirmed is a reduced one. Some or many of its potentialities are not admitted to actualization, because actualization of being implies the acceptance of nonbeing and its anxiety. He who is not capable of a powerful self-affirmation in spite of the anxiety of nonbeing is forced into a weak, reduced self-affirmation. He affirms something which is less than his essential or potential being. He surrenders a part of his potentialities in order to save what is left.[19]

The schizoid self undergoes erosion and withers because the real ("inner") self is cut off from the world that is necessary for its nourishment and growth (figure 2). The false self may be thought of as an "agent" for the real self, but an agent that keeps all the proceeds for itself. The actions of the false self do not gratify the real self, and it is possible for the real self to remain ontically starved while the false self gives every indication of well-being.[20]

In the preceding chapter, we considered the notion that self is brought into being through the dialectical integration of elements from the interior and exterior worlds—i.e., through a synthesis of *contemplation* and *action*. The self becomes less than it might have become if either world is neglected or overemphasized relative to the other. If the exterior world is shut down to a considerable degree, one may come to live like a hermit. If the interior world is shut down to a considerable degree, one may come to behave like an animal. (Recall what we said in the preceding chapter about the Schlegels and the Wilcoxes in Forster's *Howards End*, and about Gerlach in Sartre's *The Condemned of Altona*.) Schizoid splitting may be thought of as one particular way of short-circuiting this synthesis. In the schizoid self, the self withdraws, in a manner of speaking, from the body. *Action* is restricted to the body as false self, and there is no meaningful interaction between this *action* and the real self. *Contemplation* is restricted to the real self and is cut off from the false self and its dealings with others—from the behavior of the false self. In the schizoid self, the persona is interposed between the interior and exterior worlds, so that the dialectical synthesis of self is impeded. This results, necessarily, in a diminution of self. To recall Kierkegaard's metaphor, the schizoid self is hindered in moving either *from* the "spot" or *at* the "spot," and, therefore, has diminished *actuality*.

It was Jung who first used the word "persona" to describe the splitting of the self into two parts.[21] "Fundamentally," he said, "the persona is nothing real: it is a compromise between individual and society as to what a man should appear to be."[22] Jung believed that the neurotic and psychotic behavior associated with splitting was due to the conflict between the persona and the unconscious.*

> To the degree that the world invites the individual to identify with the mask, he is delivered over to influences from within . . . An opposite forces its way up from inside; it is exactly as though the unconscious suppressed the ego with the very same power which drew the ego into the persona. The absence of resistance outwardly against the lure of the persona means a similar weakness inwardly against the influence of the unconscious. Outwardly an effective and powerful role is played, while inwardly an effeminate weakness develops in the face of every influence coming from the unconscious. Moods, vagaries, timidity, even a limp sexuality (culminating in impotence), gradually gain the upper hand.[23]

According to Jung, neurosis or psychosis would occur if a "masked" person had either a normal consciousness confronted by an unusually strong unconscious or a weak consciousness that was unable to keep back the flow of unconscious material.[24] The task of the therapist was to probe the unconscious to find the archetypal basis for the persona. A cure could begin once this was discovered and made known to the patient.

Where Jung probed the unconscious to uncover the unconscious choice made in response to some archetypal drive, Laing, an existentialist very much influenced by Sartre, looks for the *conscious choice* that was made in response to some threat from the outside. As we saw earlier, David, lacking ontological security and any sense of autonomy, chose a mask that

---

* This is an inappropriate identification with the persona, grounded in inauthenticity. In Jungian psychology, the persona functions normally as a kind of trial self that, eventually, can be integrated through individuation.

shielded his real self from the pressures of his situation. According to Laing, this choice was *conscious* but *unrecognized* by him. The task of existential psychoanalysis, whose principal initiators were Sartre,[25] Ludwig Binswanger, and Medard Boss, is to *bring to light* the choice made by the patient that caused the splitting to occur. To do this, the analyst examines the entire network of the patient's relations with others—especially the relations with his immediate family—in the hope of finding what pressures led him to make the initial inauthentic, "self-preserving" choice, the choice that caused the schizoid person to *deny* his Being to *preserve* his Being.[26]*

THE PERSONA: OUR PROTECTION AND OUR UNDOING

We all wear masks at times. It is not possible to be authentic—to be a genuine or real self—in every encounter with others, or to respond

---

* Laing has been criticized severely from many quarters for what amounts to his glorification of the schizophrenic. In a psychotic breakdown, the persona collapses so that the real self is left nakedly on its own to face the world (reality) it shunned formerly through the persona. The real self, undernourished and unprotected, is now no match for the world, and the psyche collapses.[27]

In *The Divided Self* Laing, despite his great concern for what his patients were suffering and a degree of personal involvement that is uncharacteristic of psychoanalysts, clearly distinguished between the patient and the doctor, the insane and the sane. In his later writing, however, this distinction has become blurred, and he seems to be saying that the schizophrenic is an ontic hero in an insane world. In a review of Laing's *The Facts of Life*, Bruno Bettelheim summarized what he took to be Laing's position this way: "While Freud taught us the need to bridge, through understanding of the unconscious, the abyss that separates the normal person from one who is mentally deranged, and how to use this bridge to reach him, befriend him and bring him back into our world, Dr. Laing believes that we ought to join him on the other side of the abyss; and having done so, it would be best if we would burn the bridge behind us."[28]

No matter how strongly one may agree with Laing that it was the alienating influence of a family or a society that drove a person to madness, it must be recognized that his reverence for the schizophrenic state is based on a false premise, and, indeed, is inconsistent with much of his own thinking. First, splitting comes about through an *inauthentic choice*, even though this choice may have been made under psychic duress. The *authentic* response to a potentially alienating or schizophrenogenic pressure would be to reject it and overcome it, not submit to it. Second, once splitting has occurred, there is the possibility, through "self-cure" or therapy, of healing the psychic breach, and re-annealing the self. Madness represents a *failure* of the self to deal authentically with an alienating situation. If madness is overcome, the psychotic state may be judged, in retrospect, as a *stage in the return* to authenticity and psychic health. In no way may the psychosis *in itself* be seen as anything other than an ontic failure.

authentically to every pressure we feel. Sometimes it is necessary to "petrify" ourselves temporarily to survive. We may diminish our humanness to preserve ourselves from embarrassment and pain, or, in a pinch, just to get through the day. And in some circumstances it is necessary to "petrify" others as well, to see them as merely a means to an end. If someone has snubbed, hurt, or betrayed us, we may turn them to stone in self-defense.

We are not our genuine lives, Ortega reminded us.[29] Most of our opinions and ideas are not "ours." They are not the genuine property of the real or radical self in the sense that Kierkegaard meant of adding possibility to necessity to achieve the *actuality* of the self (the "spot"). Rather, they are *appropriated* by us from our culture—from parents, friends, colleagues, lovers, and from books, films, and so forth. Shakespeare told us that the world is a stage, and that we are all actors on that stage. Many of our best lines are not our own.

But there is a great difference between a self that is ontologically secure and autonomous making the concessions to authenticity (and humanness) that are required for survival, and a self that functions for the most part through a false self, or persona, as we saw in the case of David. In the first instance, there is little or no psychic damage, while in the second instance psychic damage may become extensive. It is possible to put on a mask in response to certain pressures without causing a schizoid split in the psyche. This will be the case when the ontologically secure and autonomous real self is just temporarily *protected* by the mask of a false self, and not permanently *subsumed* in it.

Having given some idea of the mechanism by which the self is lost in schizoid splitting, we turn now to two films by Ingmar Bergman, whose principal characters live, in varying degrees, through false selves. We will examine the effects that splitting and schizoid erosion have had on their own lives, their relations with others, and on their careers.

In all his films up to and including *Winter Light*, Bergman was concerned—perhaps obsessed would be a better word—with the relation of man to God. Bergman's father had been a clergyman and was a strong influence on his son. In many of the early films, Bergman portrayed a stark and brooding Swedish Protestantism as an integral part of his milieu. But sometime after *Winter Light* (1961), he underwent what amounted to an anti-conversion[30] that was, in many ways the antithesis of the Christian's "leap" of faith:

The only life that exists for me is this life, here and now, and the only holiness that exists is in my relations with other people. And outside, nothing exists. When I realized that, when I began to understand that everything happens here and now in the world around me, it gave me a marvelous feeling of relief and security. I found a new power with which to do my work, and there was a new beginning for me. No, I don't believe in any afterlife because *this* life gives me everything I need; the cruel, beautiful, fantastic life. For me, the meaning of everything is in life itself. I don't need any other.[31]

With the religious element of his life totally eradicated, Bergman took up in his films, as an atheist, the existential themes of freedom, the limitations of reason, the anxiety of death and of the Void, and, most forcefully, the question of the authentic vs. the inauthentic self. In *Persona* (1965), *Scenes from a Marriage* (1974), and *Face to Face* (1976), he presents characters who fail before our eyes, people who should not have failed, people who had every opportunity and *did all the right things*. These men and women are attractive, from affluent families, and are well educated. They have achieved recognition as theatrical performers, university professors, lawyers, psychiatrists, and physicians. Yet in each film, one or more of the principal characters collapses at what appears to be the height of his or her powers, as if the ground underneath had suddenly given way. In *Persona* a beautiful and nationally acclaimed actress suddenly ceases to speak; in *Scenes from a Marriage* a man and a woman, who a short time earlier had considered their marriage idyllic, agonizingly come to realize that it is anything but so; and in *Face to Face* a psychiatrist, who has a successful practice and what she sees as a good relationship with her husband, attempts suicide for no apparent reason.*

In these films, we come to see that the principal characters collapse as the result of having pursued success—whether as a son or daughter, husband or wife, psychiatrist, lawyer, and so forth—largely through a false self or persona that accommodated itself to the requirements and pressures of each role. At the same time, the real self became disembodied in the way that Laing describes. Cut off through this schizoid splitting

---

* I have worked from the filmscripts, which differ in some respects from the films. This is particularly true of *Persona*.

from full participation with the exterior world, the real self chafed and suffocated, while the persona achieved its goals and collected its rewards. And then, unexpectedly, when the persona sustained a blow that in most cases could have been withstood by an ontologically secure and autonomous self, or, when the false self was simply not strong enough to assume any further roles, the persona collapsed, leaving the withered and unprepared real self to face a newly impinging reality. Bergman knows as well as Laing that the inauthentic choice of self can bring death to life.

BERGMAN'S *FACE TO FACE*

In *Face to Face* Jenny Isaksson is a psychiatrist who is filling in for the summer as the supervisor of a psychiatric clinic in a large Swedish hospital. Her husband, a successful businessman, has just left to spend three months in the United States. Jenny moves in with her grandparents, who have a large apartment near the hospital (Jenny was raised by them after her mother and father were killed in an automobile accident). At a party she meets Tomas Jacobi, a middle-aged gynecologist, who is divorced. After the party, they have dinner together and then go back to Jacobi's house, where they engaged in some verbal sparring about a possible assignation. Jenny is not persuaded and returns by taxi to her grandparents' apartment. At dawn, she receives a call from someone she does not know, but somehow realizes that the call is coming from the house that she and her husband have vacated for the summer. She returns to the house and finds Maria, a highly volatile patient whom she has been treating at the clinic, curled up on the floor, unconscious, apparently from a drug overdose. Two men enter the room, and while the older man holds Jenny down, the younger man tries, without success, to rape her. After the men leave, she calls an ambulance for Maria and then calls Jacobi to confirm a date for a concert that evening, without saying anything about the incident with the two men. Then, at the concert, something suddenly begins to stir inside Jenny that she has never felt before:

> [She] has to close her eyes, she must go into herself. But she discovers at once that this is not the place to be. Something is going on there that frightens her and makes her giddy. No, not there. She can't go there. As long as she keeps still, watching Tomas's hand with half-closed eyes, all is well. As long as she has the self-discipline

not to turn inward, all is well. It's a matter now of minute by minute, hour by hour.

She knows instinctively that the longer she can put off what is going to happen at any moment, the better chance she has of clinging to the reality that is gradually disintegrating.[32]

Triggered by the shock of the attempted rape, Jenny's false self is beginning to crumble. The mask is disintegrating, and with it, her hold on reality. When she speaks of going into herself, she is talking about making contact, for the first time, with her real self that is now partly unmasked and vulnerable. Jenny is frightened of this inward flight into unknown territory and tries to prevent it by keeping her attention riveted on what is happening in the concert hall. She is having a breakdown.

Two days later, apparently on the spur of the moment, Jenny decides to take her life by swallowing an entire bottle of Nembutol tablets. But first, she dictates this explanation to her husband into a tape recorder:

. . . I realize suddenly that what I'm going to do in a little while has been lurking inside me for several years. Not that I've consciously planned to take my life, don't think that. I'm not so deceitful. It's more that I've been living in an isolation that has got worse and worse—the dividing line between my outer behavior and my inner impoverishment has become more distinct. I remember last Whitsun, for instance. You and I and Anna went for a ramble in the forest. You and Anna thoroughly enjoyed yourselves. I made out it was wonderful too, and said how happy I was, but it wasn't true. I wasn't taking in anything of all the beauty surrounding us. My senses reported it, but the connections were broken. This upset me and I thought I'd try to cry but the tears wouldn't come.

This is only one example picked at random, but the more I think back, the more I remember. I stopped listening to music, as I felt sealed up and apathetic. Our sex life—I felt nothing, nothing at all. I pretended I did, so that you wouldn't be anxious or start asking questions. But I think the worst of all was that I lost touch with our little girl. A prison grew up all around me, with no doors or windows. With walls so thick that not a sound got through, walls that it was useless to attack, since they were built from materials I supplied myself.

> I think you should explain all this to our daughter. You should explain it very thoroughly, you must be unflinchingly truthful. We live, and while we live we're gradually suffocated without knowing what is happening. At last there's only a puppet left, reacting more or less to external demands and stimuli. Inside there is nothing but a great horror.[33]

Jenny's explanation to her husband sounds very much like one of Laing's cases from *The Divided Self*. She speaks of "an isolation that has got worse and worse"—the isolation of her real self. She sees that the dividing line between her outer behavior (persona) and her inner impoverishment (her ontologically insecure, unautonomous real self) has become more distinct. She has no real contact with herself—i.e., no contact with her real or "inner" self—and none with the real selves of others (see figure 2). Her senses "report" the impressions of a beautiful day, but, as she says, the connections to her real self have been broken. She cannot even cry. Jenny is a truly disembodied self. And, as a disembodied self, sex means nothing to her.

The metaphors she uses to describe how she feels are those of the self experiencing what Laing calls engulfment and implosion: "A prison grew up all around me, with no doors and windows"; and, "We're gradually suffocated without knowing what is happening." Jenny is also experiencing the anxiety associated with petrification, the turning of oneself into a thing: "At last there's only a puppet left, reacting more or less to external demands and stimuli. Inside there is nothing but a great horror."

Jenny swallows the Nembutol. She loses consciousness and enters a dream state that, not surprisingly, seems about as "real" as her conscious life. When, during this time, Jacobi is unable to get through to her on the telephone, he becomes worried and goes to her grandparents' apartment. (They had left the day before for a vacation.) He finds Jenny unconscious and has her taken to the clinic by ambulance. There the doctors bring her around, and it becomes clear that she will recover. After a few days at the hospital, Jenny is composed and able to explain, at least in general terms, how her false self came into being.

> We act the play. We learn our lines. We know what people want us to say. We lie. In the end it's not even deliberate.[34]

> I've tried to live like everyone else. And I've failed. Do you think I
> don't see that myself? I have no words to say what I mean.[35]

Jenny is giving here a classic description of the making of a false self.
The imagery in her description is that of the stage and the mask—"act,"
"play," "lines." She is not speaking of a momentary compromise made to
get through a difficult situation. She is describing a *lifelong compromise with
the real self* and the becoming of a disembodied person through schizoid
splitting. She has lived by conformity and surrendered her real instincts.
Her entire life amounts to what Laing calls "the deliberate cultivation of a
state of death-in-life as a defense against the pain of life."[36]*

In the Preface to the filmscript of *Face to Face*, Bergman says of Jenny
that she is "a stifling, static combination of mapped-out qualities and
patterns of behavior," who "realizes in a flash that she is a conglomera-
tion of other people and of the whole world."[37] (Recall what we said
earlier about Dick Diver from *Tender Is the Night*.) Her lack of self-
knowledge up to the time of her breakdown is particularly ironic in view of
her profession. "Despite her wide knowledge," Bergman says, "she is, to a
pretty great extent, mentally illiterate (a common ailment with psychiatrists, one could almost call it an occupational disease). Jenny has always
been firmly convinced that a cheese is a cheese, a table is a table, and, *not
least*, that a human being is a human being."[38] As a disembodied self,
Jenny functions as a thing, a Sartrean In-itself. The persona *is* a thing,
static and dead. The dynamic real self—the Sartrean For-itself—eludes
her both in herself and in others. (This is the basis for Bergman's analogy
between how Jenny sees a person, and a cheese or a table.)

Jenny has an inauthentic notion of death, which she describes in words
that could have been taken from Heidegger's *Being and Time*. Mikael, a
homosexual groupie whom Jenny met at the same party where she met
Jacobi, asked Jenny if she was afraid of death. "No," she replied, "I don't
think so. I'm like most people, I suppose, who regard death as something
that happens to others but never to yourself."[39] And in the hospital, she
says to Jacobi: "I've followed the principle that now I'll make up my mind
to feel like this and I feel like this. I decided I'd never be afraid of death

---

* The choices of an inauthentic self made by Jenny throughout her life that led to schizoid
splitting are *conscious* choices, although she does not *recognize* this until now. The process of
psychic disintegration that culminates in her breakdown, however, occurs unconsciously.

and the dead. I decided to ignore the fact that people died every day, every moment. Death didn't exist any more except as a vague idea, and that was that."[40] By "deciding" to ignore death, Jenny undercuts reality by superimposing her will on her condition. Not only does Jenny deny death as a *process* that is overtaking her second by second, she denies her death as a certain *future event* as well. Jenny refuses to see the meaning of her death to her life, and to experience the existential anxiety (dread) that comes with recognizing this reality, an anxiety that is one of the starting points for authentic existence (Heidegger's Being-towards-death). Thus, she opens the way for a neurotic perversion of this "healthy" anxiety that is self-destructive, as Tillich described in *The Courage to Be*. She reminds us of Camus's Caligula who, because he would not accept the limitations of the absurd, imposed on his subjects conditions even more cruel and destructive than the absurd itself.

Jenny now understands how her false self has come into being and how her real self suffocated in the process. Just before swallowing the Nembutol, she says to her husband in the tape recording: "It may even be that this [the breakdown] is a recovery from a lifelong illness" (her inauthentic self). But she does not yet know how to go about constructing a real self. She takes the evasive attitude of business as usual. "If you force everything to be as usual," she says to Jacobi, "then it *will* be as usual . . . that's how it is with me anyway."[41] Again, she asserts her will to deny the reality of her situation.

It is Jacobi who gives her the first intuition of her real self, and she resists it—violently:

JACOBI:	The world begins and ends with yourself. That's all there is to it.
JENNY: *(Bursting out)*	I can't talk about that!
JACOBI:	You must try.
JENNY:	I can't, I won't!
JACOBI:	There's no avoiding it. You must try.
JENNY:	Leave me alone. Let me be. My head's aching. Can't you give me a shot or something? *(Bangs her head against the wall)* It's more than I can bear. I can't go on.

JACOBI:	You must. *Nothing is more important!*
JENNY:	Let me be. You're hurting me. (*Weeping*) Leave me in peace. Let me go for Christ's sake! You have nothing to do with me. Go away.
JACOBI:	Jenny, *please.* Jenny it's important for me too. You can't just slink away.
JENNY:	I feel so sick.
JACOBI:	Lie down. Breathe deeply.
JENNY:	I can't live with this.[42]

Jacobi is trying to make Jenny feel her *reality*, to force her to get inside herself. But she is terrified of this excursion into herself, as she was during the first moments of her breakdown. (Recall that to avoid this interior flight, Jenny fought to keep her attention riveted on Jacobi and on the music.) The very suggestion that she look inward causes her pain and *makes her sick*; she cannot even "talk about" it. This is what Laing characterizes as the anxiety of implosion, the anxiety that the false self, which has been constituted as a negation of reality, will be annihilated by the entrance of reality. And with the mask of the false self now partially torn away, Jenny "can't live" with the prospect of reality impinging on her diminished real self. She is still, as Bergman said, "mentally illiterate"—an ontic basket case. Her mandate is nothing less than to be reborn to reality.

Jacobi doesn't feel real himself, but he is at least able to define his unreality and the character of the reality to which he aspires:

JACOBI:	I wish that someone or something would affect me *so that I can become real.* I repeat over and over: Let me become real one day.
JENNY:	What do you mean by real?
JACOBI:	To hear a human voice and be sure that it comes from someone who is made just like I am. To touch pair of lips and in the same thousandth of a second know that this is a

pair of lips. Not to have to live through the
moment needed for my experience to check
that I've really felt a pair of lips. Reality
would be to know that a joy is a joy and
above all that a pain has to be a pain.
(*He is silent*)

JENNY: Please go on.

JACOBI: Reality is perhaps not at all what I
imagine. Perhaps it doesn't exist, in fact.
Perhaps it only exists as a longing.[43]

Jacobi longs to be what Laing calls an embodied self, a self that is,
within the limitations of its dynamic nature, coincident with itself, a self
that has, as Kierkegaard defined it, *actuality*. He seems to recognize
intuitively that reality is illusive and precarious, that it can be experienced
only through a continuing synthesis of elements from the interior and
exterior worlds, and that this synthesis can occur only when the psyche is
intact, i.e., unsplit. The only character in *Face to Face* who has reality and
actuality is the sybaritic Elisabeth (Mikael's patron and lover). "I've
come to the conclusion that I'm grateful," she says. "*Humbly* grateful, if
you know what I mean. Not only for this with Mikael but because I still
have myself. *I know* that it's *my* feelings and sensations, since there's no
gap between myself and what I experience."[44] No one else in the film
could make this statement. Elisabeth is the sole embodied self. Unlike
Jacobi, who says he needs a moment to confirm that he has actually
experienced something, there is no "gap" between what Elisabeth feels
and what she is. The gap that separates Jacobi from his experience is the
disjunction between his real self and his false self—his "inner" self and his
persona (figure 2).

Throughout the film, Jenny sees visions of a spectral woman with one
eye gouged out. She cowers from the apparition, obviously an inverted
symbol of the reality she eludes. *Face to Face* ends with Jenny meeting this
woman, *now real*, at a crowded intersection—face to face. Jenny takes the
woman by the arm, and escorts her across the street.*

---

* This scene and the scene cited earlier where Jenny makes the tape recording that

BERGMAN'S *PERSONA*

It was in *Persona*, which preceded *Face to Face*, that Bergman first examined how the creation of a false self, or persona, could lead to the destruction of the real self.

During her final appearance in a production of *Electra*, Elisabeth Vogler, a well-known and highly regarded actress, suddenly ceased speaking her lines. She refused a cue from anyone else on the stage and just stood mute for a minute. Then, as if nothing had happened, she flawlessly resumed her performance. When the curtain fell, Elisabeth apologized to the cast for the lapse. Her only explanation for the silent interval was, "I got this fit of laughter."

She went home, had supper with her husband, and retired for the evening. The next morning, she would not get out of bed, speak to anyone, or even move. When *Persona* opens, Elisabeth has neither spoken to nor had any real contact with anyone for three months, and is in a mental hospital. Alma, an attractive nurse in her mid-twenties, has been assigned to take care of her. Elisabeth has been given every conceivable test, and, according to her doctor, is "perfectly healthy, both mentally and physically." The doctor feels that Elisabeth's silence is just another role, one played to avoid having to continue playing any of her previous life-roles, which she now finds distasteful.

To the extent that she sees Elisabeth's life as a series of roles, the doctor's analysis is correct. But she does not understand the psychic damage that this role playing has caused. "I think you should keep playing this part," she tells Elisabeth, "until you've lost interest in it. When you've played it to the end, you can drop it as you drop your other parts." To say that Elisabeth is "perfectly healthy, both mentally and physically," is to deny that she has a real problem. As a result of schizoid splitting, Elisabeth has had a breakdown, and no one, not even her doctor, realizes it. Elisabeth, we are told, feels "a vast melancholy, a petrified pain." At times, she becomes "immobile, lethargic, almost extinguished." These are unmistakable symptoms of what Laing calls petrification, the hardening of the self under siege. The mask of Elisabeth's false self—her roles—has collapsed, leaving her diminished and suffocated real self exposed to a reality that it cannot cope with. She is locked inside herself

continuation

---

explains to her husband why she is planning to take her life are in Bergman's filmscript of *Face to Face*, but not in the film itself.

and is incapable of participating in the world outside her. Because her exterior world has shut down, the dialectical synthesis of elements from this exterior world with elements from the interior world—a synthesis necessary if the self is to create and maintain its Being—has ceased. She is, ontically speaking, less than human. In the parlance of existential psychoanalysis, she has suffered a schizophrenic breakdown and is acutely ill.

The doctor feels there is no point keeping Elisabeth in the hospital. She suggests that Elisabeth and Alma go to live in her summer house, an isolated cottage near the sea, where, away from the pressures of the city, Elisabeth could play her role to completion. The two women go off together to the summer house. Elisabeth remains silent, but the apathy that she showed in the hospital abates somewhat. Patient and nurse take long walks, go fishing, and cook together. As if to compensate for Elisabeth's silence, Alma is voluble about herself. She talks to Elisabeth as a girlfriend and even describes, in great detail, a casual sexual encounter with a teenage boy on a deserted beach. Elisabeth responds only with nods and smiles.

We begin to see that although Alma is an excellent nurse (she had the highest marks in her class), she has a rather tenuous sense of her identity. She says to Elisabeth: "I'll marry Karl-Henrik [her fiancé] and we'll have a couple kids that I'll bring up. That's all decided, it's in me somewhere. I don't have to work things out at all, how they're going to be." We could say that Alma lives from the outside in, passively, for the most part by reaction to other people and to events. Karl-Henrik tells her that she lives like a "sleepwalker." Just before leaving for the cottage, Alma went to see one of the films in which Elisabeth had a starring role, and, later, standing in front of a mirror, it occurs to her that they look very much alike. "I think I could turn myself into you," she says to Elisabeth, "if I really tried. I mean inside. Don't you think so?" For someone like Alma, who lives from the outside in, it is not surprising that similar appearances— personae—should suggest the possibility that one interior life could be transformed into another.

Elisabeth's husband comes to visit her unexpectedly. But he sees Alma first and speaks to her *as if she were Elisabeth*, pouring out his pain and his guilt. Alma remonstrates—"Mr. Vogler, I'm not your wife"—but then assumes the part of Elisabeth wholeheartedly, while Elisabeth stands by in silence. Vogler asks Alma/Elisabeth: "Do you like being with me? Is it good with me?" and she answers, "You're a wonderful lover darling. You know that, my love." Elisabeth, who is standing behind her husband during this exchange, moves toward Alma, kisses her on the mouth, strokes her breasts, and mutters endearing words to her. Alma allows this to happen without any protest. Vogler embraces Alma/Elizabeth, mumbling words that are unintelligible and meaningless. Elisabeth, Alma, and Vogler lose momentarily all sense of their own identity and autonomy. They cease being separate selves.

Some time shortly after this episode, Alma finds Elisabeth sitting at a table dressed in her nurse's uniform. As Alma speaks, Elisabeth mimics her:

ALMA:	Now I've learned quite a lot.
ELISABETH:	. . . learned quite a lot.
ALMA:	Let's see how long I can manage.
ELISABETH:	. . . how long I can manage.[45]

Elisabeth is repeating the last words of Alma's sentences, just as a child who is learning to speak repeats the last words of its mother's sentences. She is even dressed in her "mother's" clothes. Elisabeth is beginning to come out of her partly catatonic, petrified state. Somehow, most likely through transference,* Alma's impersonation of her in the conversation with her husband has catalyzed a rebirth of her real, or "inner," self. Elisabeth's first sentences are garbled and reflect the shattered reality she is now beginning to experience.

   The failure that never happened when it should, but which came unexpectedly at other times and without warning. No, No, now it's another sort of light, which cuts and cuts, no one can protect themselves.[46]

---

   * A term used in psychoanalysis to indicate a redirection of feelings and desires from one object to another. In this case, Elisabeth seems to have identified with Alma's impersonation of her, generating what might be thought of as a psychic seed crystal around which her existential rebirth could begin. Ferenczi, one of Freud's closest collaborators, said that transference was the "self-taught [attempt] on the patient's part to cure himself" (S. Ferenczi, "Introjection and Transference," Chapter 2 in *Contributions to Psychoanalysis* [London: Phillips, 1916], p. 47).

Elisabeth is speaking in the language of what Laing calls "schizophren-ese." The "failure" that she says should have happened is the deserved failure of the false self—the persona—that succeeded and collected the accolades. The failure that came "without warning" is her breakdown, which began during her last performance of *Electra*. The light that "cuts and cuts" is the reality that has forced its way through her crumbling persona, the light that is illuminating her real self, which is struggling so hard to be reborn. From the ashes of a breakdown, Elisabeth is beginning her existential rebirth.*

At the end of the film, the doctor brings us up-to-date on Elisabeth's condition: "Early in December Elisabeth Vogler returned to her home and to the theatre, both of which welcomed her with open arms. I was convinced all along that she would go back. Her silence was a role like any other. After a while she no longer needed it and so left it." Which, of course, completely misses the point. The doctor still believes that there was never anything "wrong" with Elisabeth, that her silence was a voluntary escape from the pressures of the other roles she had played all her life. The doctor has been going by the book, and her "book" appears not to have included any scenario for Elisabeth's problem. And this is a very telling point: she has *no name* for what broke Elisabeth's psyche and, finally, broke Elisabeth.

SCHIZOID SPLITTING . . . A CULTURAL DISEASE

Schizoid splitting is so much a part of the ethos of Western society that it goes largely undiagnosed and untreated. In a word, Elisabeth's problem is inauthenticity. Her conscious choices to become other than herself—i.e., inauthentic, disembodied, and unactualized—made throughout her life in a society that rewards this kind of self-abrogation generously, bring her, finally, to a state of death-in-life.

Elisabeth in *Persona*, Jenny in *Face to Face*, and Marianne and Johan in *Scenes from a Marriage* (see Chapter 8) are marginal selves by virtue of the schizoid erosion of self. As horrible as the consequences are, their schizoid

---

* The real self that is exposed by the tearing away of the persona may be thought of as the psychic counterpart of a premature birth. Special support systems are required to bring both the premature infant and the person who is experiencing an existential rebirth to the point where they can function normally on their own.

splitting goes unrecognized and untreated *as such.* Elisabeth recovers *in spite of* her doctor's misinterpretation of her illness. That Elisabeth and Jenny have breakdowns and are hospitalized distinguishes them only by degree from Marianne and Johan, who do not. The false selves of Elisabeth and Jenny crumble precipitously, exposing their real selves to a reality that they are unprepared to cope with. The false selves of Marianne and Johan, on the other hand, collapse gradually, revealing a considerable degree of psychic erosion. Without the props of their false selves, their marriage soon fails.*

We have given here examples of schizoid splitting that could be considered extreme. Bergman's characters pay very heavily for their inauthentic choices of self. While many people today have experiences that parallel those of the characters we have just seen, many more pay a lesser, although still considerable, price. In Western society, schizoid splitting seems to be as endemic as high blood pressure or high cholesterol. We seem almost eager to relinquish ourselves to security and success. We set our sights on long-range goals and leave ourselves behind. But, as Jung said, the persona is "nothing real." The false self is a mask without tenure; it does not remain intact forever. And once it begins to disintegrate, the real self must pay the price. Dr. Alvin Goldfarb, a psychiatrist at Manhattan's Mt. Sinai Hospital, put it this way: "Our acculturation is such as to produce emotionally dependent people [i.e., people who are ontologically insecure and unautonomous]. They are chronically depressed on a relatively controlled level. The symptoms surface as they lose their protectors [masks] and begin to develop feelings of helplessness."[47] Goldfarb is describing here the neurotic manifestations of schizoid splitting and the price in psychic pain that the ontologically insecure, unautonomous marginal self must pay for its inauthenticity. Kierkegaard recognized that mental anguish, what he called "hysteria of the spirit," was symptomatic of a self that had lost itself, and that this symptom demonstrates there *is* a center of self, unknown and uncared for.[48]

---

* When we proposed the analogy of a moving picture to illustrate the phenomenological method in Chapter 4, we had not yet planned to use characters from Bergman's films as examples of schizoid splitting. In the analyses of *Face to Face* and *Persona*, we have, in effect, put this analogy into practice: by "stopping" the films during key episodes and attempting to uncover the significance of the "phenomena" of which these episodes are composed, we are employing the phenomenological method.

One very common way for the ontologically insecure person to avoid the difficult task of developing a real self is to choose a false self through the work he does. In the next chapter, we will examine the consequences of the self splitting itself as an accommodation to the requirements and the rewards of work.

7

The Search for Self and the Loss of Self in Work

> You can't eat for eight hours a day nor drink for eight hours a day nor make love for eight hours a day—all you can do for eight hours is work. Which is the reason why man makes himself and everybody else so miserable and unhappy.
>
> —William Faulkner

> . . . the ability to do nothing demands courage and intelligence of a high order.
>
> —Henry Miller

Even after acquiring financial security and recognition, most people elect to continue working. There is more money to be made, or there are more buildings to design, or more books to write. The drive to succeed, to achieve some external goal, is a strong one. But there is another driving force that comes from within. The dynamic self, the Sartrean For-itself, is never static or complete, and must be reconstituted from moment to moment through choice and action. A state of self that satisfies us today may very well not suffice for tomorrow. We are, as Heidegger said, always "ahead of ourselves." The synthesis of *contemplation* and *action* that *is* the self requires some form of the activity we call work. If we do not occupy a certain amount of our time with work, boredom will overtake us. As Faulkner noted, one cannot eat, drink, or make love for eight hours a day.

WORK AS DIVERSION

After completing the case of "The Red-headed League," Sherlock Holmes is complimented by Dr. Watson on the solution of the crime. "It saved me from ennui," Holmes replied. "Alas! I already feel it closing in upon me. My life is spent in one long effort to escape from the commonplaces of existence. These little problems help me to do so."[1] Holmes fights off boredom through his work. When he is not working, he feels the weight of his existence too heavily; the world is too much with him.

James Bond has the same problem:

> The blubbery arms of the soft life had Bond round the neck and they were slowly strangling him. He was a man of war and when, for a long period, there was no war, his spirit went into a decline . . . [He] woke . . . and was disgusted to find that he was thoroughly bored with the prospect of the day ahead.[2]

Pascal felt that man's natural condition was inconstancy, boredom, and anxiety. To alleviate boredom and anxiety, he said in the *Pensées*, we seek diversion. To take our minds off our condition, we look for distraction in sport and in work:

> . . . I have often said that the sole cause of man's unhappiness is that he does not know how to stay quietly in his room. A man wealthy enough for life's needs would never leave home to go to sea or besiege some fortress if he knew how to stay at home and enjoy it. Men would never spend so much on a commission in the army if they could bear living in town all their lives, and they only seek after the company and diversion of gambling because they do not enjoy staying at home.[3]

> What people want is not the easy peaceful life that allows us to think of our unhappy condition, nor the dangers of war, nor the burdens of office, but the agitation that takes our mind off it and diverts us. That is why we prefer the hunt to the capture . . . The hare itself would not save us from thinking about death and the miseries distracting us, but hunting it does so.[4]

As a diversion, work may take either of two forms. If work takes us out of a stifling lassitude, it may become a starting point for the authentic creation of self. It may serve as a "mediator" between Nothingness and Being, i.e., as a means through which Being (self) may come into being. But work, as diversion, may take a second form. Instead of diverting the self from boredom, work may divert the self *from itself*. This is an escape from self and leads to a diminution of self.

In Hemingway's *A Farewell to Arms*, Rinaldi, a surgeon, after treating the casualties from a particularly intense battle, feels the strain and fatigue of war more than ever before and cries out in exasperation, "To hell with the whole damned business." But when Frederick Henry says to him, in effect, OK, to hell with it, Rinaldi replies: "No, no . . . You can't do it. You're dry and you're empty and there's nothing else . . . Not a damned thing. I know when I stop working."[5] Through work, Rinaldi keeps the Void at bay. He is at his "best" when conditions force him to work hardest. He is an excellent example of someone who uses work as a diversion from self. For him, work is not a "mediator" between Nothingness and Being, but a means of rejecting Nothingness (the Void) as the medium through which Being may come into being. It is not his *self* that Rinaldi places over and against the Void, but his *work*. He lacks ontological security. He cannot take his anxiety of the Void "into himself," as Tillich says, and therefore remains permanently anxious and alienated. His "courage" is merely the courage to do his work, nothing more. Even when he is working, Rinaldi does not enjoy life as Holmes and Bond seem to when they are pursuing criminals and foreign agents. It is only through his work that Rinaldi is able to even tolerate his existence. For him, work is a diversion from self that leads to no enhancement of self, only to a holding action against anxiety. Rinaldi is a marginal self by virtue of default, the failure to become.

WORK AS BEING AND HAVING

How does work lead to the enhancement or to the diminution of self? We can begin to penetrate this question by recalling the distinction that Marcel made between Being and Having.[6] Broadly, Being is what *I am*, Having is what *I have*. In the strictest sense of the term, I can only *have* something whose existence is independent of me. Having entails different degrees of externality. Having a car implies a greater degree of externality than, say, having an idea. It is tempting to say that the car is totally external to me, but this is not so. My reasons for selecting a specific car go beyond the consideration of it as a means of transportation. The car must fulfill certain aesthetic and social needs, which are, of course, interior needs. Marcel describes the relation between the external and the internal components of Having this way:

> . . . I find myself confronted with things: and some of these things have a relationship with me which is at once peculiar and mysterious. These things are not *only external*: it is as though there were a connecting corridor between them and me; they reach me, one might say, underground. In exact proportion as I am attached to these things, they are seen to exercise a power over me which my attachment confers upon them, and which grows as the attachment grows.[7]

Sartre, too, distinguishes between Being and Having. For him, Having (possessing) is an attempt by the contingent For-itself to appropriate the non-contingent In-itself, so as to become, in effect, its own non-contingent foundation, an absolute, a deity—an In-itself-For-itself. According to Sartre, however, it is the essence of man to be contingent, and when he tries to deny or circumvent this limitation of his condition, when he tries to identify with what he imagines to be an absolute—either through religion, work, love, or whatever—*he loses himself as a man*. This, Sartre says, is man's "useless passion." "The desire *to have*," he maintains, "is at bottom reducible to the desire to be related to a certain object in a certain *relation to being*."[8] In other words, the For-itself, through what it possesses and creates, tries to overcome the limitation of its contingency and become an In-itself-For-itself. "The 'mine' [is] a relation of being intermediate between the absolute internality [and contingency] of the *me* and the absolute externality [and non-contingency] of the *not-me*."[9]

Existentially, i.e., in life, Being and Having are inseparable. They are complementary components of the self and are in touch with each other through what Marcel calls a "connecting corridor." Being requires Having to sustain it. A person needs certain things, both utilitarian and aesthetic, to survive. One cannot do without food, clothing, and shelter at all, and one cannot do without many other things very well. The contingent For-itself constantly desires and needs to be filled up by all kinds of things, through many modes of Having. But the "connecting corridor" that makes it possible for Being to be nourished by Having also allows for Being to be *displaced* by Having. In the attempt to secure a non-contingent foundation through Having, the For-itself may relinquish itself. If a person forms a fanatical attachment to a possession, which may be anything from a car to an idea, his self may become *incorporated* in the possession. Being is then absorbed by Having, and the For-itself is reduced to a kind of human In-itself.

Work is a specific mode of Having. The product of work, whether it be an architect's building, a bricklayer's wall, a writer's book, or a director's film, is external to its creator and is, therefore, a *possession*. But this possession is inextricably bound to the self that created it. While one is working, the Having of the creative act may impinge upon the Being of the creator through the "connecting corridor." The creator may be nourished and fulfilled by his creation for as long as he and it last. At the same time, however, he risks being subsumed in what he is creating (or has created), just as anyone who owns something may become subsumed in his possession. By "creation," we mean not only the work an artist does, but whatever is created or made in any kind of work.

The project of the authentic self is to become itself. In work, however, *the self may relinquish its becoming to Having*, i.e., Having may take the place of becoming. According to Marcel, "the self disappears in the full exercise of an act, of any creation whatever."[10] The self only reappears, he says, when there is a "check" in creation, i.e., when the creator *breaks* with what he is doing.[11] This break is temporary and does not imply a rejection of either the process or the product of work. It merely allows a breathing space, during which becoming may assert itself against the Having of creation.

Through any kind of work, we try to go beyond ourselves—"ahead of ourselves," as Heidegger said—and that is how it should be. But work has the potential of taking the self away from itself, of absorbing the self, of being transformed into a substitute for self. As we saw in Chapter 3, this is what happened to Roquentin in Sartre's *Nausea* while he was writing his biography of the Marquis de Rollebon. If the self is to "survive" its work, it must, at some point, break with it, and reassert itself *as itself*. While working, a person temporarily relinquishes a part of himself to what he is doing. The more he gives himself over to work, the more he risks shutting down the "connecting corridor" between what he is doing and what he is, of allowing his Being to become encroached upon by the Having of his work. "Our possessions," Marcel says, "eat us up."[12] And so it is with the work we do. Through the Having (possessing) of work, the For-itself may try to become an In-itself-For-itself, and thus lose itself. This is what we mean by shutting down the "connecting corridor" between Being and Having. To prevent this, there must, as Marcel says, be a periodic "check" in the creative process, a break with it, in which the For-itself takes stock of its contingency and finitude. At this point, becoming may reassert itself against Having.

I have recognized for some time that when I read or write for three or four hours at a stretch, I am doing a certain violence to my body *by neglecting it*. Reading and writing are purely cerebral and sedentary activities. They involve only the realm of *contemplation* and have no component in the realm of *action*. As I work, I feel that I am acquiring self in the realm of *contemplation*. At the same time, however, I recognize that I am going into hock to the *action* pole of the dialectic. I have found that by swimming for about a half-hour as soon as possible after finishing a session of work, I can pay back the debt to *action* incurred during the period of contemplative labor. I can break with work as a possession and *reassert myself*. I have often thought that, for me, the highest point of what I am trying to evoke in these pages as self occurs not at my desk or in the pool, but during the eight-minute walk, in the late afternoon, going to and coming from the gym. On the way over, the contemplative "high" that comes with the afternoon's work is at its peak. In the pool, a new "high," that of the body asserting itself in and against the water, develops. On the way back, I experience the mixing of the two "highs"—the contemplative and the physical.

I believe that Forster must have had something very much like this mixing of states in mind when, as narrator in *Howards End*, he replies to Aunt Juley's question of whether truth (reality) was to be found "halfway between" the *prose* and the *passion* (a dialectical pair similar to *action* and *contemplation*, as we showed in Chapter 5): "No," Forster answers, "truth, being alive, was not halfway between anything. It was only to be found by continuous excursions into either realm, and though proportion is the final secret, to espouse it at the outset is to insure sterility."[13] "Only connect the prose and the passion . . ."[14]

The "higher" the work one does, the greater is the risk that the autonomy of the worker will be surrendered in its execution. Thus, Marcel says, the philosopher, in his work, is less autonomous than the scientist, and the scientist less autonomous than the technician.[15]* "A man *is* a

---

*Marcel distinguishes between what he calls a "problem" and a "mystery." A problem is

genius, but *has* talent."[16] A genius must make a greater effort to break with his creation than a man who merely has talent, because the product of a genius's creation is more intrinsic to his self. Genius inheres more deeply in the self than talent and thus encroaches upon the self more forcibly.

Kierkegaard is a perfect example of the genius whose growth as a man was compromised by his work. Kierkegaard *lived* the dialectic of the finite and the infinite that he wrote about. "All my work," he said, "has been at the same time my own development: in it I have become conscious of my idea, of my task." "In a sense, I have produced my entire *oeuvre* as if I had done nothing but copy out, every day, a definite portion of a book already printed."[17] There was an essential congruence between what Kierkegaard wrote and what he was, between the books and the man. His Being and the Having of his work were essentially the same thing. But he could not break with his work as Marcel says is necessary if the self is to be fully realized. This is the principal reason why Kierkegaard felt he had to end his engagement to Regine Olsen, a girl he really loved. Once he began to write his books, he worked so feverishly that he knew he would not take the necessary time away from his work to be Regine's husband. Kierkegaard made no provision for his body in the dialectic he lived. He paid the price for this omission, first, in the pain he suffered when Regine married someone else, and, finally, with his life itself. In 1855 he collapsed on a street in Copenhagen and died a few weeks later, physically burned out at forty-two by a vocation that *was* his life. He was, from all appearances, a willing martyr to his work. He concludes his largely autobiographical *The Point of View for My Work as an Author* by saying, in anticipation of his death, that he "historically died of a mortal disease, but poetically died of longing for eternity, where uninterruptedly he would have nothing else to do but to thank God."[18]

"Man," Goethe said, "can find no better retreat from the world than art, and man can find no stronger link with the world than art."[19] The

continuation

---

something that is "before me in its entirety." The work that the scientist (and technician) does is in the realm of the problematic because it is pursued as something outside him and separate from him. That is why a scientist's work is said to be objective. With a mystery, on the other hand, one cannot separate himself from his attempt to come to grips with it. A mystery is a "problem which encroaches upon its own data." Because the work of the philosopher is in the realm of mystery, he surrenders more of his autonomy in its pursuit than the scientist, who can remain outside of and detached from the subject of his investigation.

result of this polarity of possibility will depend upon whether the artist (or any other worker) can keep open the "connecting corridor" between the Having of his art and his Being. Lists of the great artists who relinquished themselves to their work—and destroyed themselves in the process—have been compiled many times.

Ingmar Bergman has said that he became an artist to satisfy what he calls a "hunger" for life that he could not satisfy in life itself.[20] Bergman works toward self through his films, i.e., toward his Being through the Having of his artistic creation. As we saw in the preceding chapter, he is concerned in his films with people who have a great deal of difficulty becoming themselves. We may assume that he has had similar difficulties, first, trying to find a satisfactory relationship with God, and then, later, coming to terms with what it means to be an authentic self in a world without God. While making several of his films, Bergman became so totally involved in the project that, when the film was completed, he had to spend time in a mental hospital to recover from exhaustion. Thus, the self that Bergman creates in part through his work is temporarily diminished by that work. While working on a film, the "connecting corridor" between Being (his self) and Having (the film he is making) closes down, and the equilibrium is displaced toward Having. Being, for a time, takes a back seat to the Having that will ultimately enhance it. Although the film that Bergman creates is not a real world, it is a *real possession*. As Marcel says, Bergman "disappears" in the exercise of his art, and only reappears when the film is completed—i.e., when he breaks with it. Recalling Goethe's remark on the relation between art and life, Bergman's filmmaking is first a "retreat" from the world and then, later, a "link" with the world.

Bergman recognizes that his art is a compensation for something that he is missing in life itself. He also recognizes that some people are able to live more successfully and fully than he:

> There are poets who never write, because they shape their lives as poems; actors who never perform, but who act out their lives as high drama. There are painters who never paint, because they close their eyes and conjure up the most superb works of art on the back of their eye-lids. There are film-makers who live their films and would never abuse their gift by materializing them in reality.[21]

Bergman's film characters are stand-ins for Bergman and for the people who have been closest to him. He puts them in situations that he has faced himself to see what *they* will do. Through his imagination, he creates a world that is not real, but reflects the reality of his own experience. Because Having is tangible, while Being is not, Bergman can get a hold on and incarnate something of his fluctional Being through the characters he creates. He can make them do what he cannot do, or he can have them discover something of which he himself has only a vague intuition.

Bergman began making films in the early 1940s. Around 1965 he said that the "hunger" that was the initial motivation for his filmmaking began to "ease off" and was transformed into something else—"curiosity." The "hunger" that Bergman felt gradually became satiated because he was ontically filled up by the Having of his art. The characters he created *found him.* "Now, to be completely honest," he says, "I regard art (and not only the art of the cinema) as lacking importance."[22] We must be careful not to take Bergman too literally here. What he means is that he no longer feels the urgency of making films as he did before. The *need* that drove him to work at such a frenetic pace for twenty years has been lessened by the acquisition of self through the Having of his art. Now, with a more complete and secure self, the "hunger" for artistic creation that he once felt has been reduced to a "curiosity." To some degree, Bergman can now "live" his films and find presence in life itself.

WORK AND ALIENATION

Although there is a certain ontological necessity to the polarity of Being and Having, there can be little doubt that what has been characterized as the mind-matter split in Western culture has augmented this polarity. When we speak of the split between mind and matter, we are giving a name to the gap that separates what a man is from what he *has* and *does.* With the coming of the Industrial Revolution, the gap between a man and the work he did was made wider than ever before. The mass mechanization of common work brought to the ordinary citizen the consequences of the mind-matter split that began with the philosophizing of Plato and Aristotle. Because of the new machines—the god of Reason turned into hardware—industrial workers lost most of the control over how they did their work and over the product of their work. The principal considerations became those of maximum production and progress. It was not so much that the machines took over as it was that the workers gave in to and accepted the new imperative, the new deity. There is a passage in D. H. Lawrence's *Women in Love* that makes this clearer than anything else I have read. Gerald Crich took control over the mine from his sick father and immediately began reforms to achieve maximum production and profit. His father had been generous to the workers and had given them some say in the operation of the mine. But Gerald quickly saw that this altruism cost money and reduced efficiency. He brought in mining engineers who redesigned the plant, and shaved every corner, even making the miners buy their own tools and pay for their sharpening. The men had to work harder, and the work was deadening.

But they submitted to it all. The joy went out of their lives, the hope seemed to perish as they became more and more mechanised. And yet they accepted the new conditions. They even got a further satisfaction out of them. At first they hated Gerald Crich, they swore to do something to him, to murder him. But as time went on, they accepted everything with some fatal satisfaction. Gerald was their high priest, he represented the religion they really felt. His father was forgotten already. There was a new world, a new order, strict, terrible, inhuman, but satisfying in its very destructiveness. The men were satisfied to belong to the great and wonderful machine, even whilst it destroyed them. It was what they wanted. It was the highest that man had produced, the most wonderful and superhuman. They were exalted by belonging to this great and superhuman system which was beyond feeling or reason, something really godlike. Their hearts died within them, but their souls were satisfied. It was what they wanted. Otherwise Gerald could never have done what he did. He was just ahead of them in giving them what they wanted, this participation in a great and perfect system that subjected life to pure mathematical principles. This was a sort of freedom, the sort they really wanted. It was the first great step in undoing, the first great phase of chaos, the substitution of the mechanical principle for the organic, the destruction of the organic purpose, the organic unity, and the subordination of every organic unit to the great mechanical purpose. It was pure organic disintegration and pure mechanical organisation. This is the first and finest state of chaos.[23]

The gap between what a man is and what he does, if it becomes wide enough, may lead to alienation, as we saw in Chapter 2 and Chapter 5. When the polarity between Being and Having becomes sufficiently strong, the self is displaced from the "center" of the body and becomes "disembodied," as Laing says. This opens the way for the creation of a false self. We would like to describe how, when Having becomes separated from Being in work, a false self, or work persona, may come into play.

THE WORK PERSONA

We have already said that Hemingway's Rinaldi and, to a lesser degree, Sherlock Holmes and James Bond are marginal selves by default because they use their work as a diversion from self. Although they have become alienated and diminished relative to what they might have become, they are, nevertheless, authentic. They make no pretense of being other than they are. To recall Sartre's term, there is no "bad faith" involved in their diversion from self through the work they do. They *circumvent* their ontological insecurity, but they do nothing to *mask* it and show no signs of psychic splitting.

Work is one of the most accessible ways for the ontologically insecure person to mask himself, to *deny* his Being in order to *preserve* his Being. It is easier to succeed in work than it is to be a success in life. In *Nashville* Robert Altman captures the paradox of the professional strength and personal weakness that is a hallmark of the marginal self in the character of the country singer, Barbara Jean. Barbara Jean is what we think of these days as a "superstar." She has the world of country music at her feet, but falls into a neurasthenic swoon the minute she leaves the stage. Through work, the insecure and contingent For-itself may try to become a non-contingent In-itself-For-itself as a means of avoiding itself.

A certain degree of role playing is essential if we are to survive and succeed in this world. But when a person lives primarily *through* the role of his career or profession, he may create a false self. We live in a culture that values work—and especially success at work—very highly. There is a great tendency in Western culture to define the self through the professional, economic, and social statuses we achieve. In *The Greening of America* Charles Reich argued that statuses are replacing money as the goal of work, that they are becoming new forms of wealth:

A job, a stock certificate, a pension right, an automobile dealer's franchise, a doctor's privilege of hospital facilities, a student's status in a university—these are typical of the new forms of wealth. All these represent *relationships* to organizations, so that today a person is identified by his various statuses: an engineer at Boeing, a Ford dealer, a Ph.D. in political science, a student at Yale.[24]

A status is, to a considerable extent, a false self, or persona. And, as Jung reminded us, the persona is "nothing real." In one of his frequent book reviews, John Kenneth Galbraith expressed this idea very trenchantly:

> Like the head of General Motors the politician is meant for extinction the day he leaves office. The glow that was thought to be an attribute of his personality when he was a cabinet officer, senator, governor or ambassador was, in fact, a small property [i.e., prop or mask] on temporary loan from the government. The loan is foreclosed the day he is fired, is counted out by the ballots or—in those rare cases when it happens—resigns.[25]

It is easy to live through things that are external to us because we are by nature social and transcendental creatures. The defining of self through statuses, and the excessive concern with how we appear in the eyes of others, are not aberrations unique to this century, although they have probably become more pronounced in this century. In *The Sickness unto Death*, completed in 1848, Kierkegaard observed:

> By seeing the multitude of men around it, by getting engaged in all sorts of worldly affairs, by becoming wise about how things go in this world, such a man forgets himself, forgets what his name is . . . does not dare to believe in himself, finds it too venturesome a thing to be himself, far easier and safer to be like the others, to become an imitation, a number, a cipher in the crowd.[26]

Although work belongs to what Kierkegaard calls the ethical stage on life's way—the point where one makes choices and commitments—the work persona has a strong component in what he calls the aesthetic stage or mode. The aesthete, according to Kierkegaard, is someone who "expects everything from without." The aesthetic mode is typified in the extreme by the epicurean and the romantic. Any form of art may become a means of losing the self if one lives through it for long periods of time, and *disappears* in it. A person who listens to music, goes to the theatre, or reads novels must, at some point, break with the artistic experience and reassert himself, just as the artist must reassert himself by breaking with the product of his creation. The aesthete is not so much nourished by art as absorbed by it. In the "Third Quartet" Eliot wrote, " . . . you are the music while the music lasts."*

Kierkegaard denounced the aesthetic attitude toward life because, he said, the conditions upon which the aesthete bases his happiness and sense of well being lay "outside the individual or . . . in the individual in such a way that it is not posited in the individual by himself." In other words, the self is prevented from becoming itself because it is chosen *outside* itself. The authentic self "has its center within itself," but the aesthete "has his center in the periphery." Kierkegaard maintained that the aesthete is "eccentric" (not at the center of himself), and that his mood is always eccentric. Kierkegaard's notion of the "eccentricity" of the self is very close to Laing's notion of the disembodied self.

When one lives through his work in such a way that the work persona is cut off from the real self—what Kierkegaard called the "center"—the real self does not receive what we have already referred to as the "proceeds" of the persona's activity, and it becomes diminished. In this case, self is not lost merely through default to work as with Hemingway's Rinaldi, Sherlock Holmes, and James Bond, because a false self is interposed

---

*In his eulogy for Jennie Tourel, Leonard Bernstein noted that the singer was able to overcome her sense of isolation (alienation) from the world only during the moments when she shared her art by communicating with an audience:

The paradox of Jennie: so richly endowed, surrounded by loving friends, gallant admirers, and adoring fans. Yet she was never free of the always shocking awareness of isolation—except in those few thousand minutes of her life when she was transported by the bliss of communication through her art. That communication was her credo: the maximum penetration to human sensibilities; yet an hour later she was isolated. She lived her life on the assumption that "no man is an island"; but she also knew, and so often told me she knew, that every man *is* an island.[27]

between the real self and the world. With the work persona, the Having of work is cut off from the Being of the real self, so that the real self becomes isolated from the world that is necessary for its nourishment.* This is what we mean by the schizoid erosion of self. In the terms of Kierkegaard's metaphor of the "spot," the self remains mired in *necessity* (what the self already is) because the *possibility* (what the self is not but may become) that could be furnished through work is not added *at* the "spot," since it is out of its reach. When this occurs, the diminished real self, which cannot be done away with entirely, experiences psychic pain, as we saw at the end of the preceding chapter. When Kierkegaard said of the aesthete that his mood was always eccentric, he was alluding to this pain, the pain of the dispossessed, inauthentic self.

In the preceding chapter, we saw how much pain accompanied the collapse of the false selves of Bergman's Jenny Isaksson (*Face to Face*) and Elisabeth Vogler (*Persona*). A growing number of people in our time are experiencing similar pain, as the buttresses of their false selves fall away. Dr. Daniel Levinson, a psychologist at Yale, has given the name "mid-life crisis" to this syndrome.[28] In *Passages* Gail Sheehy presents the case histories of a number of men and women, each of whom she interviewed in depth, who have gone through this kind of crisis. We will now consider one of her case histories, that of an architect to whom she gives the pseudonym Aaron Coleman Webb, and show how his crisis can be understood as the consequence of the collapse of a false self, one that has been fashioned, as we said, from the outside in.[29]

In real life the pseudonymous Aaron Webb is, according to Sheehy, one of the most prolific and successful architects of our time. He has received as much recognition and as many accolades as any career can possibly bring. But suddenly, at the age of forty, he begins to feel that he is "collapsing internally."

It is clear from the interview that Webb has always used work as a bulwark against life. "I really wanted to achieve a kind of professional mastery," he says, "which would make me immune to anybody's control, to get into a leverage position of such dimension that no one would be able to criticize me. And, to a large extent, I achieved that." Webb is a

---

*The body, according to Marcel, is the *interface* between Being and Having. My body is not entirely external to me, in fact, *I am in it*. We both *are* and *have* a body. When the persona masks the real self, the body ceases to be the true interface between one's interior and exterior worlds, and between oneself and others (see figure 2 in Chapter 6).

classical example of the talented and ambitious man who attains the whole world, but leaves himself behind in the process. He has denied himself to preserve himself. He has tried to become "immune" to life itself. In Sartre's terminology, he has tried to become his own non-contingent foundation, an In-itself-For-itself.

I have always used my work as a substitute for solving problems in my life. It began when I married. I packed my life with activity in order to avoid major personal decisions. What I do is *give up* autonomy by creating a high-demand situation, so that I must always jump from project to project, never really allowing time to think about what I'm doing it all for. Since I turned 40, it's become clearer to me that the reason I do this is [that] I really haven't wanted to scrutinize what my life is all about.

Webb has lived not only *for* his work, but *through* it as well. He has interposed his work between his real self and the world.* In the terms of Marcel's distinction between problem and mystery, he has avoided the mystery of his life by concentrating on the problems of his work. It is difficult to judge from what he says in the interview whether the primary mechanism of his self-loss has been default or schizoid erosion, but there is some indication that splitting has occurred. Webb is a textbook example of a marginal self. He had succeeded, until he was forty, in keeping his real self under wraps. Because his real self offered no distraction to his career, he probably advanced faster and farther than if he had taken it into consideration. (Kierkegaard knew that this was the way to "succeed.")[30] There was no *connection*—Marcel's "connecting corridor"—between the work he did and his real self. Work became a substitute for self, and he never broke with it, as Marcel feels one must if the self is to reassert itself over the Having of its creation. Through his work, Aaron Webb became alienated and estranged from himself.

------

*We must contrast this with the case of Kierkegaard, who *lived* the dialectic he wrote about. For Kierkegaard, work and life were the same thing, while with Webb work became a *substitute* for life. There was an essential congruence between Kierkegaard's Being and the Having of his work, while with Webb there was an almost total separation. Kierkegaard became present through the work he did, Webb alienated.

Webb feels the inadequacy of his real self most intensely just before going to sleep: " . . . closing his eyes, in the instant between realms when outer achievements must be let go, Aaron Coleman Webb is alone with that sense of internal collapse." The Having of work does not fortify the self against the Void when the loss of consciousness through impending sleep *forces* one to break with that work. Like Hemingway's characters, Webb feels the terror of the Void most strongly at night. His "sense of internal collapse" is one of the symptoms of the implosion of the real self that occurs when the false self begins to crumble, as Laing says.

The real self, diminished and starved as it is, cannot be done away with entirely. With Webb, at some point during his fortieth year, his real self asserts itself, and begins to give him trouble. "Just the idea of stopping to investigate [this real self]," he realizes, "is an indication that something has changed." For Webb, the recognition that there *is* a real self is the starting point of an authentic existence. As Sheehy says, he will not let himself run away into work anymore, drown himself in alcohol, or pursue a different kind of escape through drugs. Webb's dilemma is, Where do you go from the top? The trembling structure of his unautonomous false self will no longer adequately mask and support the emerging real self, which now demands attention. He will have to give up, to some extent, what he has achieved externally—to break with it, as Marcel says—if the rebuilding of his real self is to begin. Sometimes, as the song says, you have to fall to rise again.

> I don't know what I want to do. It's a time of confusion for me, great personal confusion. What I really have to learn for myself are the feelings of passivity, dependence, weakness, frailty—all the things that are abhorrent to me on the intellectual level. As a counterweight to that, I must permit myself to acknowledge my own aggression, my punishing quality—all the rest of that. I can't pretend any more that the duality of roles does not exist.

Webb is speaking here of facing up to his finitude, those facets of Nothingness in his Being that must be acknowledged and dealt with if he is to begin an existential rebirth. Up to now, he has lived entirely in the outer world, the world of *prose* ("the world of telegrams and anger"), like the Wilcoxes in Forster's *Howards End*. But his crisis has forced him to see that there *is* an interior world, the world that Forster called *passion*. Aaron

Coleman Webb's mandate now is to "connect" the *prose* and the *passion*, to open the "connecting corridor" between the extraordinary Having of his work and his newly emerging real self. By giving up the comforting illusion of the In-itself-For-itself, he can begin to become an authentic For-itself.

As he tells us, Webb packed his life with activity because he did not want to scrutinize what his life was all about. For a long time, he succeeded at this ploy. But many other people try to do this and do not succeed. In *The Sickness unto Death*, Kierkegaard describes the despair of someone who decided he would be either Caesar or nothing,* and failed to become Caesar:

> . . . he is not in despair over the *fact* that he did not become Caesar, but he is in despair *over himself* for the fact that he did not become Caesar. This self which, had he become Caesar, would have been to him a sheer delight . . . this self is now absolutely intolerable to him. In a profounder sense it is not the fact that he did not become Caesar which is intolerable to him, but the *self* that did not become Caesar is the thing that is intolerable; or, more correctly, what is intolerable to him is that he cannot *get rid* of himself [emphasis added].[31]

The (real) self will not disappear entirely. Not even despair can burn it up. And that, Kierkegaard tells us, is how we can be sure there *is* a real self.

In 1935, when he was thirty-nine, F. Scott Fitzgerald was in Hollywood, trying to write for the movies—and having a bad time of it. *Esquire* Magazine was paying him a retainer of two hundred dollars a month, but he had written nothing for them. Arnold Gingrich, *Esquire*'s editor, went out to see Fitzgerald. As it turned out, Fitzgerald was in the midst of the worst writing block of his career, unable to do anything he felt was worthwhile. Gingrich told him that he understood, but that the accounting department did not, and suggested to Fitzgerald that he just knock something out on his typewriter—anything at all—and send it in. He

---

*"Either Caesar or nothing" (*Aut Caesar aut nullus*) was the motto of Caesar Borgia.

would tell the people in accounting that it was stream-of-consciousness stuff, too avant-garde for the magazine. But Fitzgerald showed no enthusiasm for the stopgap plan. Then it occurred to Gingrich to ask Fitzgerald to write about why he couldn't write. Gingrich went back to Chicago, and several weeks later received a manuscript from Fitzgerald entitled "The Crack-Up."[32] This was a story not only of a blocked writer, but of a divided and "cracked" self.* It was Fitzgerald's attempt to explain how he had lost the ability to write—and to live.

While there is some question as to whether Gail Sheehy's Aaron Coleman Webb came to be a marginal self primarily through default or through schizoid erosion, there is no question that Fitzgerald was brought down by schizoid erosion. "The Crack-Up" tells a story that could easily be one of Laing's case histories from *The Divided Self*. Writing about Fitzgerald, Hemingway, and several other novelists of their generation, Malcolm Cowley makes it very clear that these men lived, to a considerable extent, through a work persona: " . . . they regarded their talent as something apart from their ordinary selves. Hence, their efforts to preserve the talent were selfless, after a fashion, or at least ran counter in many cases to their material interests. A question they asked themselves was, 'How can I best live in order to produce the books that are in me?' "[33] For these writers, there had been an almost complete divorce between the Having of their writing and the Being of their real selves.

In "The Crack-Up" Fitzgerald draws a classic sketch of a self that lacked ontological security and autonomy:

> I was an average mixer, but more than average in a tendency to identify myself, my ideas, my destiny, with those of all classes I came in contact with.[34]

And speaking of the spectacular success of his first novel, *This Side of Paradise*, Fitzgerald acknowledged that

---

*Two years earlier, in 1933, Fitzgerald published *Tender Is the Night*. The principal character, Dr. Richard Diver, is an alter ego and fictional stand-in for Fitzgerald. The parallels between the blocked writer in "The Crack-Up" and Dick Diver are many and strong.

> . . . for a shy man it was nice to be somebody else again: to be "the
> Author" as one had been "the Lieutenant."* Of course one wasn't
> really an author any more than one had been an army officer, but
> nobody seemed to guess behind the false face.[35]

Thus, work (and what extraordinary work it was) became the means
through which Fitzgerald dealt with his ontological insecurity, the way he
chose to deny his Being in order to preserve his Being. A work persona
was created, and splitting—the division of the psyche into a real self and a
false self—occurred.

The "shy" Fitzgerald, who hid behind the mask of "the Author,"
admits that he consciously modeled his life on the lives of certain men
whom he looked up to, and that he, in effect, let them do his thinking for
him.

> . . . I had done very little thinking, save within the problems of my
> craft. For twenty years a certain man had been my intellectual
> conscience. That was Edmund Wilson.
> . . . another man represented my sense of the "good life," though I
> saw him once in a decade, and since then he might have been hung.
> He is in the fur business in the Northwest and wouldn't like his
> name set down here. But in difficult situations I had tried to think
> what *he* would have thought, how *he* would have acted.[36]

In his life Fitzgerald was an imitator, fashioning himself from the
outside in. He put his originality, creativity, and, may we say, his
authenticity into his writing. But because he lived and worked through a
false self, the Having of his art was cut off from the Being of his real self,
which then withered from lack of nourishment. Unlike Bergman, Fitzgerald's fictional characters never *found him*. At what must have been close to
the lowest point of his decline, Fitzgerald realized that there was no
longer anything he could call "I," and that his diminished real self could
no longer even support the mask of "the Author."

---

*Fitzgerald wrote *This Side of Paradise* almost immediately after returning from the First
World War.

> So there was not an "I" any more—not a basis on which I could organize my self-respect—save my limitless capacity for toil that it seemed I possessed no more. It was strange to have no self—to be like a little boy left alone in a big house, who knew that now he could do anything he wanted to do, but found that there was nothing that he wanted to do.[37]

Fitzgerald felt that he had become "an unwilling witness of an execution, the disintegration of [his] own personality." But from this nadir he began a painful climb to recover the lost "I." In 1940 he was well into another novel, *The Last Tycoon*, when he died from a heart attack. He was forty-four.

WORK AND PRESENCE

We have seen how self may be lost either through default (the failure to become), when work is used as a *diversion from self*, or through schizoid erosion (the result of interposing a work persona between the real self and the world), when work is used as a *substitute for self*. In both cases, the self becomes alienated from itself and from the world. We will see now how work may enhance the self when the "connecting corridor" between the Having of work and the Being of the worker is kept open. This kind of work leads to the presentation of the self to itself and to the world, i.e., to presence.

Fitzgerald said there were times when he did not know whether he was real or a character from one of his novels. Because he severed the tie between the "I" and "the Author"—the real self and the work persona—he had trouble distinguishing his greatly diminished real self ("I") from the literarily very real characters he created. Another writer, Jorge Luis Borges, does not have this problem. In a brief but extraordinary sketch that he calls "Borges and I," he examines the dichotomy between the writer and his work. Unlike Fitzgerald, he not only *knows* there is a difference between what he is and what he creates but also *lives* with this distinction clearly in mind.

> The other one, the one called Borges, is the one things happen to. I walk through the streets of Buenos Aires and stop for a moment,

perhaps mechanically now, to look at the arch of an entrance hall and the grillwork on the gate; I know of Borges from the mail and see his name on a list of professors or in a biographical dictionary. I like hourglasses, maps, eighteenth-century typography, the taste of coffee and the prose of Stevenson; he shares these preferences, but in a vain way that turns them into the attributes of an actor. It would be an exaggeration to say that ours is a hostile relationship; I live, let myself go on living, so that Borges may contrive his literature, and this literature justifies me. It is no effort for me to confess that he has achieved some valid pages, but those pages cannot save me, perhaps because what is good belongs to no one, not even to him, but rather to the language and to tradition. Besides, I am destined to perish, definitively, and only some instant of myself can survive in him. Little by little, I am giving over everything to him, though I am quite aware of his perverse custom of falsifying and magnifying things. Spinoza knew that all things long to persist in their being; the stone eternally wants to be a stone and the tiger a tiger. I shall remain in Borges, not in myself (if it is true that I am someone), but I recognize myself less in his books than in many others or in the laborious strumming of a guitar. Years ago I tried to free myself from him and went from the mythologies of the suburbs to the games with time and infinity, but those games belong to Borges now and I shall have to imagine other things. Thus my life is a flight and I lose everything and everything belongs to oblivion, or to him.

I do not know which of us has written this page.[38]

"Borges" is the man who writes books, has readers, teaches at the university, and gets mail. "I" is the man who takes walks, and likes architecture and coffee. "Borges" is caught up in what Walker Percy in *The Moviegoer* calls the "vertical search," the search of the intellectual or the artist. "I" is pursuing the "horizontal search," i.e., just being himself. "Borges" is the Having of Jorge Luis Borges, while "I" is his Being. Borges knows that "Borges" will last as long as the books he writes, but that "I" is perishing even as he immortalizes this recognition in words. Little by little, he is handing everything over to "Borges." "I" tried to shake off "Borges" by writing about something different, but "Borges" eventually (and inevitably) took that also. At the end, "I" will give everything to "Borges."

Borges lives the dialectic between "Borges" and "I"—Having and

Being—and is truly present to himself and to the world. He feels himself to be distinct from his writing, yet because the "connecting corridor" between the writer and the man has been kept open, the man is enriched by the achievements of the writer. With Borges, unlike Fitzgerald, there is no false self interposed between the man and his work that would prevent the transformation of Having into Being. Borges has accepted his finitude and has no illusions of becoming an In-itself-For-itself through his work.

In *Zen and the Art of Motorcycle Maintenance*, Robert M. Pirsig examines the relation between the Being and the Having of work by casting these antinomies in the terms of Zen meditation (the interior world, *contemplation*, essentially pure Being) and motorcycle maintenance (the exterior world, *action*, principally Having). This is another way of specifying what we have been referring to all along as the mind-matter split—the separation of a man from his thoughts and from the work he does—that leads to alienation. Pirsig sees the dialectical integration of Being and Having in these terms:

> The real cycle you're working on is a cycle called yourself. The machine that appears to be "out there" and the person that appears to be "in here" are not two separate things. They grow toward Quality or fall away from Quality together.[39]

In Chapter 1, we saw that the "Quality" that Phaedrus, the protagonist of Pirsig's novel, came to recognize as the goal of his search was the "wholeness and oneness of life." Quality, as Phaedrus says, is the *relationship* between a man and his experience, a relationship that we have been calling presence. A man has a sense of presence when he feels that he *belongs* to the world. One may become present to himself and to his world through the work he does when the distinction between "out there" and "in here" disappears.

> . . . you can actually *see* this fusion in skilled mechanics and machinists of a certain sort, and you can see it in the work they do. To say that they are not artists is to misunderstand the nature of art. They have patience, care and attentiveness to what they're doing, but more than this—there's a kind of inner peace of mind that isn't contrived but results from a kind of harmony with the work in which

there's no leader and no follower. The material and the craftsman's thoughts change together in a progression of smooth, even changes until his mind is at rest at the exact instant the material is right.

We've all had moments of that sort when we're doing something we really want to do. It's just that somehow we've gotten into an unfortunate separation of those moments from work. The mechanic I'm talking about doesn't make this separation. One says of him that he is "interested" in what he's doing, that he's "involved" in his work. What produces this involvement is, at the cutting edge of consciousness, an absence of any sense of separateness of subject and object. "Being with it," "being a natural," "taking hold"—there are a lot of idiomatic expressions for what I mean by this absence of subject-object duality, because what I mean is so well understood as folklore, common sense, the everyday understanding of the shop. But in scientific parlance the words for this absence of subject-object duality are scarce because scientific minds have shut themselves off from consciousness of this kind of understanding in the assumption of the formal dualistic scientific outlook.[40]

Pirsig's observation that a mechanic or a machinist finds it easier to achieve presence through his work reminds us of Marcel's claim that the scientist is less autonomous in his work, i.e., he gives up more of himself to it than the technician does. Work done with tools and machines has less inherent power to alienate the worker from himself than the more abstract and theoretical work a scientist does. The work of the scientist requires a greater separation between "out there" and "in here." The mechanic is more *grounded* in his work, through what Pirsig calls the "folklore, common sense, [and] the everyday understanding of the shop." This is not to say that a scientist may not find the same kind of harmony in his work—many scientists do—only that the *pull* toward alienation is greater in his case. In *The Courage to Be* Tillich gives this description of what it is like when a scientist overcomes the alienation inherent in his work, when he keeps open the "connecting corridor" between the Having of his investigation and his own Being: "The scientist loves both the truth he discovers and himself insofar as he discovers it. He is held by the content of his discovery."[41]

Pirsig gives another illustration of the "out there–in here" dichotomy of work and interior experience by distinguishing two ways in which one may approach the climbing of a mountain.

To the untrained eye ego-climbing and selfless climbing may appear identical. Both kinds of climbers place one foot in front of the other. Both breathe in and out at the same rate. Both stop when tired. Both go forward when rested. But what a difference! The ego-climber is like an instrument that's out of adjustment. He puts his foot down an instant too soon or too late. He's likely to miss a beautiful passage of sunlight through the trees. He goes on when the sloppiness of his step shows he's tired. He rests at odd times. He looks up the trail trying to see what's ahead even when he knows what's ahead because he just looked a second before. He goes too fast or too slow for the conditions and when he talks his talk is forever about somewhere else, something else. He's here but he's not here. He rejects the here, is unhappy with it, wants to be farther up the trail but when he gets there will be just as unhappy because then *it* will be "here." What he's looking for, what he wants, is all around him, but he doesn't want that because it *is* all around him. Every step's an effort, both physically and spiritually, because he imagines his goal to be external and distant.[42]

One can lose himself climbing a mountain almost as easily as in a production line or in a library. The climber who imagines his goal to be external and distant has put the Having of his search *in front* of him, rather than allowing it to *enter into* him. He has blocked the "connecting corridor" between the Having of his activity and his Being. It is not the destination that is primary, but the Quality of the getting there—the degree of presence one achieves.

Erica Jong, the author of *Fear of Flying*, has described how she feels when she writes:

My passion was for the pen, the legal pad (on which I was writing), and the ecstasy of watching my scrawl cover the pages. It is the sort of trance saints speak of—a blissful, heightened state in which you feel at once utterly alone and in harmony with the universe. It has something in common with the childhood bliss of coloring or making paper dolls or building models. And it has something in common with meditation. And it certainly has something in common with sex. Just what, I don't know. I do know that after writing for several hours, I feel high and happy and psychically released, as after sex.[43]

Jong compares the "heightened state" she experiences while writing with the mystical experience of the saints and the psychic release that follows sex. Her phrase, "utterly alone and in harmony with the universe," is perhaps as good an expression of what it means to be present as we can hope for.

When a person works in such a way that the Having of work, whatever kind of activity it is, becomes separated from the worker, he becomes alienated (separated) from himself and from his world. This is what happened with F. Scott Fitzgerald and Gail Sheehy's Aaron Coleman Webb. If the Having of work is initially separated from the self, but, somehow, later joined to it, the self may still be augmented, as we saw with Bergman and his filmmaking. When there is no separation between the worker and what he is doing, when, as Pirsig says, there is no distinction between "out there" and "in here," the worker becomes present to himself and to his world. As we have seen, this is the case with Borges, the mechanic whom Pirsig knows, and Erica Jong.

8

The Search for Self and the Loss of Self in Love

God created man, and, finding him not sufficiently alone, gave him a female companion to make him feel his solitude more keenly.

— Paul Valéry

Camus felt that there was an inherent gap between what people ask of the world and what they could expect to receive from it. He used the word "absurd" (which literally means discordance) to describe the state of disjunction between what is desired and what is given. Men and women are equally mortal and share the same longing for meaning, familiarity, clarity, unity, cohesion, and the absolute. Both live in a world that often seems deaf to their needs. But in addition to the gap that separates what men and women both require from a universe that is sexually indiscriminate, there is another gap that separates men and women from what they want and need from each other.

To understand fully the need of men for women and of women for men, we would first have to conceive of an androgynous self—i.e., a species that had all the characteristics of the male and female—and then imagine this sexually non-contingent, "spherical" species split into two "hemispherical" parts, each of which is incomplete and therefore contingent for completion upon a partner of the opposite polarity. It almost seems as if, through some perversity of nature, sexual absurdity has been superimposed on the metaphysical absurdity of existence itself. "Sex," Berdyaev said, "is one of the chief causes of human solitude. Man is a sexual being, that is half a being, divided and incomplete."[1]

LOVE: THE ONTOLOGICAL NEED

Before we can hope to understand what love is, we must come to terms with the need that ineluctably drives every man toward a woman and every woman toward a man. Sartre has characterized the self (the For-itself) as lacking its own foundation, of being dependent upon the world and others for its nourishment and continuance. According to Sartre, the For-itself *proceeds through lack* and acts out of what he calls an "ache for being." The project of the For-itself is to become its own foundation, complete, a non-contingent In-itself-For-itself. We have already seen how the For-itself may attempt this completion through belief in a transcendent divinity and through work. We must consider now the consequences of the fact that the For-itself has sexuality, that each self is, sexually, only *half* a self. Through the love of a woman, a man seeks his own sexual foundation—his sexual completion—as Augustine finally sought completion in the love and praise of God, and as Gerald Crich in Lawrence's *Women in Love* initially sought completion in perfecting the operation of his father's mine.

There is a strong element of coincidence between Camus's statement of man's absurd condition and the nostalgia this condition gives rise to, and Sartre's description of the lack in the For-itself and its need for completion. Through the beloved, the lover attempts not only to satisfy himself sexually, but to complete the circuit between himself and existence. Through love, we attempt to close the gap of Camus's absurd condition and fill the "hole of being at the heart of being" in Sartre's For-itself. The lover, according to Sartre, seeks the totality of Being, an absolute, the supreme value. The beloved is the means, or *intermediary*, through which the lover tries to become complete.

Perhaps our best chance to understand what the possibilities for love are is to try to understand why love fails, as we must admit it so often does. Sartre is our chief pathologist of love. In several dozen rather murky pages in *Being and Nothingness*, and in his very popular play *No Exit*, Sartre, as if performing an autopsy, sets down what amounts to an ontology of failed love. His lovers fail because, in the hope of completing themselves, they try to appropriate the freedom of the other which, for Sartre, is tantamount to appropriating the other's essence. The lover (the For-itself) "devours" the beloved (who, to the lover, is an In-itself) to become his or her own foundation (an In-itself-For-itself). Sartre believes that in love "it is the Other's freedom which founds my essence."[2] I cannot, he says, overcome my sexual contingency and become my own foundation without taking away from another person her freedom. According to Sartre, *the mere fact of wanting someone to love me* deprives the other of her freedom.[3] He believes that any attempt at love is doomed at the outset, that there can be "no dialectic"[4] in my relations with a potential beloved, that, in short, love is impossible. For Sartre this attempt at completion, like the belief in God itself, is a "useless passion." The problem of the lover remains, therefore, "without solution."[5]

If all this sounds harsh and "hopeless," we may be assured that it is what Sartre intends. The question arises: In a consideration of love, why go to so much trouble to examine the thought of someone who clearly does not believe in it? The answer is that however we may feel about the possibilities of love between men and women, we must admit that in most cases what begins as love eventually turns into the kind of rapacious situation that Sartre describes. From the experiences of the families we grow up in and from the families we ourselves create, we must acknowledge that Sartre's sparring lovers are rather accurate reflections of our parents, ourselves, and our friends. The simple fact is that in most love relationships hell *does* become the other person, and for pretty much the reasons that Sartre gives. We *do* try to take away the freedom of the other for our own aggrandizement, to "devour" the beloved for our own sustenance. And the other tries to do the same thing to us. Naturally, there is conflict (what Sartre calls the clash of "alien freedoms"). Reading Sartre on love, we come to feel the fire and smell the brimstone of hell.

DIALECTIC AND PRESENCE

We must be grateful to Sartre for describing the ontological need that draws men and women together, and for his characterization of the corpse that most love eventually becomes. But if we suspect that a dialectic between a man and a woman *is* possible, we must look elsewhere for insight into it. Sartre has the right to his denial, but if one senses the possibility of love he owes it to himself to go beyond that denial.*

---

*We should point out that although Sartre is pessimistic about love on paper, he seems to have had a rather successful experience with it. Of Simone de Beauvoir, his friend (although

Martin Buber's greatest contribution to the understanding of love is his articulation of the dialectic that Sartre repudiates. What Sartre has done for the corpse of love, Buber does for its flourishing body. Buber understands the "appropriative" love that Sartre sees as the only relationship possible between a man and a woman. He calls this the *I-It* relation. *I-It* is a mode of Having*; the lover is the subject, and the beloved is an object that is to be possessed. Each is a "severed I," wallowing, as Buber says, "in the capital letter."[6] *I-It* is not a relationship, but a *disrelationship*. There is no dialectical third term, no "between." Buber's *I-It* is another way of specifying what Sartre called the appropriation of the In-itself by the For-itself.

But an *I* may assume another stance vis-à-vis the other. If an *I* approaches the other in the mode of relation rather than in the mode of Having, there is reciprocity rather than appropriation. When an *I* approaches another person in this way, a person is perceived not as an *It* but as a *You*. Unlike *I-It*, *I-You* is a relationship, and there *is* a dialectical third term, a "between." In the *I-It*, the other is held as an object. But in the *I-You*, Buber says, "there is no metaphor but actuality."[7] "Love does not cling to an I, as if the You were merely its 'content' or object; it is *between* I and You" (emphasis added).[8]

The world of *I-You* does not require relinquishing the *I*, but rather giving up the solipsism and the security of the "severed I" for something fuller and more risky.

What has to be given up is not the I, as most mystics suppose: The I is indispensable for any relationship, including the highest, which always presupposes an I and a You. What has to be given up is not the I but the false drive for self-affirmation which impels man to flee from the unreliable, unsolid, unlasting, unpredictable, dangerous world of relation into the having of things.[9]

---

continuation

not always exclusively) for almost fifty years, Sartre has said: "I've found in her everything I could possibly want" (see Acel Madsen, *Hearts and Minds* [New York: William Morrow, 1977]). This discrepancy is puzzling. Perhaps by constantly keeping in mind the worst that could become of their love, and thus allowing it to remain contingent (what is currently being called "open"), he and de Beauvoir were able to avoid it.

*Recall the distinction made in the preceding chapter between Being and Having.

The *I* of *I-You* is not the same *I* as that in *I-It*. As an *I* of encounter and actuality, it is an *expanded I*. And it is only by participating in a *You* that the self can approach wholeness. The self *requires* a *You* to become a (whole) *I*.

> The concentration and fusion into a whole being can never be accomplished by me, can never be accomplished without me. I require a You to become; becoming I, I say You.[10]

The "between" that is created when an *I* becomes related to another as a *You* is a part of Husserl's Life-World, the world that precedes thought, explanation, and understanding. "The heart," Pascal said in the *Pensées*, "has its reasons that reason does not know." The dialectical third term of *I-You* is preconscious and ineffable. This is what Buber means when he says that there is no metaphor for it but actuality. It simply *is*.

> Nothing conceptual intervenes between I and You, no prior knowledge and no imagination; and memory itself is changed as it plunges from particularity into wholeness.[11]

While the *dis*relation of *I-It* alienates the *I* from the other, from himself, and from the world (hence, Buber's "severed I"), the self becomes present through the relation of the *I* to the *You*. Most of the time, we experience the world as unordered and opaque; we are separated (alienated) from much of it. But during moments of presence, the world does seem to take on an order. What is usually unstructured now falls into place for us, and we see ourselves as having a part in the scheme of things. For a while the absurd yields to unity and clarity. We feel at home. These moments are evanescent, but we are enlarged for having had them. "They leave," Buber says, "no content that could be preserved, but their force enters into the creation and into man's knowledge . . ."[12]

There is a passage in Fitzgerald's *The Great Gatsby* that exemplifies how an *I*, when it is at the peak of its relation with a *You*, feels present and at one with the world. The narrator is describing how Gatsby felt the night he fell in love with Daisy:

. . . One autumn night, five years before, they had been walking down the street when the leaves were falling, and they came to a place where there were no trees and the sidewalk was white with moonlight. They stopped here and turned toward each other. Now it was a cool night with that mysterious excitement in it which comes at the two changes of the year. The quiet lights of the houses were humming out into the darkness and there was a stir and bustle among the stars. Out of the corner of his eye Gatsby saw that the blocks of the sidewalks really formed a ladder and mounted to a secret place above the trees—he could climb to it, if he climbed alone, and once there he could suck on the pap of life, gulp down the incomparable milk of wonder.

His heart beat faster and faster as Daisy's white face came up to his own. He knew that when he kissed this girl, and forever wed his unutterable visions to her perishable breath, his mind would never romp again like the mind of God. So he waited, listening for a moment longer to the tuning-fork that had been struck upon a star. Then he kissed her. At his lips' touch she blossomed for him like a flower and the incarnation was complete.[13]

On that evening, Gatsby's love for Daisy brought him not only the woman he worshiped, but the world itself. Through Daisy, he enlarged himself so that he could hear "the tuning-fork that had been struck upon a star."

One tends to trust Buber's delineation of the *I-You* relation because he recognizes—as we recognize from our own experience—that it invariably collapses, at least temporarily, into the *dis*relation of the *I-It*. In the relationship between any two people who love each other, there is a perpetual oscillation between *I-You* and *I-It*.

It is not the relationship that necessarily wanes, but the actuality of its directness. Love itself cannot abide in a direct relation; it endures, but in the alteration of actuality and latency. Every You in the world is compelled by its nature to become a thing for us or at least to enter again and again into thinghood.[14]

Gatsby's self-deluding love for Daisy was doomed from the start. But even with love that endures, there are times when one lover, and then the other, will turn the beloved into an object. The "between" evaporates temporarily, and the *You* becomes an *It*. Love is never constant: it is made and broken and remade many times. How often have we heard lovers we know, and those in novels, plays, and films, say to their partners in a moment of anger, "I hate you"? With *I-You* lovers, the change in the polarity of feeling may come about when, because of some strain, the accustomed "between" vanishes, leaving one or both with a temporarily shrunken, uncompleted, and alienated *I*. With *I-It* lovers, the change from "love" to "hate" may occur when one becomes frustrated in the attempt to appropriate the other. When the "feeding" of the For-itself on the In-itself is interrrupted, so that the secure foundation of the In-itself-For-itself crumbles, the painful contingency of the For-itself returns. When the beloved withdraws his sustenance, "I love you" (i.e., I am getting what I need from you) may quickly change to "I hate you" (i.e., You're not giving me what I want).

When one partner in an *I-You* relation withdraws from the union, the other partner is, as we said, left with a shrunken, uncompleted *I*. The "ache for being" that was palliated by the beloved returns and is felt even more painfully than before the union, since loss has now been added to the original lack. In *The Sickness unto Death* Kierkegaard speaks of the young girl who is in despair because her lover has left her or has died. She is in despair, Kierkegaard says, not over her lost lover but over *herself*: "This self of hers, which, if it had become 'his' beloved, she would have been rid of in the most blissful way, or would have lost, this self is now a torment to her when it has to be a self without 'him' . . ."[15] Kierkegaard is being somewhat cynical here—his emphasis is always on the isolated individual, and he is implying that a certain loss of self, not merely change and expansion, is inevitable in union—but he makes the point that after one lover from an *I-You* relation has withdrawn, the other is thrown back on and "stuck" with himself in a new way. The "ache for being" of the disappointed lover longs to be palliated again, if not by completion with another lover, then at least by regaining that much of himself as he had before union with, and separation from, the other. During a period of frustrated love, the self goes into escrow. *The disappointed lover wants his self back again.*

LAWRENCE'S WOMEN IN LOVE: "I-IT" AND "I-YOU"

In Lawrence's *Women in Love*, there are excellent characterizations of both the *I-It* and the *I-You* relations: the affair between Gerald and Gudrun is strictly *I-It*, and that between Birkin and Ursula is distinctly *I-You*.

As we saw in the preceding chapter, Gerald first tries to find fulfillment and completion through his work at the colliery. For a time his "ache for being" is assuaged by his efforts to fine-tune the operation of the mine. Efficiency and maximum production become absolutes that fill his self. The mine is literally a *Deus ex machina*, a God of the machine. Gerald has indentified with an absolute, and with his desire for completion realized, he feels at home in the world.* But when he and the efficiency experts he hired succeed in turning the mine into an instrument of perfection that is capable of functioning without him, the circuit of completion is broken, and Gerald is confronted again with his "uncompleted" self. He is no longer a part of the process of perfection. Once again he feels a "vacuum" in the "very middle of him." When the mine no longer offers Gerald a road to completion, the "ache for being" returns. At this point Gerald turns to Gudrun. He abandons the search for a complete self through work and initiates a search for completion through love.

Gerald's affair with Gudrun is an excellent example of what Sartre means by two lovers trying to "appropriate" one another. Each sees the other as a total "otherness" that could be added to his or her self, so that he or she might become complete. Each sees the other as a means to completion, an *object* to be used for his or her emotional and physical gratification. There is no complementarity or union in their relation. In Buber's terms, there is no "between," no *You*, only two *Its*. In the continuing struggle between Gerald and Gudrun, first one is victorious, and then, when the balance shifts, the other is.

> Sometimes it was he who seemed strongest, whilst she was almost gone, creeping near the earth like a spent wind; sometimes it was the

---

*Lawrence's description of the yearning for "completion" is similar to Sartre's assertion that the project of the For-itself is to become an In-itself-For-itself through work, love, belief in God, etc. Buber characterizes the *I-It* and the *I-You* to distinguish between two *modes* of completion through love.

reverse. But always it was this eternal see-saw, one destroyed that the other might exist, one ratified because the other was nulled.[16]

The relation between Gerald and Gudrun lacks presence. "They cannot," as T. H. Adamowski points out in an incisive essay on *Women in Love*, "move from a sense of their insertion in otherness to a delight in each other."[17] They are paradigms of Sartre's doomed lovers. They remind us, too, of the eternally scrapping lovers in plays and films as diverse as Strindberg's *The Dance of Death*, Eliot's *The Cocktail Party*, Albee's *Who's Afraid of Virginia Woolf?*, Miller's *After the Fall*, and Bergman's *Scenes from a Marriage*. Periods of "love," when each receives from the other what he or she requires for completion, alternate with periods of "hatred," when each (or both) becomes frustrated in the drive for completion. The "eternal see-saw" that Gerald and Gudrun ride is a perfect metaphor for the protagonists of Sartre's *No Exit*, who conclude that "hell is other people." For each pair of lovers in Sartre's play, hell is *each other*, or, more to the point, the frustration caused by the failure of each to "appropriate" the other.

Where Sartre feels that every attempt of the self to complete itself through the other in love is doomed—i.e., that there can never be a "between"—Lawrence, like Buber, believes that the self *can* achieve completion (wholeness) through love and sexuality. For him, sexuality is the road to complete and perfect Being. Lawrence knows that it is a difficult road, and that few are able to follow it: Gerald and Ursula could not. (Sartre denies that there *is* such a road.) In *Women in Love* Lawrence contrasts the appropriative, Sartrean, *I-It* "love" of Gerald and Gudrun with a very different kind of relationship between Rupert Birkin and Gudrun's sister Ursula. Where Gerald and Gudrun try to achieve completion *at the expense of each other*, Ursula and Birkin seek perfection in and through each other. Their goal is mutuality. Gerald and Gudrun remain separate and unmerged in their pursuit of completion. Ursula and Birkin approach *unity*. Their merging is all the more remarkable because each insists on preserving his and her freedom and sense of self as far as is compatible with union. Birkin tells Ursula that theirs is "the perfect relation . . . we are free together."[18] He feels their love is a

paradisal entry into pure, single being, the individual soul taking precedence over love and desire for union, stronger than any pangs of emotion, a lovely state of free proud singleness, which accepted the obligation of the permanent connection with others, and with the other, submits to the yoke and leash of love, but never forfeits its own proud individual singleness, even while it loves and yields.[19]

Birkin and Ursula strive for the ideal of perfection, which embraces the paradoxes of separateness in unity and freedom in commitment. Lawrence asks:

Why could they not remain individuals, limited by their own limits? Why this dreadful all-comprehensiveness, this hateful tyranny? Why not leave the other being free, why try to absorb, or melt, or merge? One might abandon oneself utterly to the *moments*, but not to any other being.[20]

Lawrence implies here that the lover—an *I* vis-à-vis a *You*—may keep his or her identity just as it was prior to love. But later, as his relationship with Ursula ripens, Birkin comes to realize that he has become a *different I*, an *expanded I*. The dialectical merging of the lovers has generated something new, a "third term." This is what Buber means by the "between."

It was something beyond love, such as a gladness of having surpassed oneself, of having transcended the old existence. How could [Birkin] say "I" when he was something new and unknown, not himself at all? This I, this old formula of the age, was a dead letter.

In the new, superfine bliss, a peace superseding knowledge, there was no I and you, there was only the third, unrealised wonder, the wonder of existing not as oneself, but in a consummation of my being and of her being in a new one, a new, paradisal unit regained from the duality. How can I say "I love you" when I have ceased to be, and you have ceased to be: we are both caught up and transcended into a new oneness where everything is silent, because there is nothing to answer, all is perfect and at one. Speech travels between the separate parts. But in the perfect One there is perfect silence of bliss.[21]

In the love of Birkin and Ursula, neither *I* is lost, but each is transcended and transfigured. Through the *You* of the other, each *I* becomes complete. And they merge not only with one other, but with existence itself. They become *present*. "Everything is ours," Ursula tells Birkin. Their love is a part of Husserl's Life-World, the world that precedes thought, explanation, and understanding. " . . . they delighted in each other's presence, pure presence, not to be thought of, even known."[22] Because they have come to each other with no trace of a persona, Birkin and Ursula are able to return to "the pre-personal self of the body"[23] and reach "the very stuff of being." During sex with Birkin, Ursula completes the circuit of perfection:

> This was release at last. She had had lovers, she had known passion. But this was neither love nor passion. It was the daughters of men coming back to the sons of God, the strange inhuman sons of God who are in the beginning.
>   . . . She traced with her hands the line of his loins and thighs, at the back, and a living fire ran through her, from him, darkly. It was a dark flood of electric passion she released from him, drew into herself. She had established a rich new circuit, a new current of passional electric energy, between the two of them, released from the darkest poles of the body and established in perfect circuit. It was a dark fire of electricity that rushed from him to her, and flooded them both with rich peace, satisfaction.[24]

In sex Birkin and Ursula seem to touch existence itself. The circuit of perfection that each completes for the other links them to a kind of (immanent) divinity. We are reminded of Heraclitus's greeting to his visitors: "For here too there are gods present . . ."[25]

In their love for each other, Birkin and Ursula become true inhabitants of the Life-World. They are beyond the ideas and theories about love that had once distracted them. Early in the novel, Birkin says to Hermione:

> There's the whole difference in the world between the actual sensual being and the vicious mental-deliberate profligacy our lot goes in for. In our night-time, there's always the electricity switched on, we watch ourselves, we get it all in the head, really. You've got to lapse out before you can know what sensual reality is, lapse into

unknowingness, and give up your volition. You've got to do it. You've got to learn [not to be] before you can come into being.[26]

Ortega has pointed out that the language of love, i.e., the words that people who love each other say to each other, is not the creation of the lovers themselves, but what he calls a "usage," a pattern of words learned from what they have heard or read about love. "We understand, more or less," he says, "the ideas that we want to express by what we say, but we do not understand what *what* we say says, what is meant by *what* we say, in itself—that is, by our words."[27] This is another way of saying that what is "between" two people who love each other takes place in the Life-World, and that the language of love may actually become a *barrier* to union. Presence and perfection can occur in love only when, as Camus said in *A Happy Death*, "the mind denies the mind," and we return to the preconscious state from which ideas and words originate.

Lawrence knows that the state of "perfection" that Birkin and Ursula have achieved will not remain at this level indefinitely, and that their most heightened moments—when they make love—will not always have the same incandescence. Near the end of the novel, Ursula recognizes that their relationship has changed. Now, even during sex, there is always some part of each lover that will not merge and yield to perfect congruence. The dialectical "between" is dynamic and always dependent upon the *I*'s who generate it. Each *I* constantly threatens to impinge upon the "between" it has helped create. Ursula

knew [Birkin] loved her; she was sure of him. Yet she could not let go a certain hold over herself, she could not bear him to question her. She gave herself up in delight to being loved by him. She knew that, in spite of his joy when she abandoned herself, he was a little bit saddened too. She could give herself up to his activity. But she could not be herself, she *dared* not come forth quite nakedly to his nakedness, abandoning all adjustment, lapsing in pure faith with him. She abandoned herself to *him*, or she took hold of him and gathered her joy to him. And she enjoyed him fully. But they were never *quite* together, at the same moment, one was always a little left out.[28]

Perhaps Birkin and Ursula come as close to completion and "perfec-tion" as any lovers can. Their love has changed because *they* have changed, as they *had* to change. It has survived the tarnishing of the ideal to reality. They are, finally, willing to settle for what they can have, implicitly accepting the limits of *any* love relationship.

LOVE AND AUTHENTICITY

One of love's greatest snares is that the lovers change, as we just saw with Birkin and Ursula. The self is not static, but dynamic. We are never fully ourselves, but perpetually "ahead of ourselves" (Heidegger) and "on the way" (Marcel). A year from now, it may not be possible for me to love the woman I love today. I will have changed, and she will have changed. During the course of a year, she or I—or both of us—may change in such a way that I can no longer look upon her as a *You*. The question is this: Can I make a commitment to a woman I desire now, knowing full well that in the future, *when I am no longer the same person who made the commitment*, I will still be required to honor it? Marcel has stated this dilemma very well:

> At the moment of my commitment, I either (1) arbitrarily assume a constancy in my feelings which it is not really in my power to establish, or (2) I accept in advance that I shall have to carry out, at a given moment, an action which will in no way reflect my state of mind when I do carry it out. In the first case I am lying to myself, in the second I consent in advance to lie to someone else.[29]

If I make a commitment to a woman I desire and assume that my feelings toward her will remain constant, I am betraying myself because the promise binds not only the person I am today, but the person I may become a year from now, or five years from now, or ten years from now. Sartre has distinguished between sincerity and authenticity. To be sin-cere, he says, is to represent ourselves to others—and to ourselves—as we *really are* at a given moment. But, he maintains, it is impossible to be sincere because our Being is a *becoming*. We *must* assume roles in order to postulate a self that we can grow into and become. To be authentic, on the other hand, is to refrain from deliberately assuming a *false* role, from misrepresenting ourselves either to ourselves or to each other (Sartre calls this misrepresentation "bad faith"). We cannot be sincere, but we *can* be authentic.

In love, the dilemma of commitment and change cannot be overcome, only lived with (and against). For a commitment of an *I* to a *You* to be authentic, it must be made in "good faith" and maintained in "good faith." The replacing of the traditional "until death do us part" with "as long as there is love" in the marriage ceremony acknowledges the dilemma of making a commitment in the face of ineluctable change. An authentic commitment can be made with the latter promise because it denies what Buber calls "that false drive for self-affirmation which impels man to flee from the unreliable, unsolid, unlasting, unpredictable, danger-ous world of relation into the having of things."[30] We long for stability and permanence (as "enjoyed" by the In-itself). But, as Sartre reminds us, this is not the true condition of the For-itself.

As we have said, the lover seeks in the beloved not only sexual completion, but the whole world. Stendhal has suggested a metaphor that is of great help in understanding what goes on in the imagination of the lover. In the winter at the salt mines near Salzburg, the miners used to throw the bare branches of a tree into an abandoned shaft that had filled with water. For several months, the branches remained submerged in the salt water, which then receded, leaving them covered with a deposit of shining crystals. The original branch was no longer recognizable. In the sun, the transfigured branch looked like something from a fairy tale; it would delight an adult as easily as a child. Now, Stendhal tells us, love is that way also. When we love someone, we *imagine* perfections in the beloved that are like the scintillating ice crystals that cover the branch. What we could think of as the salt water of our imagination contains all the characteristics we would like the beloved to possess, and, when we encounter a woman whom we desire, she begins to "crystallize" before our eyes.[31] To a great extent, we see in the beloved what we *want* to see, what it is to our advantage to see. And just as warmer weather will inevitably melt the crystals that have transfigured the branch, reality will, sooner or later, "thaw" what the imagination has crystallized around the beloved. This "thawing" is the basis for the disillusion that so many lovers eventually suffer.

Most people are not as heroic as Lawrence's Birkin and Ursula when it comes to the choice of a partner for sexual completion. Most of what is called love is motivated more by *need* than anything else. Very few people have the courage to stand alone for any length of time without a "love partner." Ortega felt that love was an attempt to overcome the solitude that each of us feels when he is without a partner. But to overcome this solitude in a way that will augment and enrich us—in order that there be what Ortega calls a "we," which is the same as Buber's "between"—the partner must be someone who the lover feels is, ontically, *on his own level*. In *Man and People* Ortega shows that there is an increasing degree of relationship between a man and, say, a stone, a tree, a donkey, a dog, and another man (or woman). While I may admire a stone or a tree, they are inanimate, and incapable of having any relation with me. A donkey or a dog may have a limited relation with me—the donkey may pull a cart in which I ride, and I may take a walk or sit by the fire with a dog—but whereas the animal may respond to me and I to it, the animal may not, to use Ortega's terms, "cor-respond" to, or "co-exist" with, me, i.e., respond to me *on my own level*. In order to co-exist with another, I must have approximately the same degree of *inwardness* as the other. The stone and the tree have no inwardness whatever, while the donkey has some, and the dog somewhat more. But it is only with *another person* that I can share my inwardness fully and overcome my solitude. Only with another person can there be what Ortega calls an "inter-twining of existences."

All animals of a given species have the same degree of inwardness and may therefore mate satisfactorily with any other member of the species. Man, however, is a conscious animal, and each man and woman is capable of a different degree of inwardness. For a specific person, *any* other person will not necessarily do. But the "urge to merge" is one of the strongest human drives. Sartre has described its orbit as "two against the world." Very few people have the patience and the courage to wait beyond a certain point for someone with whom they could have Ortega's "we" and Buber's "between." Real love, Buber reminds us, is risky, dangerous. What most people are willing to settle for in a "love partner" is security (the In-itself-For-itself), and they want it as quickly as they can get it, with whomever they can get it from. In most cases, what is called love is at bottom an attempt *to get rid of the self* (recall Kierkegaard's remark about the young girl who had lost her lover), to deny one's Being in order to preserve one's Being, as Laing describes it.

Someone who has set his or her sights on a partner who gives every indication of being able to provide the required security will go to almost any length to rationalize the choice, even if it means rejecting a potential partner for whom there is a greater feeling. Listen to how Rosalind, in Fitzgerald's *This Side of Paradise*, tries to end her relationship with the quixotic Amory Blaine so that she may marry the more sound and wealthy Dawson Ryder. Although this exchange between Rosalind and Amory is somewhat melodramatic, it is an archetype of the nest-feathering rationalization:

ROSALIND:	Amory, if you don't sit down I'll scream.
AMORY: (*Sitting down suddenly beside her*)	Oh, Lord.
ROSALIND: (*Taking his hand gently*)	You know I love you, don't you?
AMORY:	Yes.
ROSALIND:	You know I'll always love you—
AMORY:	Don't talk that way; you frighten me. It sounds as if we weren't going to have each other. (*She cries a little and rising from the couch goes to the armchair.*) I've felt all afternoon that things were worse. I nearly went wild down at the office—I couldn't write a line. Tell me everything.
ROSALIND:	There's nothing to tell, I say. I'm just nervous.
AMORY:	Rosalind, you're playing with the idea of marrying Dawson Ryder.
ROSALIND: (*After a pause*)	He's been asking me to all day.
AMORY:	Well, he's got his nerve!
ROSALIND: (*After another pause*)	I like him.
AMORY:	Don't say that. It hurts me.
ROSALIND:	Don't be a silly idiot. You know you're the only man I've ever loved, ever will love.
AMORY: (*Quickly*)	Rosalind, let's get married—next week.

ROSALIND: We can't.

AMORY: Why not?

ROSALIND: Oh, we can't. I'd be your squaw—in some horrible place.

AMORY: We'll have two hundred and seventy-five dollars a month all told.

ROSALIND: Darling, I don't even do my own hair, usually.

AMORY: I'll do it for you.

ROSALIND: (*Between a laugh and a sob*)   Thanks.

AMORY: Rosalind, you *can't* be thinking of marrying someone else. Tell me! You leave me in the dark. I can help you fight it out if you'll only tell me.

ROSALIND: It's just—us. We're pitiful, that's all. The very qualities I love you for are the ones that will always make you a failure.

AMORY: (*Grimly*)   Go on.

ROSALIND: Oh— it *is* Dawson Ryder. He's so reliable, I almost feel that he'd be a—a background.

AMORY: You don't love him.

ROSALIND: I know, but I respect him, and he's a good man and a strong one.

AMORY: (*Grudgingly*)   Yes—he's that.

ROSALIND: Well—here's one little thing. There was a little poor boy we met in Rye Tuesday afternoon—and, oh, Dawson took him on his lap and talked to him and promised him an Indian suit—and next day he remembered and bought it—and, oh, it was so sweet and I couldn't help thinking he'd be so nice to—to our children—take care of them—and I wouldn't have to worry.

AMORY: (*In despair*)	Rosalind! Rosalind!
ROSALIND: (*With a faint roguishness*)	Don't look so consciously suffering.
AMORY:	What power we have of hurting each other!
ROSALIND: (*Commencing to sob again*)	It's been so perfect—you and I. So like a dream that I'd longed for and never thought I'd find. The first real unselfishness I've ever felt in my life. And I can't see it fade out in a colorless atmosphere!
AMORY:	It won't—it won't!
ROSALIND:	I'd rather keep it as a beautiful memory— tucked away in my heart.
AMORY:	Yes, women can do that—but not men. I'd remember always, not the beauty of it while it lasted, but just the bitterness, the long bitterness.
ROSALIND:	Don't!
AMORY:	All the years never to see you, never to kiss you, just a gate shut and barred—you don't dare be my wife.
ROSALIND:	No—no—I'm taking the hardest course, the strongest course. Marrying you would be a failure and I never fail—if you don't stop walking up and down I'll scream!

(*Again he sinks despairingly onto the lounge*)

AMORY:	Come over here and kiss me.
ROSALIND:	No.
AMORY:	Don't you *want* to kiss me?
ROSALIND:	To-night I want you to love me calmly and coolly.
AMORY:	The beginning of the end.

ROSALIND: (*With a*
burst of insight)   Amory, you're young. I'm young. People excuse
us now for our poses and vanities, for treating
people like Sancho and yet getting away with it.
They excuse us now. But you've got a lot of
knocks coming to you—

AMORY: And you're afraid to take them with me.

ROSALIND: No, not that. There was a poem I read
somewhere—you'll say Ella Wheeler Wilcox and
laugh—but listen:
"For this is wisdom—to love and live,
To take what fate or the gods may give,
To ask no question, to make no prayer,
To kiss the lips and caress the hair,
Speed passion's ebb as we greet its flow,
To have and to hold, and, in time—let go."

AMORY: But we haven't had.

ROSALIND: Amory, I'm yours—you know it. There have
been times in the last month I'd have been
completely yours if you'd said so. But I can't
marry you and ruin both our lives.

AMORY: We've got to take our chance for happiness.

ROSALIND: Dawson says I'd learn to love him.

(Amory *with his head sunk in his hands does not move. The life seems*
suddenly gone out of him.)

ROSALIND: Lover! Lover! I can't do with you, and I can't
imagine life without you.

AMORY: Rosalind, we're on each other's nerves. It's just
that we're both high-strung, and this week—

(*His voice is curiously old. She crosses to him and taking his face in her*
hands, kisses him.)

ROSALIND: I can't, Amory. I can't be shut away from the
trees and flowers, cooped up in a little flat,
waiting for you. You'd hate me in a narrow
atmosphere. I'd make you hate me.[32]

Rosalind is certainly right when she tells Amory that he has "a lot of knocks coming." The point of all this seems to be, as Amory realizes, that she is not willing to take them with him. Scarlett O'Hara suffered privation and then swore that she would "never be hungry again." Rosalind swears that she'll never be hungry—*ever*. Telling Amory that she loves him, and that giving him up is "the hardest course, the strongest course," is pure Sartrean bad faith.

LOVE AND THE MARGINAL SELF

So far, our discussion of the *I-You* relation has focused on the "between" that is established when two people love each other. It is obvious that this "between" can be no stronger than the *I*'s who generate it. We must look now at what makes it possible—and impossible—for an *I* to relate to another as a *You*.

We have distinguished two mechanisms through which the self may be lost and the *I* diminished: first, self may be lost through *default* when a person repeatedly backs away from the decisions and actions (what Jaspers called "boundary situations") that are necessary if a viable self is to be created; second, self may be lost through what we are calling *schizoid erosion* when a false self (persona) is interposed between the real self, and the world and others. When psychic splitting occurs, the real self is cut off from the world and does not receive the sustenance from reality that is required for its growth. No matter how well the persona appears to be functioning, the "proceeds" of its activity are not passed on to the real self. While the persona appears to be flourishing, the real self may be dying.

We would now like to consider how an *I*, when reduced either through default or schizoid erosion, can be rendered incapable of an *I-You* relation. A person may become so reduced—so marginal—that his or her *I* is insufficient to generate a "between" with another. We can think of no better way to characterize this insufficiency of self than to examine the situation of Johan and Marianne in Bergman's film, *Scenes from a Marriage*.[33]

The film opens as Johan and Marianne are being interviewed for a magazine article that will portray them as an ideal married couple. To all outward appearances, they are perfectly suited to each other and to their middle-class life. They are successful and well adjusted, and not a little smug about how satisfactorily things have worked out for them. Johan, forty-two, is an associate professor at the Psychotechnical Institute. Marianne, thirty-five, is a lawyer specializing in divorce cases. They have two pre-teenage daughters, to whom they are devoted. Their family is an extended one. They visit their parents regularly, and the grandparents occasionally take care of the children so as to give Johan and Marianne time to be together. There have never been any serious disagreements or arguments between them. During the ten years they have been married, every disparity has been made light of and smoothed over.

But then Marianne becomes pregnant again. Johan cannot understand why she wishes to continue with the pregnancy, and so, for the first time, they are having a disagreement. "This is serious, Johan," Marianne says. *"The whole of our future's at stake.* Suppose we now do something irrevocable. Suppose it's crucial and we don't know it is." After some thought, Marianne agrees to have an abortion. The decision is painful, but she accepts the consequences, and their lives go on much as before.

But not exactly. For the first time since they have known each other, Johan and Marianne have experienced a rift, a crack in the surface of what had previously appeared to be flawless and rooted in terra firma. They realize now, if only vaguely, that the bond between them is not absolute. Johan asks: "Can the scheme of things be so treacherous that life suddenly goes wrong? Without your knowing how it happens. Almost imperceptibly."

In the first scene, Marianne tells the interviewer that the couple has had an ideal sexual partnership. But later, Marianne and Johan admit to each other that this is not so. Marianne is not greatly shaken by the acknowledgment, and rationalizes their lack of enthusiasm for sex by saying that they work too hard and are tired in the evenings. Her rationalization recalls a remark that Camus makes about the marriage of Grand and Jeanne in *The Plague*: "The common lot of married couples. You get married, you go on loving a bit longer, you work. And you work so hard it makes you forget to love."[34]

Marianne's dissatisfaction remains minor, but Johan's becomes acute. He begins an affair with Paula, a student in her early twenties, whom he met at a convention. He loves the girl, and although he suspects that the relationship will not last, he takes a leave of absence from the Institute and goes to Paris to live with her. On the evening before he leaves, he says to Marianne:

> Do you know what I'm most fed up with? All this fucking harping on what we're supposed to do, what we must do, what we must take into consideration. What your mother will think. What the children

will say. How we had best arrange the dinner party and shouldn't
we invite my father after all. We must go to the west coast. We must
go to the mountains. We must go to St. Moritz. We must celebrate
Christmas, Easter, Whitsun, birthdays, namedays, the whole fuck-
ing lot.[35]

It is clear that Johan and Marianne have been living their lives from the
outside in, rather than from the inside out. They have done what they
were *supposed* to do to successfully fill roles as husband and wife, son and
daughter, parents, and professionals. Even holidays and vacations are
occasions for role playing. Their identification with the appurtenances of
living has been so complete that they have never developed an adequate
sense of themselves, either as individuals or with each other. Their lives
are perfect examples of what Heidegger called "everydayness"; they are
almost totally inauthentic. Neither has developed an *I*, so there was never
any *possibility* of a "between." Johan has had enough of his role. "I
intend," he says, "to behave like a cad, and what a relief!"

We see just how "unreal" Marianne has been rendered by her role
playing in an episode early in the film when she talks with a client, Mrs.
Jacobi, who wants a divorce after twenty years of marriage. The description that the woman gives of the stifling relationship with her husband is
very similar to the situation between Marianne and Johan. "I go around,"
Mrs. Jacobi tells Marianne, "with a mental picture of myself. And it does
not tally on a single point with reality." But from the way Marianne
speaks to the woman, it is clear that she does not see the connection
between what Mrs. Jacobi is telling her and the problems that she and
Johan are having. Her law clients and their troubles are a part of her
professional life, and, since this is a role just as her marriage is a role, there
is no interaction between or carryover from one to the other. Because
Marianne lives a series of roles rather than a life, she cannot integrate
what she hears in her office with what happens in her home. Both roles are
estranged from her real self, such as it is.

As he expected, Johan's affair with Paula does not go well. She is jealous
of what he still feels for Marianne and even of his visits with the children.
Marianne, meanwhile, has had several lovers of her own, none of whom
offers anything but temporary comfort. She is frequently depressed. But
while Johan is in Paris, she is coming to know herself, or, at least as a start
in that direction, that she does not know herself, a notion that previously
would have been inconceivable to her. She has kept a diary, and reads this
excerpt to Johan during one of his visits:

Yesterday I was suddenly seized by an almost reckless gaiety and for the first time all this year I felt the old lust for life, the eagerness to know what the day would bring . . . Suddenly I turned around and looked at the picture of my school class, when I was ten. I seemed to be aware of something that had been lying in readiness for a long time but beyond my grasp. To my surprise I have to admit that *I don't know who I am*. I haven't the vaguest idea. I have always done what people told me. As far back as I can remember I've been obedient, adaptable, almost meek. Now that I think about it. I had one or two violent outbursts of self-assertion as a little girl. But I remember also that Mother punished all such lapses from convention with exemplary severity. For my sisters and me our entire upbringing was aimed at our being *agreeable*. I was rather ugly and clumsy and was constantly informed of the fact. By degrees I found that if I kept my thoughts to myself and was ingratiating and farsighted, such behavior brought its rewards. The really big deception, however, occurred during puberty. All my thoughts, feelings, and actions revolved around sex. I didn't let on about this to my parents, or to anyone at all for that matter. Then it became second nature to be deceitful, surreptitious, and secretive. My father wanted me to be a lawyer like himself. I once hinted that I'd prefer to be an actress. Or at any rate to have *something* to do with the theater. I remember they just laughed at me. So it has gone on and on. In my relations with other people. In my relations with men. The same perpetual dissimulation. The same desperate attempts to please everybody. I never thought: What do *I* want? But always what does *he* want me to want? It's not unselfishness as I used to think, but sheer cowardice, and what's worse—utter ignorance of who I am. I have never lived a dramatic life, I have no gift for that sort of thing. But for the first time I feel intensely excited at the thought of finding out what exactly I want to do with myself. In the snug little world where Johan and I lived so unconsciously, taking everything for granted, there is a cruelty and brutality implied which frightens me more and more when I think back on it. Outward security demands a high price: the acceptance of a continuous destruction of the personality . . .[36]

This excerpt from Marianne's diary reads very much like one of Laing's case histories in *The Divided Self*. But surprisingly, Marianne does not show signs of schizoid splitting. Although her development has occurred largely from the outside in, she is remarkably "together." The playing of numerous life-roles to achieve acceptance and security has caused what she recognizes as a "continuous destruction of [her] personality," yet she copes reasonably well with the pressures of a disintegrating marriage. Marianne is a marginal self by virtue of default. She has simply failed to do what is necessary to create a self, an *I*. But when the illusion of a "between" in her marriage is destroyed, she turns toward herself and discovers through the pain of isolation that there *is* such a thing as an *I*. Now she clearly understands the difference between the real self and the false selves (personae) she has been living through.

Marianne feels that the inauthenticity of their marriage—she calls their relationship that "masked thing"—could be rectified, and that she and Johan could meet each other as "the people we *really* are." (What she means is as the people, the *I*'s, they could become.) "I've considered you far too much during our married life," she tells Johan. "I think consideration killed off love. Has it struck you that we never quarreled?" Whenever the substance for an argument did arise, it was easier to keep peace, save face, and sweep the difficulty under the rug, than to vent it. The habit of neither admitting nor confronting the frustrations they felt started early in their marriage: "All that mattered just then," she says, "was for you to get your Ph.D. So truth had to take a second place." Self was sacrificed to the requirements of work, and the authenticity of the moment was subordinated to a future goal. The opportunity to grow at Jaspers's "boundary" was never taken.

The language in Marianne's diary is truly extraordinary. She is feeling the slowly emerging exhilaration that comes when the self, formerly estranged from itself, approaches coincidence with itself. Now that the masks have been removed, she is coming in touch with herself. In experiencing the "reckless gaiety" and "the old lust for life," she is experiencing what Parmenides called *aletheia* (the Greek word for truth), the "unhiddenness" of Being.

In contrast to Marianne, Johan is neurotic. In playing his life-roles, he has undergone psychic splitting and is deeply schizoid. During the year he and Paula live in Paris, he deteriorates further. At one point he remarks that at the time he should be in the "prime" of his life he feels like a "corpse." Later, when he ends an affair with Eva, one of his colleagues at the Institute, she angrily points out his diminishing sexual power and reminds him that during his last checkup his doctor told him that he had shrunk almost two inches. Johan's physical contraction parallels his ontic contraction.

In the final scene, which occurs about ten years after the interview which opens the film, Marianne and Johan are both married to other people. But they meet again and spend a night together "in a dark house somewhere in the world." Marianne's new husband is a successful doctor, who spends almost all his time at his work. His emotional needs are minimal, and he and Marianne have reached an uneasy accommodation. She is not particularly dependent on him and tells Johan that she could live just as easily with any other man who attracted her. Her situation is not ideal, but she has come to terms with life. She has learned how to cope and how to survive.

Johan has not done as well. His new wife is more a mother than a wife. According to Johan, she "isn't interested in the truth," and has "arranged the marriage to our mutual convenience." Johan has not grown at all. "I'm a middle-aged boy who never wants to grow up," he says to Marianne. "I have found it very hard to grasp that I'm a child with genitals . . . I don't *want* to mature, you see. That's why Anna is a good wife." Johan's underdevelopment as a self precludes anything but a rudimentary union with *any* woman. For him there can be only dependence and effacement. He has nothing to love with, and nothing to be loved for. Unlike Marianne, he cannot generate an *I*.

During the night they spend together in the final scene, Marianne wakes up screaming from a nightmare. She has dreamt that she was walking along a road, sinking into soft sand, and trying to reach out to Johan. But she had no hands, only stumps below the elbows, and could not touch him. It occurs to her now that it is "too late," that they have "missed something important." And then comes the most painful revelation: " . . . I have never loved anyone. I don't think I've ever been loved either." While Marianne is developing an *I*, it is not the kind of *I* that can reach out to another and generate a "between." The patterns of a lifetime are not easily changed. Some deficiencies can never be made up.

Although Johan never acquires a significant degree of selfhood, he does achieve considerable self-insight. He says to Marianne:

> I'll tell you something banal. We're emotional illiterates. And not only you and I—practically everybody, that's the depressing thing. We're taught everything about Madagascar and the square root of pi, or whatever the hell it's called, but not a word about the soul. We're abysmally ignorant, about both ourselves and others. There's a lot of loose talk nowadays to the effect that children should be

brought up to know about brotherhood and understanding and coexistence and equality and everything else that's all the rage just now. But it doesn't dawn on anyone that we must first learn something about ourselves and our own feelings. Our own fear and loneliness and anger. We're left without a chance, ignorant and remorseful among the ruins of our ambitions. To make a child aware of its soul is something almost indecent. You're regarded as a dirty old man. How can you ever understand other people if you don't know anything about yourself?[37]

While Johan has learned a great deal about himself, he cannot make the transition from insight to self-actualization. He cannot accept and live with what he calls "the complete meaninglessness behind the complete awareness." He wants something to "long for," something to "believe in." As with Camus, his nostalgia has no object. But unlike Camus, he cannot accept the absurd and transcend it. He remains paralyzed in his awareness. Johan has touched what Jaspers called the "boundaries" of his existence, but he cannot function within them. Marianne, on the other hand, does not confront meaninglessness directly, but nurtures a primitive life instinct. She says to Johan: "Unlike you, I stick it out. And enjoy it. I rely on my common sense. And my feeling. They cooperate. I'm satisfied with both of them. Now that I'm older I have a third co-worker: my experience." Marianne is learning to live in the Life-World. But Johan remains alienated because he cannot go beyond his understanding to presence.

Johan is, in many ways, a prototype of the man who reached middle age during the 1960s and 1970s. And because his and Marianne's way of life has been considered exemplary here—recall the magazine interview with which the film opens—what is being characterized is not just a marriage, but an entire culture. The emotional illiteracy that Johan and Marianne come to recognize in themselves after so much time and so much pain is not unique to them, but affects, as Johan says, "practically everybody." It is a kind of ontic epidemic. What Johan is saying is that everything in the present culture—family life, work, education, socializing with friends— seems geared to *prevent* the development of self, in favor of fulfilling a function or role.

The crisis that led Johan and Marianne to self-awareness was precipitated by an unwanted pregnancy, although it probably would have followed any serious problem that could not have been swept under the rug. When their illusion of harmony and solidity was dissolved by the acid of crisis, i.e., when the masks came off, they were confronted with their diminished selves—marginal selves—selves inadequate to the demands of their situation. Furthermore, there was no possibility of making any appeal to a transcendent divinity. As in Bergman's other recent films, the presence of God is not felt at all in *Scenes from a Marriage*. Johan and Marianne are completely on their own in a homeless world. They awake from self-delusion to take their place in a world, recalling Camus's phrases, "without illusions and lights," to live "without appeal."

Marianne sees, literally, in the sense of the Greek *aletheia*, her way to an authentic and realistic, although not totally satisfying, existence. Johan is defeated because he remains stuck on the boundaries of his awareness. He has come a long way toward authenticity, between asking "Can the scheme of things be so treacherous that life suddenly goes wrong?" and crying out, *de profundis*, "I refuse to accept the complete meaninglessness behind the complete awareness." He is experiencing a bad case of existential shock. He does not have what Tillich called "the courage of despair," the courage to take meaninglessness into himself and evolve a meaning for his life *in spite of* the absence of any absolute meaning. Tillich has described how repressed existential anxiety may be transformed into psychological (neurotic) anxiety, and it seems that this transformation has taken place in Johan. He has been awakened from sleep to despair, one of the starting points for authentic existence, but he cannot take the next step. Like so many people now, he cannot become an *I*, and be present. He cannot overcome his marginality.

9

Richard Nixon:

A Paradigm of the Marginal Self

> There can be a mystique about a man. You can look him in the eye
> and know he's got it. This guy's got it!
>
> —Nixon describing Spiro Agnew (in 1968)

I n every man's life there is a certain incongruence between his real self
and the face he presents to the world, his persona. But with Richard
Nixon there has always been the nagging feeling that there was
nothing behind the persona, that the mask was all there was. Trying to
figure Nixon out, a number of journalists, historians, even a novelist or
two, have touched on the idea of a diminished self. With the help of some
of this material, we will attempt to explain Nixon, the man and the
politician, as a paradigm of the marginal self.

Nixon's persona is, and always has been, his career. In "Horatio Alger
in the White House" (*Harper's*, September 1972), Richard Poirier tried to
measure the man against the office. He argued that Nixon was a product
of the Horatio Alger tradition ("fixation on merit and the self-made man")
and compared him to Fitzgerald's Jay Gatsby, who, "like most American
heroes, has a personal taste for bareness while being inspired by extraordinary visions of the future." In the Alger sense, "self-made" means that

---

This chapter was expanded from an article, "Mask in a Mirror: The Fictional Richard
Nixon," that appeared in *The Nation* (July 6, 1974).

someone starts with "nothing" (without money, position or education—
unless, of course, acquired Abe Lincoln style) and, through perseverance,
ends up with at least money and position. The term "self-made" has an
ironic, indeed inverted, meaning here, because it refers to a goal which has
been approached and attained without any provision for the acquisition of
self. What is "made" is not a "self," but a fortune, a career, or a
reputation. Poirier writes that "throughout every aspect of his career
Nixon has been at once the actor and the director of a play in which the
self has been made up, fashioned for the attainment of a goal." Precisely.
Nixon has been *made up*, not made.

Poirier notes that in the tradition of the American self-made man, "the
position attained is made to substitute for personal attributes sacrificed in
order to attain it . . . and, as a consequence, Nixon's concern for the
respect due to his office and the respect due to the United States sounds
less like a call to grandeur [as with de Gaulle, ironically one of Nixon's
idols] than a claim for psychic disability pay." In July 1962, shortly before
he was defeated for governor of California, Richard Nixon was heard to
say that it took an awful lot to embarrass him. Poirier writes that "he was
willing to accept, even to court, personal humiliations that could be
calculated to further his public ambitions." We need only recall the
Checkers speech during the 1952 campaign to see how ready he was to
permit the further erosion of an already marginal self. Where there is little
self, there is little self-respect, and one cannot lose what one does not have.

Reviewing the Mazo and Hess biography *Nixon: A Political Portrait* for
The New York Times Book Review in 1968, Milton Viorst wrote that "what
emerges is not a man with feelings and beliefs, but an actor on the stage of
history, for whom someone else might have written most of the lines."
Poirier sees a similarity between Nixon's use of language and that of
fictional Horatio Alger heroes such as Fitzgerald's Gatsby, Cooper's
Deerslayer, and Faulkner's Sutpen of *Absolom, Absolom!*:

> When they speak or act it is not freely or gregariously, as if their
> personalities were in any way larger than their "designs," but rather
> the other way around, as if they were compelled by them. Acutely
> uncomfortable in free human interchange, their language is stilted;
> their human enthusiasms, like Nixon's for sports, ring false; and in
> the tension of personal encounters that can't be managed by the
> remote control of prepared rhetoric, they can appear awkward to the
> point of ludicrousness. One such instance, when Nixon talked to

some soldiers in Vietnam, is taken verbatim by Gore Vidal [in *An Evening with Richard Nixon*] from *Newsweek*:

NIXON: And where are you from?

SOLDIER: Texas.

NIXON: Texas! I'll be darned. Think the Cowboys can beat the Packers this year?

SOLDIER: I hope so, sir.

NIXON: They've lost their quarterback, you know. And where are you from?

SOLDIER: Chicago.

NIXON: Chicago! Have you seen the Cubs this year? They might take it all. Are you a Cub or a White Sox fan?

SOLDIER: I'm a Yankee fan, sir.

(Nixon stares unhappily at the black soldier. Neither can think of anything to say.)

NIXON: Do you ever get any black-eyed peas or collard greens out here?

BLACK SOLDIER (stunned):   I'm from Boston.

Embarrassing? Self-destroying? Richard Nixon was, in a sense, a fictional President—a fictional self. Watergate reads like fiction. As Garry Wills puts it: "Every gesture of White House virtue now prompts laughter, as Nixon steals David Frye's act—no one, henceforth, can rival him in mocking Nixon."

Nixon often spoke and acted as a disembodied self. Douglas Hallett, once a member of Charles Colson's staff, wrote in *The New York Times Magazine* (20 October 1974): "Awkward remarks popped up constantly like his 'This-is-a-great-day-for-France' comment at President Pompidou's funeral or his 'Do-you-like-your-job?' question to a policeman who had suffered an accident during one of Nixon's Florida campaign tours and was awaiting an ambulance. Once, a woodcarver was ushered into the Oval Office to present the President with a chair he had fashioned from a single piece of wood. When Nixon sat down in the chair, according to one of those present, it collapsed into pieces. Picking himself off the floor, the President asked, as if nothing had happened, 'Well, how do you go about doing this kind of work?' Most memorable of all, at least to me, was shaking hands with Nixon. Each time I did, I had the eerie, even frightening feeling that nobody was there; face-to-face, hands clasped, yet no feeling, no feeling at all.''

There has always seemed to be a lack of integration in the Nixon psyche. Writing in *The New York Times Magazine* (9 June 1974), Emmet John Hughes tells of asking a longtime friend and Congressional colleague of Nixon's how Nixon could have been bullish about the stock market, at a White House dinner for some fifty of the nation's industrial and corporate leaders, just two days before the planned invasion of Cambodia, when he must have anticipated the fall in the market that followed. Hughes says that the answer from Nixon's friend came without the slightest hesitation: "There is nothing to be puzzled about. This is completely in character. Dick only focuses on—he only *sees*—what or who is directly in front of him at any given moment. He faces whatever *it* is as if it were standing alone. Or he tells *them* whatever he thinks they ought to hear so as to get the immediate effect he wants. He just doesn't make the kinds of *connections* you might expect. This is the way Dick's mind works. It's simply the way he is.''

Nixon has always had trouble with the press. Writing in *Esquire* (April 1974) about the relations of Nixon and his two predecessors with news-papermen and television commentators, David Halberstam says that Nixon's problem with the media comes from the "conflict between the intense privacy of the inner man and the immense public demands of the public career." Stated in Jungian terms, the conflict is between a marginal self and a constantly embattled persona. Nixon presents himself to the world as the mask of his office. When reporters try to get under the mask—back to the self—they are met with resistance and resentment, because Nixon's marginal self cannot cope with that probing, cannot adequately explain and justify a persona which is not derived from the self, but is a separate creation. Halberstam maintains that reporters are always measuring a man in terms of character, looking for the man behind the politician, but, that with Nixon they do not find him. "No one likes being covered constantly," he says, "none of us likes our face in the mirror unless we own the mirror." And for one who doesn't own the self behind the face (persona) that appears in the mirror, that coverage must be intolerable.

What better way for Nixon to hinder self-revelation than to have had Ronald Ziegler speak for him? Could there have been a more suitable exponent of the Nixon persona and, concomitantly, a better indication that the Nixon self barely existed? In *1984* George Orwell looked ahead to a time when a Draconian government would make the viable self an impossibility, and gave the language reflecting that situation a name— Newspeak: "Ultimately it was hoped to make articulate speech issue from the larynx without involving the higher brain centers at all. This aim was frankly admitted in the Newspeak word *Duckspeak*, meaning 'to quack like a duck.'"

In the *Esquire* article, Halberstam asked parenthetically whether the departures of Herbert Klein and Robert Finch were hastened because they got along so well with newsmen. If they got on with the newsmen, Halberstam postulated, Nixon may have felt they were talking, and if they were talking, that they were revealing, and if they were revealing, that they were being disloyal. The Nixon persona, lacking the support of and continuity with the marginal Nixon self, would resent and fear *any* revelation not made specifically to advance the persona. Nixon is not in touch with and does not know what there is of his self.

During the final months of his Presidency, Nixon seemed to court the phlebitis condition that plagued him as a vehicle of annihilation. Before leaving for the Mideast early in the summer of 1974, he had swelling and pain in his left leg. In Salzburg, on the way to Cairo, the condition worsened, and his physicians, Major General Walter Tkach and Rear Admiral William Lukash, begged the President to cancel the trip. They warned him that by continuing he was risking death, that the clot in his leg could break away and travel through the lungs to his heart. Nixon rejected the advice and ordered the doctors to say nothing about his condition. Not only did Nixon continue the trip but, as John Osborne reported in *The New Republic*, he made no effort to limit the activities, mostly ceremonial, that aggravated the phlebitis: standing for hours in reception lines, riding in restriction in motorcades, climbing up rough slopes over jagged rocks, walking under a prostrating sun near the Egyptian pyramids. Nixon planned and followed through with the Mideast trip to generate favorable copy for his floundering Presidency. He had to preserve the mask of his office at any cost. If he was endangering his life (and what there was of his real self), that price had to be paid, just as while he was President the price of some 25,000 additional American lives had to be paid to preserve "respect for the Presidency" by achieving "peace with honor" in Vietnam.

This was not the first time Nixon had disregarded the advice of his doctors. After being released from the hospital following a bout with viral pneumonia during the summer of 1973, Nixon, then just beginning to feel the agony of the rapidly unfolding Watergate scandal, told the White House staff, which had gathered to welcome him back, that he had no intention of taking his doctors' advice to ease up: "I just want you to know what my answer to them was and what my answer to you is. No one in this great office at this time in the world's history can slow down. This office requires a President who will work right up to the hilt all the time. That is what I have been doing. That is what I am going to continue to do . . . I know many will say, 'But then you will risk your health.' Well, the health of the man is not nearly as important as the health of the nation and the health of the world." What Nixon meant was that the preservation of his self was not as important as the preservation of the Presidential persona. With his Presidency under heavy attack, he would work day and night to hold together the crumbling mask. Nixon's disregard for his health brings to mind something that Kierkegaard—that champion of the self—wrote in *Either/Or* about the apparent lack of concern shown by many in the face of death: " . . . so many live on in a quiet state of perdition . . . they outlive themselves . . . they live their lives, as it were, outside of themselves [their real selves, that is] . . . and they are not alarmed by the problem of their soul's immortality [or, their body's mortality], for they are already in a state of dissolution before they die." Ontically never having had life, the embattled President did not experience the "normal" (Kierkegaardian, Heideggerian) dread that comes with the prospect of physical annihilation.

In an article for the *Saturday Review* (23 September 1972), based on his book *The Presidential Character: Predicting Performance in the White House*, James David Barber analyzed and categorized the attitudes toward their work of a number of Presidents from Woodrow Wilson to Richard Nixon. Barber makes the initial distinction between negativists and activists—activists believe the President must be an energizing force, and they practice that belief in their daily lives—and further subdivides the activists into active-negative and active-positive Presidents: "Active-positive Presidents—recent examples are Franklin D. Roosevelt, Harry Truman and John Kennedy—experience the office as an opportunity not only to implement social reform but also to fulfill themselves personally. They value productiveness highly and adopt flexible approaches toward achieving their goals. They exude confidence and the sense of enjoying the power of the Presidency."

"By contrast," Barber continues, "active-negative Presidents—Lyndon Johnson, Herbert Hoover and Woodrow Wilson, for example—start out strong and flexible but wind up defeated and rigid. *They experience in the office a basic contradiction between intense effort and low emotional reward for that effort.* In fact, the harder they work, they worse they feel. They are hyperambitious, compulsive, endure-today-to-enjoy-tomorrow types. Deeply unsure of themselves, they feel aggressive and suspicious toward those around them" (emphasis added).

After observing him in office for one term, Barber felt that Nixon would take his place among the active-negative Presidents. In fact, Nixon seems to have been an active-negative type throughout his career, as exemplified by a quotation from the Halberstam article cited previously: "In 1959, when he met Khrushchev at the famed kitchen debate, he was at his absolute best. Khrushchev caught him by surprise—Nixon was, after all, the Soviet leader's host at the American exhibition and yet the verbal dialogue, some of it threatening and insulting, was initiated by the Russian. Under instant pressure, Nixon handled himself with skill and balance, in all an intelligent, tempered performance. One of his finest hours. He thereupon went back to the American Embassy and came completely apart, drinking very heavily. He did not know himself, he did not know how well he had done."

Barber further says of active-negative Presidents that, although they come across as adroit political realists, they eventually endanger themselves and perhaps even the country by taking a stand on "principle" and sticking to it regardless of the consequences. There are the familiar examples of Wilson and his League of Nations and Johnson and the war in Vietnam. Richard Nixon has *never* stood on principle (except perhaps the negative principle of anti-communism), but came close to it with his evocation of executive privilege when asked to provide witnesses and documents for the Watergate investigation. Nixon's "principle," in this case, did not emanate from any requirement of the self—ordinarily the source of what we think of as principle—but rather from the requirements of the embattled persona. It is a supreme and telling irony that the closest Richard Nixon ever came to taking a positive stand on anything, after more than a quarter century in public life, was in defense of what was to be revealed as a lie. As for Barber's prediction that an active-negative President Nixon might be willing to sacrifice the best interests of the nation in defense of a "principle," the military alert over the Arab-Israeli war in October 1973 is a chilling recollection.

In an effort to understand how Richard Nixon became what he is, Barber looked back to his childhood in Whittier, California, and found several traumatic experiences which could have engendered Nixon's pessimism and crisis-haunted view of life. There were at least three near-fatal injuries and illnesses, the sudden death of two brothers, and severe economic insecurity. But perhaps more important for this discussion is Nixon's relationship with his parents, who were very different kinds of people, and who made very different emotional demands on the boy. His mother, to whom he developed strong ties, was emotionally restrained to the point that she would not permit herself even to feel anger, much less express it. His father, on the contrary, according to the description of a local cleric, was "brusque, loud, dogmatic, strong-willed, emotional and impatient." Barber concludes: "The contrast thrust Richard into the mediator role, not only in practical terms but, more importantly, in emotional terms. He took the part of the responsible son, adapting his mood now to his mother's long silences, now to his father's diatribes. In that highly charged atmosphere he struggled to pattern himself after both parents; there was little room for developing an identity [a self] of his own."

This analysis offers a satisfying—though certainly not definitive—explanation of the origin of Nixon's self-persona disjunction. In fact, it reads much like a case history from Laing's *The Divided Self*, but with one important difference. Although the conflict the young Nixon experienced was potentially schizophrenogenic—capable of inducing a schizoid split—there is nothing in Richard Nixon's public or private life to suggest psychic splitting. From all available evidence, it seems that the persona (substitute self) has had very little competition from the "real" self and represents a relatively stable psychic entity. In Nixon's case, there was simply too little self to cause any significant trouble. The "real" self defaulted to the persona, handing over everything to this false self, and remained unsplit because it was too slight an entity to put up a fight. Nixon lived *through* the mask: he fought all his battles with it, won his victories with it, and suffered his defeats with it. He is a marginal self by virtue of default, of *default to the persona*.

In *The Future Is Now*, a biography of George Allen, coach of the Washington Redskins and a longtime friend of Richard Nixon, William Gildea and Kenneth Turan quote Allen on the subject of achievement: "The achiever is the only individual who is truly alive. There can be no inner satisfaction in simply driving a fine car or eating in a fine restaurant or watching a good movie or television program. Those who think they're enjoying themselves doing any of that are half dead and don't know it. *I see no difference between a chair and the man who sits in the chair unless he is accomplishing something*" (emphasis added).

This could as easily have been said by Nixon. What it reveals is the total lack of value given to the state of Being, or *existing*, as contrasted to doing, or *achieving*. When one is achieving one is also, of course, existing. A distinction is to be made, however, between an achievement and the enhancement of self which may or may not accompany it. Allen's claim that there is no difference between "a chair and the man who sits in the chair unless he is accomplishing something" denies the very idea of self. This disclosure may contribute to the understanding of how Richard Nixon's "accomplishments" failed to augment his self, and, far more important, how that marginal self failed to influence his "accomplishments." For Allen and Nixon, there can be no "inner satisfaction" in anything that is not an "achievement" because for them there is no inner self. For this kind of man, it is as though the tie between the achievement and the achiever were severed. The "connecting corridor" that Marcel felt could link the Having of work with the Being of the worker never existed for Richard Nixon.

In "Richard Nixon's Seventh Crisis" (*The New York Times Magazine*, 8 July 1973), Garry Wills argued that Watergate (and all that the word now encompasses) was motivated by a need for Nixon—from the beginning of his career an outsider and insurgent—to have something to fight *against* in order to secure his hold on the Presidency. He had the 1972 election wrapped up from the start, but because he could not really possess the Presidency—even though he was the President—the insurgent mounted a counterinsurgency effort *against himself*, either directly, or indirectly through his assistants, authorizing the burglary of Watergate, the break-in of Daniel Ellsberg's psychiatrist's office, the "dirty tricks" against Muskie, Humphrey, and McGovern, the (largely unneeded) illegal campaign contributions, and all the rest.

This analysis by Wills—certainly our most incisive interpreter of Richard Nixon—can be taken a step further, and the Nixon "outsider-insider" dichotomy seen as a consequence of the marginal Nixon self and the disjoined persona. Because Nixon could not experience satisfaction from *being* President, he had to continue *achieving* the office he already had. As with his friend George Allen, it was not enough to sit in the chair—in this case the chair behind the desk in the Oval Office—and *be* President. The Presidency had to be re-achieved, re-accomplished and retaken from, or more precisely, at the expense of, the (marginal) Nixon self, its only real rival. Watergate was, as Wills says, "the perfect expression of our outsider's inability simply to possess, to find peace inside." And what "outsider" means here is that Nixon is outside of, disjoined from, his self.

Another manifestation of Nixon as "outsider-insider" is found in the *Saturday Review* article by James David Barber cited earlier. Barber notes

Nixon's striking self-consciousness and penchant for self-dramatization (reacting to the rejection of the Haynsworth and Carswell nominations by denouncing the Senate on television, the "ego trips" to Peking and Moscow, the bravura television announcements of his first Cabinet, and the release of edited transcripts of the White House tapes), and writes that "in these self-dramatizations Nixon becomes part of his audience, perpetually watching and correcting his own performance and managing his own feelings." He cites an account by Nixon of his arrival at the airport in Caracas during the stormy South American tour in 1958: "The minute I stepped off the airplane, while getting the salute, I cased the place. (I always do that when I walk out.) I looked it all over and watched the kind of crowd, thinking, where will I make an unscheduled stop, where will we move out and shake hands and so forth . . . we walked down the steps from the airplane, and I quickly made a few mental notes and decisions. As we trooped the line I decided not to wave to the crowd, but to ignore it since they were showing disrespect for their flag and their national anthem as well as ours."

Even more distressing than the familiar facts of Nixon's career is the apparent absence from any of his decisions or actions of ethical or moral considerations. During the last years of the war in Vietnam, as the justifications of our involvement there wore thin and finally became absurd, Nixon kept insisting on what he called "peace with honor." To Nixon, "honor" meant not losing face, the persona, the mask. He *could not* be the first American President to preside over what he considered a military defeat, because the marginal self of this essentially destroyed man could not absorb and withstand that blow to the face. The moral arguments cut no ice with him and did not impinge on the process of his deciding to continue the war. His self, from which any morally motivated act would have had to originate, was simply too weak to compete with the drive to perpetuate the mask. Richard Nixon is not, as has so often been alleged, an immoral man; he is an *amoral* man.

From all evidence, Nixon does not seem to be particularly religious. But upon being elected, he was quick to invite prominent religious leaders to the White House for "prayer meetings" and to be photographed with them. Though brought up a Quaker, he seems to have had no particular preference for the denomination of these services—Billy Graham, Cardinal Cooke, and various rabbis appeared regularly at the White House— and the choices seem to have been made to achieve identification with the largest number of religiously inclined voters. It is interesting to compare

Nixon's "ecumenical" approach to worship with those of his two immediate predecessors. John Kennedy attended Sunday Mass regularly, which, as a Catholic, he was required to do. Lyndon Johnson rarely went to his own church but occasionally accompanied his daughter Lucy (who was then taking instruction to become a Catholic) to Mass. One somehow never felt that Johnson was doing this to get votes.

Nixon often invoked the name of God when trying to justify his actions. This was particularly noticeable in the major television addresses on Vietnam during his first term. In *The Nixon Theology* Charles Henderson tries to fathom Nixon's nominal alliance with the Almighty: "Nixon systematically appropriates the vocabulary of the church—faith, trust, hope, belief, spirit—and applies these words not to a transcendent God but to his own nation, and worse, to his personal vision of what that nation should be. Lacking awareness of the self-interest that corrupts even the best intentions and the most pragmatic policies, he allows himself a free hand to range around the world, applying American power in the firm belief that he is being counseled by the 'best angels' of his own nature; lacking a transcendent God, he seems to make patriotism his religion, the American Dream his deity. Far from returning to the 'spiritual sources' that made this country great, he accomplishes a macabre reversal of those traditions, selling the mirror image as the original."

It was apt of Henderson to use the term "mirror image," for the mirror image is never superimposable on the original. This reversal—this inversion of truth that any moral person would call a lie—has been a staple of Nixon's career from the beginning. When he ran for the Senate in California in 1948 against Helen Gahagan Douglas, he took advantage of rising anti-Communist sentiment, accusing her of being sympathetic to the Communist cause and going so far as to have the accusations printed on pink paper. (The charge remains unverified.) When he won the nomination in 1968, he chose Spiro Agnew as his running mate with the explanation that if anything should happen to the President, Agnew would be the man best qualified to replace him. (An intriguing interpretation is that the choice of Agnew was directed by a blind drive to protect the persona [his Presidency] from the threat of annihilation. By assuring that no advantageous succession would result, Nixon could reduce the chance at least of a "rational" assassination.) When he announced the appointment of his Cabinet on national television in December 1968, he justified his choices by citing the independence of these men and promised to ask their counsel. (We know how independent John Mitchell and Maurice Stans were, and what happened to Walter Hickel when he offered Nixon some advice.) When dissatisfaction with South Vietnamese President Thieu became widespread among the American people, Nixon tried to shore Thieu up by calling him "one of the four or five greatest leaders in the world." (Speaking at an antiwar rally at Johns Hopkins shortly thereafter, former Senator Ernest Gruening set the record straight on that question when he replied that Thieu was one of the four or five *worst* leaders in the world.) And when Nixon went on national television on 29 April 1974 to announce that he was turning over edited transcripts of the White House tapes to the House Judiciary Committee, he said that, read in their entirety, the transcripts would satisfy the American people that he had told the truth all along, even allowing for certain sections which could be interpreted in more than one way. (In fact, the 1,300-page volume compels the reader to the opposite conclusion: that Nixon approved of hush money for E. Howard Hunt and at least considered clemency for the Watergate burglars; that an effort was made to limit the information given to investigators; that false testimony was fabricated for potential witnesses; and that every effort was made to hold to a minimum the number of persons who could be accused of criminal action.)

The editorial page of *The New York Times* for 11 May 1974 reprinted an excerpt of a conversation between President Nixon and former Assistant Attorney General Henry Peterson from the edited transcript of the White House tapes, sandwiched between two statements made by the President shortly before and after the conversation took place. The editorial, "'Image' and Reality," is reproduced as it appeared, and needs no commentary.

The judicial process is moving ahead as it should, and I shall aid it in all appropriate ways . . . I condemn any attempts to cover up in this case, no matter who is involved.
President Nixon, public statement, April 17, 1973
***

From the White House Transcripts, April 27, 1973
Mr. Nixon: We've got to head them off at the pass. Because it's so damned—so damn dangerous to the Presidency, in a sense . . .
Mr. Petersen: Mr. President I tell you, . . . We have to draw the line. We have no mandate to investigate the President. We investigate Watergate, and I don't know where that line draws, but we have to draw that all the time.
Mr. Nixon: Good. Because if Dean is implicating the Presidency—we are going to damned well find out about it . . .
Mr. Petersen: My understanding of our responsibilities is that if it

came to that I would have to come to you and say, "We can't do that." The only people who have jurisdiction to do that is the House of Representatives, as far as I'm concerned.

Mr. Nixon: That's right . . . Now understand that this is not a grand jury thing.

* * *

I was determined that we should get to the bottom of the matter, and that the truth should be fully brought out—no matter who was involved.

President Nixon, public statement, April 30, 1973

Many who watched Nixon announce his resignation on television on 8 August 1974 must have asked, rhetorically, "But why is he resigning?" The words read by the President somehow did not connect the man on the television screen with anything serious enough to warrant his exit from office. "I would," he said, "say only that if some of my judgments were wrong—and some were wrong—they were made in what I believed at the time to be the best interests of the nation." But everyone who wrote about the White House tapes pointed out that if there was one consistent theme in the conversations between Nixon and his associates, it was the utter *disregard* for the good of the nation. Right up to the end, Nixon employed the technique of the reversal—the inversion of truth that any moral person would call a lie—and for the last time while he was President we saw the Nixon mask in a mirror, the inverted image which was not superimposable on the reality.

Near the end of his resignation address, Nixon offered, in metaphorical terms, a bathetic summary of his Presidency: "Sometimes I have succeeded. And sometimes I have failed. But always I have taken heart from what Theodore Roosevelt said about the man in the arena whose face is marred by dust and sweat and blood, who strives valiantly, who errs and comes short again and again because there is no effort without error and shortcoming, but who does actually strive to do the deed, who knows the great enthusiasm, the great devotion, who spends himself in a worthy cause, who at the best knows in the end the triumphs of high achievements and with the worst if he fails, at least fails while daring greatly." The departing President was asking the American people to believe that he had spent himself in a "worthy cause" and that he was taking consolation from the fact that he failed "while daring greatly." In other words, what had come to be known as Watergate became, in a Nixon reversal, a worthy cause and a great dare.

In *Nixon Agonistes* Garry Wills raises the question of Nixon's authenticity: "He is the least 'authentic' man alive, the late mover, the tester of responses, submissive to 'the discipline of consent.' There is one Nixon only, though there seem to be new ones all the time—he will try to be whatever people want." Is Nixon authentic? Was he authentic, for example, when he insisted on an "honorable" settlement in Vietnam? It is clear now that by "honor" he meant preserving the record of American military invincibility, a tradition which the Nixon persona could not tolerate breaking under any circumstances. (Charles de Gaulle—a monumental self if there ever was one—had no problem pulling out of Algeria when it became clear that France's cause there was lost.) If continuing the war to achieve "victory" meant the loss of some 25,000 more American lives and the virtual physical destruction of Vietnam, then, to the Nixon persona, that price had to be paid. Respect for the *Presidency* had to be maintained at all costs, just as *America* had to be kept from appearing to be "a pitiful, helpless giant" by the invasion of Cambodia in 1970. The question of authenticity in Nixon's case is not a straightforward one because there is so little self to this man—there *is* no Richard Nixon.

Bruce Mazlish, M. I. T. psychohistorian and author of *In Search of Nixon*, sees him as "an insecurely held self," but feels that a certain constancy of behavior exempts him from the judgment of hypocrisy: "Acting, role-playing, denial—these patterns of behavior have been constant throughout Mr. Nixon's life . . . Nixon is not being a hypocrite in his statements. He believes with total conviction in the role he is playing at any given moment; it is the source of his power over his audience . . . Nixon is 'genuine' and never more so than when he is acting a part, such as the aggrieved innocent man" (*Washington Post*, 26 November 1973). But Mazlish here sidesteps the central question. For when we speak of acting and role-playing, which are attributes of the persona, even though these posturings are made over a period of years and are therefore "constant," how is this constancy of persona to be related to the questions of authenticity and genuineness, which are attributes of the self? It may be that such words are simply not apposite to the analysis of a marginal self such as Nixon. Before the law he is responsible for his crimes, because there is no reason to see him as anything but sane. But it is possible that "morally" some other standard will have to be used to judge him. We are reminded of something that Margaret Schlegel said of the Wilcoxes in E. M. Forster's *Howards End*: "Perhaps the little thing that says 'I' is missing out of the middle of their heads, and then it's a waste of time to blame them." Richard Nixon has never said "I" in his life.

In both the grand jury and House Judiciary Committee investigations of Watergate, a cardinal question was what was said by the President in the Oval Office on 21 March 1974 about hush money for the original Watergate defendants. During the summer of 1973, John Dean testified that Nixon said raising $1 million to meet the demands of the defendants would be "no problem." H. R. Haldeman, however, also present at the 21 March meeting, later testified that the President immediately added "but it would be wrong." (The White House tape of the conversation apparently did not include any such qualification by the President, and Haldeman was indicted for perjury by the grand jury in February 1974). At a news conference on 22 August 1973, the President said that Haldeman's recollection of what was said at the meeting was accurate, and added that he [Mr. Nixon] recalled saying, "It is wrong, *it won't work*" (emphasis added). Here in the President's own words, in a Freudian (or perhaps Jungian) slip, the amoral self and the persona are seen as one: it is wrong *because* it won't work.

Perhaps the most incisive look into the psyche of Richard Nixon came with the change in tack of the White House defense that occurred soon after James St. Clair succeeded Charles Allen Wright as chief legal counsel. This new approach was explained by Mr. St. Clair when he said in an interview that he did not think of himself as defending Richard Nixon, but as defending the Presidency itself. In a speech to a group of Chicago businessmen on 15 March 1974, Mr. Nixon said he would not resign because he "refused to be a party to the destruction of the Presidency of the United States." Here we have the final Nixon epiphany—a marginal-self President defending a depersonalized Presidency. Having all but run out of acceptable options for his self-defense—the defense of his self, that is—the President would, in Tom Wicker's words, "have us believe that he is not so much a mortal man [a self] as a function . . . that Richard Nixon, having blended his mortality into the continuing flow of the Presidency [his persona], is above the law."

The emporer was naked. The chimera of a Nixon self was dispersed, and he was revealed as a persona, a mask, a role. Again Wicker: "Mr. St. Clair and Mr. Nixon are trying to defend Richard Nixon by proclaiming that *he is not Richard Nixon at all* but the historical Presidency, which must not be impaired" (emphasis added). Never having been quite mortal, Nixon was straining for a kind of immortality, trying to preserve his persona and his Presidency for time and for history.

And what can be said about the people who twice elected this marginal man to the highest office in the country? It seems that to ask the question is to answer it.

10
Beyond the Marginal Self

Description is one thing, prescription another. I have not presented
the phenomenon of the marginal self as a "problem" to be solved,
but as a "mystery" to be illuminated. There are no solutions as
such, no "answers." On the other hand, by holding this phenomenon up
for scrutiny, by "walking around" it so as to see it from many perspectives, we can get some notion of where the trouble lies. Something can
then be said about how this limiting state might be surpassed and
avoided.

At the end of Chapter 5, I distinguished two paths through which the
self can be lost and the marginal self can come into being. First, self may
not be developed because one fails to do what is necessary to create it in
the crucial situations we all encounter. I called this the loss of self by
default; it is the failure to become. Second, self may be lost when one lives
largely through a false self (persona), so that the real self—the vital,
spontaneous, and free component of the self—is cut off from this false self
and, consequently, from others and from the world. I used the term
"schizoid erosion" to describe the consequences to the self when people
choose, but do so inauthentically, so that what is chosen is not consonant
with what is vital, spontaneous, and free in themselves.

AN IMPLIED THERAPEUTIC

In pointing out what is "marginal" about so many people today and
presenting this against the backdrop of a phenomenology of self, I imply a
therapeutic, or, at the minimum, a direction away from the marginal self.
I would like to consider now how someone might avoid the two principal
paths through which self is forfeited and the marginal self comes into
being—default and schizoid erosion.

DEFAULT

In default, people do not become themselves, the selves they might become, because they do not use their freedom to make the choices that would create this self. In essence, default is a denial that a person is free and a turning away from the possibilities this freedom opens to him or her. To illustrate this and how it might be avoided, I would like to consider the boundary situation of being blocked, of having something (or someone) stand in my way so that I cannot do or get what I want. As explained in Chapter 5, a boundary situation occurs when one is confronted with certain limits that cannot be gotten around, reduced, or overcome.

I have a friend who is a reporter and feature writer for a local newspaper. He has worked as a jounalist for almost twenty years. During this time he has been with several prominent newspapers in major cities. He has also published a book on the breaking of a large earthen dam in West Virginia, a disaster resulting in the deaths of many people.

Since I have known him, my friend has had a good deal of difficulty doing his job. He's a fine craftsman and has a good nose for a story. He knows his business. That is not the problem. The problem is that he has trouble dealing with his editors and trouble dealing with himself. He has been married twice and divorced twice. He is an alcoholic and drank heavily for many years, although, as far as I know, he has not had a drink for almost two years. He smokes two to three packs of cigarettes a day. And he has an ulcer that erupts now and then, causing him great pain.

My friend is at odds with the values of this country and is critical of it in his casual conversation and in his writing—sometimes, I feel, to the point of paranoia. He resents authority, particularly in those people who have power over him. He says his editors often cut the best parts of his stories. To him, every story he publishes is a compromise with authority.

My friend is more than a little jaded about the profession of journalism. He tells me that every story he writes now is very much like some other story he has already written. What my friend wants to do is write fiction. He has written two novels, both unpublished. The first was taken around by an agent to several major publishers in New York, but was turned down. My friend keeps working as a journalist so he can afford to spend his free time revising his novels, hoping they will eventually be accepted for publication. Not long ago he told me he wants to change things so that instead of interviewing writers about their books, *he* will be the one interviewed.

My friend is in a boundary situation. He writes his feature stories, which are well received but give him little satisfaction, and continues to plug away at writing novels, which is gratifying, but brings him rejection from publishers. He is a recovering alcoholic, is addicted to cigarettes, and has a bad ulcer. He drives himself night and day. For the last three years, his emotional state has been relatively stable, but he knows this could change. Meanwhile, he keeps going, paying the price as he goes: there are three or four feature stories a week; interviews; freelance articles for other newspapers and for magazines; book reviews; out-of-town assignments. Through it all, he works on his novels. He believes the odds are against either book being published, but this does not stop him. He recently bought a half interest in a word processor, so he can do the revisions more easily.

My friend refuses to default. He could forget about writing novels and have a reasonably comfortable life as a journalist. He has stopped drinking, which was and continues to be very difficult for him. He knows he can't do anything about the damage he has already done to his body with alcohol, but he refuses to damage it further this way. My friend is trying to transcend the boundary situation in which he finds himself. To do this, he must hold himself open to the pain that his situation is, because it is here, at the boundary, where the possibilities for going beyond it lie. He takes responsibility for his situation, does not blame anyone else for his being in it, and does not make excuses. Implicitly, he is refusing to become marginal in the face of this situation.

As I pointed out at the beginning of the chapter, I do not see the marginal self as a "problem" to be solved, but as a "mystery" to be illuminated. There are no answers or solutions, and models for emulation do not help all that much. The most I hope to do is indicate a *direction* and point to a *state of becoming* different from that which leads to the marginal self. The marginal self is not an object or a thing. It is a way of becoming oneself, a stance vis-à-vis others and the world. To use Heideggers's language, it is a particular way of Being-in-the-world.

SCHIZOID EROSION

Chapter 6 was devoted to a discussion of the loss of self through schizoid erosion. Using Laing's model of the divided self, I showed how someone can create a false self (persona) so as to circumvent the anxiety that inheres in creating a real self. This is stating the situation in extremes, since no one is or could ever be a totally "real" self. No one is entirely authentic. What I tried to describe in Chapter 6 was a degree of inauthenticity that, for certain persons, could lead to psychopathological pain and behavioral dysfunction.

To be inauthentic in the face of a situation is to deceive oneself about what one is capable of doing in that situation, without necessarily being aware this self-deception is occurring. We do not try to deceive ourselves; we try to become secure. We deny our Being not to deny it, as Laing points out, but to preserve it, and, in doing so, we deny it. People will give up anything—including pleasure and whatever chance they have to be happy—trying to become secure, their own "foundation," to recall Sartre. The need to become secure is more basic than sex, aggression, or the desire for recognition; it subsumes all these. When people trick themselves into believing this or that will give them what they want and need, the self that is experiencing a degree of security is, at the same time, undermining, losing, and perhaps even destroying, itself. This paradox can never be escaped entirely. It is of the very essence of people that they must create themselves through (really, from) others and the world. Because they cannot always find someone or something they need to do this satisfactorily—authentically—they may deceive themselves about the meaning and value of who and what are at hand to satisfy their needs.

We do what we must to survive. The crucial point is *how* we do this. Putting on a mask, as one would when playing a role demanded by a certain situation, is not destructive if the role is recognized and lived as such. If people can keep their real feelings (real selves) from being subsumed in the role, if they can, in effect, break with the role after playing it, they will not be diminished seriously by it. But if they *live through* the role, if they cannot make a lived distinction between *it* and *them*, they are diminished through what I am calling the schizoid erosion of self.

Let us consider this illustration of how an ambiguous situation can be lived authentically and inauthentically. A woman becomes thirty, perhaps thirty-five. She is not married, or she has been divorced. She may be a veteran of many affairs of varying outcomes. She wishes to marry again; more specifically, she wishes to *be married*. She wants to be supported and to have a regular sexual partner. She wants her own home and children. She wants the "respectability" society reserves for those who are married. She has a prospect, a man who is successful professionally and could give her every material thing she wants. He is attracted to her and wishes to marry her. She is not particularly attracted to him, but recognizes he is a "good man." He is reliable. He will be good to her and to the children.

A woman in this situation who decides to marry may do so in two different ways. She may accept the fact that, for her, this marriage will be a compromise. It will not bring everything she could hope for, or be what an earlier marriage or affair may have been, but it will bring something. She can acknowledge the situation for what it is, accepting the limitations as well as the benefits. As with any compromise, there will be moments when she will find the going difficult and question whether she made the right choice. But through this, she can continue to acknowledge the situation for what it is, and not deceive herself or anyone else about what any of it means. She can be authentic in the face of a limited fulfillment of her needs. She can acknowledge and live the pain that inheres in her compromise solution.

But there is another way a woman can live the marriage we are considering here. She can constitute it as something it is not. She can trick herself into believing her husband is the love of her life and the answer to her prayers. She can deceive herself about what their relationship means and what needs it fulfills. She can live her entire life through this self-deception, which is, necessarily, a deception of her husband as well. A woman who does this is not acknowledging and living the pain that inheres in her compromise solution to her need for a husband. Through this self-deception, she may succeed for a time at keeping the pain of a not entirely satisfactory marriage at bay, but will pay the price of a diminished self, which will result, eventually, in a different and more profound psychopathological pain. I tried to show in Chapter 6 how this happened to Jenny Isaksson in Bergman's *Face to Face*.

THE SECURITY PRINCIPLE

Freud was wrong: we do not operate under a "pleasure principle," nor does the "death instinct" drive people to their destruction. Rather, we try to become secure, our own foundation, by appropriating others and the world. It seems fitting to call this the "security principle." Here is the meaning, finally, of all the choices we make and of all we do. It is inevitable that we do this because we are not our *own* foundation, and this is intolerable to us. But the security—the foundation—we strive for is frequently antithetical to the satisfaction and happiness we expect from what is sought. Paradoxically, in trying to become secure through what are often self-deceiving choices, we diminish ourselves in the process and become marginal selves. And this, necessarily, results in pain and unhappiness.

A NEW IMPERATIVE: THE HOLY INFIDEL

I began my description of the marginal self on a theological note, and so it seems appropriate to end it in the same way. I would like to recall the distinction made in Chapter 1 between the religious impulse, the need for meaning and transcendence that is ineradicable, and the Judeo-Christian (theistic) satisfaction of that impulse. In a world where theistic transcendence is no longer absolute, something less absolute will have to be recognized and lived as the *summum bonum*, the ultimate good. For the first time since the ancient Greeks, people are being confronted with their limits *as people*. They are being forced back on themselves and made to ask ultimate questions, when there are no longer ultimate answers. This is the source of the "existential shock" I described in Chapter 1.

Feuerbach understood a century ago why people have felt alienated since creating the Judeo-Christian God: they are alienated from themselves because they created a God in their own image, thus projecting the best part of their spirit outside themselves, adoring it as if it were a superior being. If God is the superior being, a person is, necessarily, an inferior being. We are now in an interim period, when God is no longer experienced as absolute, but people do not experience themselves as absolute either. They can rely fully neither on God nor on themselves. Philip Rieff showed in *The Triumph of the Therapeutic* how Christianity has lost its integrating and therapeutic power. The therapist's office has replaced the priest's confessional, and now priests, too, have therapists. If people felt alienated while in the shadow of a superior being, is it surprising they feel even more so now this absolute has been repealed, and they still experience themselves as inferior beings?

Now that the notion of sin and its attendant guilt no longer dominates us, the psychopathological pain of mental illness has become our greatest emotional scourge. Self-deception (inauthenticity) is the secular counterpart of sin, and the resulting psychopathological pain the counterpart of religious guilt. In deceiving ourselves, we "sin" against our Being, which should be our main concern, and, at the same time, we distort our relationships with others and our relation to the world.

As no Christian could be free from sin, no person can be free from self-deception. But what is inauthentic in us can be recognized and thematized and, in some instances, remade without self-deception. Only in this way can we become holy and whole. It is here the battle for a non-marginal self must be fought, and where it will be won or lost.

For the Holy Infidel, the model of sanctity is not Christ's cross, but

Sisyphus's rock. Our task is to reestablish fidelity to what is human, and become confident again in ourselves and in this more difficult, but truer—and potentially happier—world.

References and Notes

1

1. Paul Tillich, *The Courage to Be* (New Haven: Yale University Press, 1952), p. 107.

2. *Ibid.*, p. 108.

3. Walker Percy, *The Moviegoer* (New York: The Noonday Press, 1961), pp. 69–70.

4. Quoted in Robert M. Pirsig, *Zen and the Art of Motorcycle Maintenance* (New York: Bantam Books, 1974), pp. 371–72. See also Tillich, *The Courage to Be*, p. 83.

5. The quotations by Schubert Ogden, Gerhard Ebeling, Karl Rahner, and John Courtney Murray, as well as the excerpt from *motive*, were taken from the *Time* article cited in the text.

6. Philip Rieff, *The Triumph of the Therapeutic* (New York and Evanston: Harper Torchbooks, 1968), p. 26.

7. Friedrich Nietzsche, *Joyful Wisdom*, trans. Thomas Common (New York: Frederick Ungar Publishing Co., 1960). pp. 167–69.

8. Ralph Harper, *Existentialism: A Theory of Man* (Cambridge: Harvard University Presses, 1948), p. 8.

9. Jean-Paul Sartre, *Existentialism and Human Emotions*, trans. Bernard Frechtman and Hazel E. Barnes (New York: Philosophical Library, 1957), p. 57.

10. Quoted in Harper, *Existentialism*, p. 133.

11. Hwa Yol Jung, ed., *Existential Phenomenology and Political Theory: A Reader* (Chicago: Henry Regnery Company, 1972), p. xxviii.

12. Tillich, *The Courage to Be* p. 41.

13. *Ibid.*, pp. 37–38.

14. *Ibid.*, pp. 69–70.

15. Miguel de Unamuno, *Tragic Sense of Life*, trans. J. E. Crawford Flitch (New York: Dover Publications, 1954), p. 283.

16. Excerpted from Terrence Des Pres, *The Survivor* (New York: Oxford University Press, 1976), in *Harper's*, February 1976, p. 48.

17. Friedrich Nietzsche, *The Will to Power*, trans. Walter Kaufmann and R. J. Hollingdale (New York: Random House, 1967), p. 35.

18. Samuel Beckett, *Proust and Three Dialogues* (London: Calder & Boyars, 1965), p. 103.

19. Tillich, *The Courage to Be*, pp. 140–41.

20. David E. Roberts, *Existentialism and Religious Belief*, ed. Roger Hazelton (New York: Oxford University Press, 1957), p. 4. Later in his book (p. 100), Roberts summarizes the explanation that Kierkegaard gave in *Concluding Unscientific Postscript* of how Johannes Climacus, the pseudonymous author of the *Postscript*, came to be a writer. We learn a great deal here about Kierkegaard, and the revolt of the existentialists:

One day he was sitting in a café smoking a cigar. For about a decade he had been a lackadaisical student, reading much, but spending most of his time in idling and thinking which came to nothing. As he was smoking it occurred to him that he was going to become an old man without really undertaking anything, while his contemporaries were becoming prominent by benefiting mankind with various mechanical inventions and metaphysical systems that make existence easy. The thought flashed into his mind that his contribution might be, with the same humanitarian intentions as the others, to make things harder. For at a banquet where everyone has overeaten the man who fetches a vomitive may be the only one who sees what is really required.

2

1. In *Irrational Man* (Garden City, N.Y.: Anchor Books, 1962), William Barrett gives the following accounts of how Hegel and Kant dealt with the question of existence in their systems:

Hegel's peculiar offense lay not in following the tradition by leaving existence out of his system, but rather in the way in which he tried to bring it in, having begun by excluding it. At law, I suppose, this would come under the heading of a compound felony. All his philosophical predecessors, or nearly all of them, had committed the theft, but poor Hegel was caught in the act of trying to restore the misappropriated article. The means he chose were most unfortunate: he tried to bring back existence through logic. Reason, become omnipotent, would generate existence out of itself. Even here, Hegel was not really flying in the face of tradition, as it might seem; he was only giving a more audacious expression to the overinflation of reason and its powers that had been the peculiar professional deformation of almost all earlier philosophers. This conjuring up of existence, like a rabbit out of a hat, Hegel accomplished by means of his famous dialectic, the instrument Marx later turned with such devastating results upon social and economic history. We begin, says Hegel, with the concept of Being, a pure empty concept without existence; this begets its opposite, Nothing, and out of the pair come the mediating and reconciling concept that is the synthesis of both. This process goes on until at the proper stage of the dialectic we reach a level of Reality, which is to say Existence. The details of the derivation we need not go into here; what concerns us is the general structure of Hegel's argument, through which thought begets existence. It does not require much imagination to see the human implications of this sample of Hegelian dialectic [pp. 159–60].

In contrast, Kant, who preceded Hegel, declared that existence could never be conceived by reason: "Being," he said, "is evidently not a real predicate, or concept of something that can be added to the concept of a thing." Kant's response to this recognition was the diametric opposite of Kierkegaard's. He felt that existence was too general, remote, and tenuous to be the subject of fruitful consideration by the mind at all, so he left it out of his scheme, limiting his attention to what was *observable* and *measurable*:

Hence, all modern Positivism takes its cue from Kant's doctrine and discards all thinking about existence (metaphysics, as this school calls it) as pointless because existence cannot be represented in a concept, and hence thinking about it will never lead to any definite results in observation. The crossroad in modern philosophy is precisely here, and Kierkegaard takes a road leading in the opposite direction from that taken by Positivism. If existence cannot be represented in a concept, he says, it is not because it is too general, remote, and tenuous a thing to be conceived of but rather because it is too dense, concrete, and rich. *I am*; and this fact that I exist is so compelling and enveloping a reality that it cannot be reproduced thinly in any of my mental concepts, though it is clearly the life-and-death fact without which all my concepts would be void.

Kant can justly be called the father of modern philosophy, for out of him stem nearly all the still current and contending schools of philosophy: Positivism, Pragmatism, and Existentialism. The difference between Positivism and Existentialism, to confine ourselves to these two, can be seen simply as the different response to Kant's point that existence cannot be a concept [p. 162].

2. Sören Kierkegaard, *Repetition*, trans. Walter Lowrie (Princeton: Princeton University Press, 1941), p. 114.

3. Sören Kierkegaard, *The Sickness unto Death in Fear and Trembling and The Sickness unto Death*, trans. Walter Lowrie (Princeton: Princeton University Press, 1941), p. 144.

4. Sören Kierkegaard, *Concluding Unscientific Postscript*, trans. David F. Swenson and Walter Lowrie (Princeton: Princeton University Press, 1941), pp. 191–92.

5. Kierkegaard, *The Sickness unto Death*, p. 142.

6. *Ibid.*, pp. 171–72.

7. *Ibid.*, pp. 166–67.

8. Maurice Merleau-Ponty, "What Is Phenomenology?" *Cross Currents* 6, no. 1 (Winter 1956), p. 59.

9. Maurice Merleau-Ponty, *Phenomenology of Perception*, trans. Colin Smith (New York: The Humanities Press, 1962), pp. viii–ix.

10. These terms are used by Marjorie Grene in her article on Heidegger in *The Encyclopedia of Philosophy*, ed. Paul Edwards (New York: The Macmillan Company & The Free Press, 1967), vol. 3, pp. 459–65. We use them here as a complement and counterpoint to Heidegger's hyphenated terms.

11. Martin Heidegger, *Being and Time*, trans. John Macquarrie and Edward Robinson (New York: Harper & Row, 1962), p. 21. Published originally as *Sein und Zeit* in 1927.

12. *Ibid.*, p. 23.

13. Paul Ricoeur, *Husserl*, trans. Edward G. Ballard and Lester E. Embree (Evanston: Northwestern University Press, 1967), p. 212.

14. D. H. Lawrence, *Women in Love* (New York: The Viking Press, 1960), pp. 314–15.

15. Barrett, *Irrational Man*, p. 226.

16. *Ibid.*, p. 290.

17. Quoted by Richard M. Zaner and Don Ihde, eds., in *Phenomenology and Existentialism*, (New York: G. P. Putnam's Sons, 1973), pp. 174–75.

18. *Ibid.*, pp. 147–48.

3

1. Tillich, *The Courage to Be*, pp. 149–50.
2. Barrett, *Irrational Man*, p. 248.
3. Sartre, *Existentialism and Human Emotions*, p. 38.
4. *Ibid.*, pp. 22–23.
5. Jean-Paul Sartre, *The Flies*, in *No Exit and The Flies*, trans. Stuart Gilbert (New York: Alfred A. Knopf, 1947), p. 158.
6. Sartre, *Existentialism and Human Emotions*, p. 90.
7. Jean-Paul Sartre, *Existentialism*, trans. Bernard Frechtman (New York: The Philosophical Library, 1947), pp. 292–93.
8. *Ibid.*, pp. 293–94.
9. Tillich, *The Courage to Be*, p. 41.
10. Jean-Paul Sartre, interview with Michel Contat, *The New York Review*, 7 August 1975, p. 10.
11. Jean-Paul Sartre, *Nausea*, trans. Lloyd Alexander (Norwalk, Conn.: New Directions, 1959), pp. 133–34.
12. Ibid., pp. 135–36.
13. Ibid., pp. 176–77.
14. An account of this contretemps is given in the appendix ("Sartre and Camus: The Anatomy of a Quarrel" by Bernard Murchland) in *Choice of Action: The French Existentialists on the Political Front Line*, Michel-Antoine Burnier, trans. Bernard Murchland (New York: Random House, 1968). Jeanson's review of *The Rebel* appeared in *Les Temps Modernes* in June 1952. Camus's response, not to Jeanson but to Sartre ("Letter to the Editor of *Les Temps Modernes*"), along with Sartre's reply ("Reply to Albert Camus"), was published in that journal in August 1952.
15. Jean-Paul Sartre, *Situations*, trans. Benita Eisler (New York: George Braziller, 1965), p. 109.
16. This quotation and the preceding one are from Camus's first book, *L'Envers et L'Endroit* (*The Wrong Side and the Right Side*), written in 1935–36, but only published in 1958. Quoted in Henri Peyre, *French Novelists of Today* (New York: Oxford University Press, 1967), pp. 313 and 314 respectively.
17. Jean-Paul Sartre, "The Outsider," in *Literary Essays*, trans. Annette Michelson (New York: The Philosophical Library, 1957), p. 32. This essay on *The Stranger* ("The Outsider" is Michelson's translation) is truly seminal.
18. Henri Peyre, "Camus: An Anti-Christian Moralist," *Proceedings of the American Philosophical Society* 102, no. 5 (October 1958), pp. 477–82. This essay was of great assistance in preparing the section on Camus, as was Chapter 11 ("Albert Camus: Moralist and Novelist") in Peyre's book, *French Novelists of Today* (New York: Oxford University Press, 1967).
19. Albert Camus, *The Plague*, trans. Stuart Gilbert (New York: Alfred A. Knopf, 1948), p. 278.
20. Sartre, "The Outsider," in *Literary Essays*, p. 35.
21. Albert Camus, *The Myth of Sisyphus*, trans. Justin O'Brien (New York: Alfred A. Knopf, 1955), p. 15.
22. Grene, *The Encyclopedia of Philosophy*, p. 462.

We would also like to acknowledge an anthology that was valuable both for the scope of its inclusion and the accompanying critical analysis: *The Fabric of Existentialism: Philosophical and Literary Sources*, ed. Richard Gill and Ernest Sherman (New York: Appleton-Century-Crofts, 1973).

4

1. José Ortega y Gasset, *Man and People*, trans. Willard R. Trask (New York: W. W. Norton & Co., 1957), p. 60.
2. *Ibid.*, p. 86.
3. *Ibid.*, p. 86.
4. *Ibid.*, p. 87.
5. *Ibid.*, p. 88.
6. *Ibid.*, p. 87.
7. *Ibid.*, pp. 90–91.
8. *Ibid.*, p. 92.
9. Gabriel Marcel, *Being and Having*, trans. Katherine Farrer (New York: Harper Torchbooks, 1965), p. 97.
10. Ortega y Gasset, *Man and People*, pp. 97–98.
11. *Ibid.*, p. 99.
12. *Ibid.*, p. 101.
13. *Ibid.*, p. 93.
14. *Ibid.*, p. 104.
15. *Ibid.*, p. 147.
16. *Ibid.*, p. 166.
17. *Ibid.*, pp. 169–70.

5

1. *The Way of Chuang Tzu*, trans. Thomas Merton (New York: New Directions, 1965), p. 71.
2. Ortega y Gasset, *Man and People*, p. 17.
3. *Ibid.*, p. 33.
4. Simone Weil, *The Iliad, or The Poem of Force*, trans. Mary McCarthy (Wallingford, Penna.: Pendle Hill, 1956), p. 15. First published in *Politics*, November 1945.
5. Jean Anouilh, *Antigone* (in *Five Plays, Vol. 1*), trans. Lewis Galantière (New York: Hill and Wang, 1958), pp. 36–37.
6. Jean-Paul Sartre, *The Condemned of Altona*, trans. Sylvia and George Leeson (New York: Vintage Books, 1963), p. 11.
7. *Ibid.*, pp. 177–78.
8. Ortega y Gasset, *Man and People*, p. 25.
9. This discussion of the relation of fictional characters to the question of self is based on an address given by Ralph Harper entitled "The Range and the Role of

the Imagination," delivered during the Johns Hopkins Centennial Celebration on 21 February 1976.

10. André Malraux, *The Temptation of the West*, trans. Robert Hollander (New York: Vintage Books, 1961), pp. 15–16.

11. *Ibid.*, p. 59.

12. *Ibid.*, p. 63.

13. *Ibid.*, p. 87.

14. *Ibid.*, p. 19.

15. Barrett, *Irrational Man*, p. 82.

16. E. M. Forster, *Howards End* (New York: Vintage Books, 1921), p. 186.

17. *Ibid.*, p. 195.

18. *Ibid.*, p. 195.

19. *Ibid.*, p. 204.

20. John Ciardi, *How Does a Poem Mean?* (Boston: Houghton Mifflin, 1959), p. 995.

21. Forster, *Howards End*, p. 234.

22. Albert Camus, *A Happy Death*, trans. Richard Howard (New York: Alfred A. Knopf, 1972), p. 110.

23. *Ibid.*, pp. 118–21.

24. *Ibid.*, pp. 128–29.

25. *Ibid.*, p. 122.

26. Karl Jaspers, *Reason and Existenz*, trans. William Earle (New York: The Noonday Press, 1955), p. 126.

6

1. Merleau-Ponty, *Phenomenology of Perception*, p. 382.

2. Kierkegaard, *The Sickness unto Death*, p. 169.

3. *Ibid.*, p. 169.

4. Unamuno, *Tragic Sense of Life*, p. 90.

5. *Ibid.*, p. 8.

6. *Ibid.*, p. 8.

7. R. D. Laing, *The Divided Self* (Baltimore: Penguin Books, 1965). William James used the term "divided self" earlier in *The Varieties of Religious Experience* (New York: Longmans, Green and Co., 1902) to designate the discordant longings in the self for the spiritual and for the natural, for God and for Mammon (see lecture 8). This "division," however, does not involve the formation of a false self, and does not result in the schizoid erosion of self that we are describing here. In the context in which he was using the term, James considered Augustine, prior to his conversion, to be the divided self par excellence.

8. Laing, *The Divided Self*, p. 39.

9. Gerard Manley Hopkins, *A Selection of His Poems and Prose* (Baltimore: Penguin Books, 1962), p. 197.

10. Ralph Harper, *The Existential Experience* (Baltimore: The Johns Hopkins Press, 1972), pp. 28–29.

11. *Ibid.*, p. 35.

12. Laing, *The Divided Self*, p. 52.

13. *Ibid.*, p. 53.

14. F. Scott Fitzgerald, *Tender Is the Night* (New York: Charles Scribner's Sons, 1933), p. 245.

15. Laing, *The Divided Self*, p. 111.

16. *Ibid.*, pp. 70–72.

17. *Ibid.*, p. 81.

18. *Ibid.*, p. 80.

19. Tillich, *The Courage to Be*, p. 66.

20. Laing, *The Divided Self*, p. 96.

21. *The Basic Writings of C. G. Jung*, edited with an introduction by Violet S. de Laszlo (New York: The Modern Library, 1959). See particularly pp. 136–82 and pp. 380–97.

22. *Ibid., p. 138.*

23. *Ibid.*, p. 164.

24. *Ibid.*, p. 292.

25. Jean-Paul Sartre, *Existential Psychoanalysis*, trans. Hazel E. Barnes (Chicago: Henry Regnery Co., 1962).

26. Laing, *The Divided Self*, p. 150.

27. Laing gives this description of the schizophrenic experience: ". . . the very ontological foundations are shaken . . . There are no supports, nothing to cling to, except some fragments from the wreck, a few memories, names, sounds, one or two objects, that retain a link with a world long lost. This void may not be empty. It may be peopled by visions and voices, ghosts, strange shapes and apparitions" (R. D. Laing, *The Politics of Experience* [New York: Pantheon Books, 1967], p. 92).

28. *The New York Times Book Review*, 30 May 1976, p. 5.

29. Ortega y Gasset, *Man and People*, pp. 97–98.

30. See William James, *The Varieties of Religious Experience*, lectures 9 and 10.

31. *The New York Times Magazine*, 1 July 1973, p. 10. See also the interview with Bernard Weintraub ("Bergman in Exile"), Arts and Leisure Section, *The New York Times*, 17 October 1976. It is interesting to contrast Bergman's description of how he felt after severing the tie with God with that given by Sartre through his stand-in, Orestes, in *The Flies*: "Suddenly, out of the blue, freedom crashed down on me and swept me off my feet. Nature sprang back, my youth went to the wind, and I knew myself alone, utterly alone in the midst of this well-meaning universe of yours. I was like a man who's lost his shadow. And there was nothing left in heaven, no right or wrong, nor anyone to give me orders". Both Bergman and Sartre made a "clean break" with God. But where Bergman was *relieved* of the heaviest burden of his life through this new freedom, Sartre *incurred* his heaviest burden through it. We can understand this difference when we recognize that religion had been a serious problem for Bergman, but not for Sartre.

32. Ingmar Bergman, *Face to Face*, trans. Alan Blair (New York: Pantheon Books, 1976), p. 53.

33. *Ibid.*, pp. 64–65.

34. *Ibid.*, p. 100.

35. *Ibid.*, p. 83.

36. Laing, *The Divided Self*, p. 138.

37. Bergman, *Face to Face*, p. vii.

38. *Ibid.*, p. vii.

39. *Ibid.*, p. 34.

40. *Ibid.*, p. 99.

41. *Ibid.*, p. 56.

42. *Ibid.*, pp. 101–02.

43. *Ibid.*, pp. 105–06.

44. *Ibid.*, p. 27.

45. Ingmar Bergman, *Persona and Shame*, trans. Keith Bradfield (New York: Grossman Publishers, 1972), p. 91.

46. *Ibid.*, p. 93.

47. Quoted in "Is There a Male Menopause?" by Martha Lear, *The New York Times Magazine*, 28 January 1973, p. 58.

48. Harper, *Existentialism*, p. 51. See also Günter Grass, "On Stasis in Progress: Variations on Albrecht Dürer's Engraving *Melancholia I*," *American Review*, 18 (September 1973), p. 41.

7

1. Sir Arthur Conan Doyle, *The Adventure of The Speckled Band and Other Stories of Sherlock Holmes* (New York: The New American Library, Inc., 1965), p. 81.

2. Ian Fleming, *Thunderball* (New York: Signet, 1961), p. 7.

3. Blaise Pascal, *Pensées*, translated with an introduction by A. J. Krailsheimer (Harmondsworth, Middlesex, England: Penguin Books Ltd., 1966), p. 67.

4. *Ibid.*, p. 68.

5. Ernest Hemingway, *A Farewell to Arms* (New York: Charles Scribner's Sons, 1929), p. 174.

6. Gabriel Marcel, *Being and Having*, trans. Katherine Farrer (New York: Harper Torchbooks, 1965).

7. *Ibid.*, p. 164.

8. Sartre, *Existential Psychoanalysis*, p. 91.

9. *Ibid.*, p. 91.

10. Marcel, *Being and Having*, p. 152.

11. *Ibid.*, p. 152.

12. *Ibid.*, p. 165.

13. Forster, *Howards End*, p. 186.

14. *Ibid.*, p. 195.

15. Marcel, *Being and Having*, p. 131.

16. *Ibid.*, p. 173.

17. This and the preceding quotation are from Kierkegaard's *The Point of View for My Work as an Author*, as cited in Denis de Rougement's *Love Declared*, trans. Richard Howard (New York: Pantheon Books, 1963), pp. 96 and 97. For our purposes, Howard's translation of these excerpts, presumably from French, is superior to that of the translation of Kierkegaard's book directly into English (see note 18).

18. Sören Kierkegaard, *The Point of View for My Work as an Author*, trans. Walter Lowrie (New York: Harper Torchbooks, 1962), p. 103.

19. Quoted by Thomas Mann in a Preface ("Homage") to Franz Kafka's *The Castle*, trans. Willa and Edwin Muir (New York: Vintage Books, 1974), p. xiii.

20. See "The Snakeskin" in Ingmar Bergman's *Persona and Shame (The Screenplays)*, trans. Keith Bradfield (New York: Grossman Publishers, 1972).

21. *Ibid.*, p. 13.

22. *Ibid.*, p. 12.

23. Lawrence, *Women in Love*, p. 223.

24. Charles A. Reich, *The Greening of America* (New York: Random House, 1970), p. 102.

25. Quoted from a review by John Kenneth Galbraith of Malcolm Muggeridge's *Chronicles of Wasted Time* in *The New York Times Book Review*, 14 July 1974.

26. Kierkegaard, *The Sickness unto Death*, pp. 166–67.

27. Quoted from *The New York Times* (Arts and Leisure Section), 9 December 1973.

28. See Linda Wolfe, "A Time of Change," *New York* Magazine, 5 June 1972, p. 68.

29. Gail Sheehy, "Why Mid Life Is Crisis Time for Couples," *New York* Magazine, 29 April 1974, p. 31. All the quotations by Aaron Coleman Webb were taken from this article, which was adapted from Sheehy's book *Passages* (New York: E. P. Dutton, 1976).

30. Kierkegaard, *The Sickness unto Death*, p. 167.

31. *Ibid.*, 152.

32. *Esquire* published Fitzgerald's story in four parts during 1936 and 1937. The entire story is reprinted in a collection of Fitzgerald's shorter pieces: *The Crack-Up*, ed. Edmund Wilson (New York: New Directions, 1956). The account of Arnold Gingrich's meeting with Fitzgerald in Hollywood is given in the October 1976 *Esquire*, p. 65.

33. Malcolm Cowley, "The Lucky Generation," The *Atlantic*, December 1972, p. 55.

34. Fitzgerald, *The Crack-Up*, p. 71.

35. *Ibid.*, p. 88.

36. *Ibid.*, p. 79.

37. *Ibid.*, p. 79.

38. Jorge Luis Borges, *Labyrinths, Selected Stories and Other Writings*, ed. Donald A. Yates and James E. Irby (New York: New Directions, 1964), p. 246.

39. Pirsig, *Zen and the Art of Motorcycle Maintenance*, p. 319.

40. *Ibid.*, pp. 289–90.

41. Tillich, *The Courage to Be*, p. 46.

42. Pirsig, *Zen and the Art of Motorcycle Maintenance*, p. 206.

43. Erica Jong, "The Writer as Sexual Guru," *New York* Magazine, 20 May 1974, p. 80.

8

1. Nikolai Berdyaev, *Solitude and Society*, trans. George Reavey (London: The Centenal Press, 1938), p. 118.

2. Sartre, *Being and Nothingness*, p. 371.

3. *Ibid.*, p. 375.

4. *Ibid.*, p. 363.

5. *Ibid.*, p. 376.

6. Martin Buber, *I and Thou*, trans. Walter Kaufmann (New York: Charles Scribner's Sons, 1970), p. 115.

7. *Ibid.*, p. 66.

8. *Ibid.*, p. 66.

9. *Ibid.*, p. 126.

10. *Ibid.*, p. 62.

11. *Ibid.*, p. 62.

12. *Ibid.*, p. 82.

13. F. Scott Fitzgerald, *The Great Gatsby* (New York: Charles Scribner's Sons, 1925), p. 112.

14. Buber, *I and Thou*, p. 147.

15. Kierkegaard, *The Sickness unto Death*, pp. 152–53.

16. Lawrence, *Women in Love*, p. 436.

17. T. H. Adamowski, "Being Perfect: Lawrence, Sartre, and *Women in Love*," *Critical Inquiry* 2 (Winter 1975), p. 345. Quotation is from p. 362.

18. Lawrence, *Women in Love*, p. 308.

19. *Ibid.*, p. 247.

20. *Ibid.*, p. 301.

21. *Ibid.*, pp. 361–62.

22. *Ibid.*, p. 305.

23. Adamowski, "Being Perfect," p. 362.

24. Lawrence, *Women in Love*, pp. 305–06.

25. See Zaner and Ihde, *Phenomenology and Existentialism*, pp. 174–75.

26. Lawrence, *Women in Love*, p. 37.

27. Ortega y Gasset, *Man and People*, p. 224.

28. Lawrence, *Women in Love*, p. 426.

29. Marcel, *Being and Having*, p. 50.

30. Buber, *I and Thou*, p. 126.

31. Stendhal, *Love*, trans. Gilbert and Suzanne Sale (Harmondsworth, Middlesex, England: Penguin Books Ltd., 1975), pp. 284–92. See also Sartre, *Existential Psychoanalysis*, pp. 107–08.

32. F. Scott Fitzgerald, *This Side of Paradise* (New York: Charles Scribner's Sons, 1920), pp. 177–79.

33. Ingmar Bergman, *Scenes from a Marriage*, trans. Alan Blair (New York: Bantam Books, 1974). All quotations are from this text.

34. Camus, *The Plague*, p. 75.

35. Bergman, *Scenes from a Marriage*, p. 89.

36. *Ibid.*, pp. 125–26.

37. *Ibid.*, p. 152.

Index